JOB #:

Author Name:

Title of Book:

ISBN:9781930337503

Publisher:

Trim Size:6x9

Bulk in mm:13

What the Bee Knows

P.L. TRAVERS

What the Bee Knows

Reflections on Myth, Symbol and Story

Foreword by David Appelbaum

Codhill Press

NEW PALTZ ⚬⚬ NEW YORK

First published by The Aquarian Press 1989
Published by Penguin Books 1993

Copyright © P.L. Travers, 1989
All rights reserved

Reprinted by arrangement with the Trustees of
the P. L. Travers Will Trust in care of Harold
Ober Associates Incorporated

The moral right of the author has been asserted

Codhill Press edition, 2010

ISBN 1-930337-50-7

Codhill Press
New Paltz, New York 12561
www.codhill.com

Foreword

W hat the bee knows gives taste to the honey but isn't found there. The bee's knowledge concerns the invisible realm, at once inner and outer. There, the spirit dwells in its many manifestations, and there the soul travels in search of spirit. The bee knows of spirits, everyday spirits, for the most part, and occasionally a great spirit, Spirit in capitals. This is the formless essence of the invisible, its absolute authority beyond the law. At its heart, the formless cohabits with each and every thing, and with the totality, surrounding it like a nimbus, an atmosphere. At least, this is the image that the mind seeks to steady itself in relation to the void, where it meets its nothingness. So much is this deep wisdom that P.L. Travers conveys in this classic work of hers.

Bees access the primordial knowledge in their circulation through the world and its flora. It provides their pollen. They gather it and return to the hive, a fact Nietzsche likens to our greed for information. They are one with the wind, which listeth where it bloweth—which is to say, spirit. They are initiates to ancient culture whose constatements are preserved in myth, legend, fairytale, and folklore, as an excess of charge or moving force that exists over and above the telling. By recognizing the cosmoses that P.L. Travers recreates and the knowledge they contain, we pay homage to the bee, who can take it in more directly. We humans require an indirect approach in order to bypass a basic incredulity, Heraclitus says. This means lies for us moderns and post-moderns in myth—directly understood. Myth takes the soul on the circuitous journey to spirit, located at the *mysterious and empty center of our being*. There, story and tale can do the work they were devised for, to transform the tough, resistant coat of intellect into a sensitive opening to groundless existence.

In this regard, P.L.Travers remains a master. She allows the myth to circulate beneath the skin and to penetrate deeper layers where its effect is more subtle. There in the fertile darkness in which Eros is engendered, as Hesiod tells, stories blend together with everything that exists. There, all desires seek to know themselves, for this is also Plato's realm where Eros dwells, a great spirit whose other name is the life-force that moves her retellings and reflections on tradition and a source of meaning. Knowledge in the deep empowers the human spirit to rise and soar so that it is just a little lower than the angels.

What the bee knows is not far from the spirit expressed through these essays and stories. The ring of P.L.Travers' words comes from an age of great and grave imagination. It exemplifies the complex weave of characters that play a role in one single unfolding creation: the world. Each day is a day in the Great Year, where words she has written count. The Year and the Day contain the beehive, the many lives of it, the almost countless cells of life. Their wanderings are mimicked by the bees' flight, which is the very trace of the knowing spirit—of that of knowing spirit. P.L.Travers gift to us is the record of that mysterious trace of a limitless Source.

—*David Appelbaum*

Contents

The World of the Hero   11
Two Pairs of Shoes   19
Fear No More the Heat of the Sun   25
The Legacy of the Ancestors   30
If She's Not Gone, She Lives There Still   36
Letter to a Learned Astrologer   50
The Youngest Brother   59
The Primary World   65
Five Women   73
What the Bee Knows   80
The Seventh Day   91
Where Will All the Stories Go?   95
Speak, Lord   107
Name and No Name   117
Leda's Lament   129
Walking the Maze at Chartres   132
What Aileth Thee?   138
Re-Storying the Adult   141
The Hanged Man   145
Miss Quigley   147
The Way Back   151
Sip No Sup and Bite No Bit   156
Lucifer   163
Now, Farewell and Hail   166
On Unknowing   170
The Garment   174
Out From Eden   179
Le Chevalier Perdu   181
Lively Oracles   185

The Unsleeping Eye: A Fairy Tale   189
O Children of This World!   195
On Forgiving Oneself   197
Zen Moments   200
The Interviewer   203
Well, Shoot Me!   210
Monte Perdido   216
And Endless Story   219
The Black Sheep   229
A Radical Innocence   235
The Death of AE: Irish Hero and Mystic   242
Grimm's Women   257
Christmas Song For a Child   260
About the Sleeping Beauty   261
The Shortest Stories in the World   272
Admit One   282
Only Connect   285

The World of the Hero

I WILL preface what I am going to say with a few lines from e. e. cummings:

May my mind walk about freely and supple
And even if it's Sunday may I be wrong,
For whenever men are right they are no
longer young.

This gives you leave to doubt me and to take what I say simply as hint and indication and not at all as assertion. It is meant as a whisper at the inner ear and designed to touch that part of you which is not accessible to the things that are spoken of in newspapers.

But before we begin to search for the hero, I think we should take a look at the element he moves in, the world where he functions — folklore, fairy-tale, allegory, legend, parable, even nursery rhyme; for all these are as it were the principalities that together comprise the homeland of myth, the country which in the old Russian stories is called East of the Sun and West of the Moon, and for which there is no known map.

But first I think it important to clarify what I mean by that word myth. We have so betrayed and brutalized language that we have forgotten that in itself it is, in a way, mythical, in the sense that it is sacred, in its essence, a gift at some immemorial time mysteriously bestowed. Even the behaviourists are beginning to question their own theory that language is a simple human function that has evolved, over milleniums, from the grunting of bears and apes. We have lost our respect for this given treasure and now care so little to foster its growth that we have all become like Humpty-Dumpty: 'When I use a word,' he says in *Alice in Wonderland*, 'it means exactly what I mean it to mean.' This is all very well, perhaps, for somebody who is living down a rabbit hole, but not for us, if we are truly to understand each other and try to communicate ideas; we have to admit that words exist in their own right, that they have antecedents, long family trees and are not just foundlings left on a doorstep for anybody to pick up and do with as they will. If I were a hero the maiden I would set out to rescue would be language.

The word myth, for example, is largely accepted and used as something synonymous with lie. 'It's a myth,' we say, meaning something that is not to be believed, a tarradiddle, a tall story, an impossibility. Even the Concise Oxford Dictionary describes it as a 'fictitious idea'. I would rather have said 'unverifiable', but even that would not have been exact. For whether we know it or not, or wish it or not, we all — like the hero — live in myth, or rather the context of myth, as the egg yolk lives in its albumen; and if we set about it, we can verify and confirm the fact in ourselves.

If we begin to look for the origin of myths, we hear first perhaps the answer of such Victorians as Frazer of *The Golden Bough* and Andrew Lang: that they are the relics of an ancient barbaric world, the avocations, even the aberrations, of savages. But when one thinks of *Gilgamesh*, of the Chinese structures that underlie that oldest of known books, the *I Ching*, of the Hindu myths, the African and those of the American Indians, one can only say: 'What barbarians are these!' and pray to be turned forthwith into a savage.

Malinowsky, nearer the mark, called them the re-arising of primordial reality in narrative form. And Nietzsche, who in everything he did and wrote was deeply involved in the mythical process, said that myth was not merely the bearer of ideas and concepts but that it was also a way of thinking, a glass that mirrors to us the universe and ourselves. One of our own contemporaries, Robert Graves, has written that 'they are all grave records of ancient religious customs, events or ritual, and reliable enough as history once their language is understood.' And William Blake said: 'The Authors' — and he spelled the word with a capital A — 'the Authors are in Eternity.' And in eternity is where we have to leave them, I think, if we are looking for inventors. We shall never know what species of man it was that first unfolded from his own subjective understanding this Orphic and objective art. And as to the meaning of the myths, the more one studies them the more one sees that this heritage from archaic man — the rituals and concepts that guided his conscious life — miraculously survives and is ever present in the subterranean layers of ourselves. It can be tapped as one taps the waters under the earth; it can be questioned as once our forefathers questioned the oracles, seeking an answer to what, in essence, is perhaps not so different from our own question. We go to the myths not so much for what they mean as for our own meaning. Who am I? Why am I here? How can I live in accordance with reality?

Now, this problem of meaning can literally overwhelm us, particularly nowadays when there are no rituals, no rites of passage, as the ancients called them, to help us to make the transition from one stage of life to the next. One moment we're children and a moment later, as it seems, we're adolescents and then grown-ups, facing alone our own existence and all the dubiousness of things. And yet, perhaps, not so alone as we imagine. The myths have something to say here; not an absolute, not one sole word, no blanket phrase — although every religion, every tradition, to say nothing of every anthropologist, every archaeologist, and of course, every psychoanalyst lays claim to the myths as his special province, his own particular possession. 'We know', they say, in the kind of voice that makes one reach immediately for one's hat. 'We know and we will interpret. The myth means this, the myth means that; it means, of course, *our* meaning.'

Well, to be honest, so it may; but that is not the end of it. One of the characteristics of this ancient art is that it won't go into any particular pocket, it won't be coerced or owned. The myths never have a single meaning, once and for all and finished. They have something greater; they have meaning itself. If you hang a crystal sphere in the window it will give off light from all parts of itself. That is how the myths are; they have meaning for me, for you, and for everyone else. A true symbol has always this multisidedness. It has something to say to all who approach it.

One could say, I think, that the myths never were and always are and therefore they are indestructible. Wherever there are men, there are myths; and no matter where on the globe they arise, these myths have a startling likeness to one another. At some particular moment, always unknown — for they are not subject to the carbon test and can't be dated; and they may appear at different periods among different peoples — the selfsame themes seem to emerge, as though something in the psyche of a race had ripened and produced a fruit that corresponded, not in its form but in its substance, with the fruit of all other races. The fact that the same stories arise in India, the Middle East, Europe, the Americas, as well as in China and Japan, is an intimation that their proper soil and seeding-place is not in any geographical location but in man himself. This alone could ensure, if we believed it, (I'm speaking ideally and mythologically, of course) that no one on the planet need be a stranger to any other. Indeed, there is a Hindu myth that illustrates this. The high god Indra, it is said, once made a net to enclose the world, and at each knot or intersection, he fastened a little bell. If you think of a seine-net, with a bell in every knot of the string, you can see what this would mean. Nothing could move, not a man, not the wind, not a thought in the mind, without setting one bell ringing; and that one bell would set all the others going. It is a wonderfully graphic way of telling people who could not read, who received things through the ear rather than the eye, that everything is inevitably connected with everything else.

But if the myths always are, who is it that enacts them? Who sustains them? Who keeps them alive? You have only to read the *New York Times* to see the myths crowding into it with their splendid and terrible deeds. The daily disclosures in the papers show the material on which the mythmaking process inherent in man is always at work, however unconsciously — not only among poets and mystics, Boehme, Bunyan, Blake and the rest, but also, and chiefly, in the folk; and by folk I mean you and me and anyone walking in the street. Take as an instance the story of Galileo. Galileo is not a myth; he is in all the history books where you will read the undoubted fact that at a time when it was believed that the sun moved round the earth, Galileo dared to assert that the very opposite was true, that the earth moved round the sun. Under pressure, however, and on pain of death, he was forced to deny his truth. Thus he was able to save his life; but as he turned away from recanting he muttered firmly into his beard: *'Eppur si muove'* — 'Nevertheless, it moves.' The story is known to everyone. Galileo is famous for the *'Eppur si muove'*; but the recantation of his recantation has nowhere been recorded. How could it have been? The only people near enough to hear it were his inquisitors, and had they heard it, his fat would have been in the fire. He never said *'Eppur si muove'* — except, of course, in his accurate heart. But in its unconscious shaping of the hero, the folk required that it be said, the story required that it be said; the truth had somehow to be told that Galileo was not a liar. So, mythologically, Galileo was required to say it. It is a truth but it is not a fact.

Then there is the case of Lady Godiva. Everybody knows the

story: how in order to get from her skinflint husband a gift of land for the poor of Coventry, she offered to ride through the streets naked, having first taken the precaution of ordering the people into their houses and all the shutters closed. The whole of Coventry obeyed except for one man by the name of Tom who peeped at her through the crack of a door and had his eye shrivelled up for his pains. It is from him that we get the phrase 'a peeping Tom'. But the fact of the matter is that Tom did not enter the story until it was 200 years old. Gradually and mythologically, the folk must have come to realize that nakedness without an eye to observe it has no meaning whatever — like Bishop Berkeley's cow that didn't exist until somebody beheld it — and that an order without somebody to disobey it is somehow incomplete. A story can't live with a heroine only, it needs a villain to bring her to life. So, of course, the matter was at last put right and Peeping Tom now belongs to the myth. He also is true but he is not a fact.

So you see how the mythmaking mind works, balancing, clarifying, adjusting, making events somehow correspond to the inner necessity of things. It is this tension, the uncompromising insistence on both ends of the stick — black and white, good and evil, positive and negative, active and passive — that gives the myths their ambivalent power. In our Aristotelian, Apollonian world, where we constantly applaud the good, uphold law and order and stand on the side of what is right (while keeping the atom bomb in our pocket), the bloodiness of the myths, their vengefulness and brutality, their Dionysian recklessness — and, on the other hand, their splendour — are difficult to accept. They are too large for us, too mighty. Perhaps that is why we give them to children who, with their strong stomachs and their minds as yet untainted with knowledge, are more likely to understand them. To understand: for years I pondered on that word and tried to define its effect on myself. At last I came to the conclusion that what it means is the opposite of what it says; to understand is to stand under. Later I discovered that this was, in very fact, its meaning in Middle English. So, in order to understand, I come to something with my unknowing — my nakedness, if you like: I stand under it and let it teach me, rain down its truth upon me. That is, I think, what children do; they let it make room in them for a sense of justice, for the wicked fairy as well as the Sleeping Beauty, for dragons as well as princes.

This grasping of the whole stick is an essential feature of the hero. So what or rather who is the hero? We're all familiar with the paladins of myth: Theseus slaying the Minotaur and finding his way through the labyrinth by means of a single linen thread; Aeneas finding the way to the underworld with the help of a little golden twig; Daniel outfacing his pride of lions; Jonah measuring the dark in the belly of the whale. But what is the common denominator among these — and indeed, all other heroes? Could it be (and it's a question, not an assertion) that first and foremost the hero is one who is willing to set out, take the first step, shoulder something? Perhaps the hero is one who puts his foot upon a path not knowing what he may expect from life but in some way feeling in his bones that life expects something from him.

I think, too, that no hero would ever protest that he didn't ask to be born. If he isn't sure that he did ask, at least he is ready to behave *as if* he had, as if, having been given life, he is ready to answer for his life. And so he has to leave home, or safety, or his own conditioned way of thinking and feeling, and put himself, naked, at the service of whatever necessity arises: a dragon to be slain, a Gorgon beheaded, fire brought down from heaven. All the tasks are different, but if you closely examine the myths you will see that fundamentally the quest is always the same. Looked at from the point of view of the story, the hero's work is to rescue a beleaguered maiden from an unspeakable fate, to gather up some hoarded treasure after slaying a seven-headed serpent, or to fetch a cup of the Water of Life from the well at the world's end; all of these asking no less than all. But what do they mean essentially? Perhaps the myths are telling us that these endeavours are not so much voyages of discovery as of rediscovery; that the hero is seeking not for something new but for something old, a treasure that was lost and has to be found, his own self, his identity. And by finding this, by achieving this, he takes part in the one task, the essential mythical requirement: the reinstatement of the fallen world. It is a long and perilous journey back from the nadir to the zenith, from lying amid the husks and the swine to eating the fatted calf.

Now, the hero is not a god, nor even a saint, though many saints have been heroes. He has a human heart and therefore a dimension of vulnerability and the possibility of failing. The idea that there is a flaw in creation is fundamental to all myths. But only by studying them does one realize that it is *only* by the flaws, only by its imperfections (because they summon up the perfections) that creation can proceed. It is the same with the hero. Each one is a fallible man. Achilles has his inordinate pride; but where would his battle fervour be without that very pride? Lancelot, perhaps the most cherished hero in all myth, envied by men, loved by women, set out to find the Holy Grail while at the same time betraying his friend and king with the wife of his king and friend. He never saw the Holy Grail; it passed him by, by a hair's breadth, but by his heroic faithfulness to his own unfaith he not only sustained his place at the Round Table but was its brightest ornament. And his son, Galahad (or his own unsullied part, perhaps) was the one who found the Grail. Ulysses, whom one might call Lancelot's runner-up in popularity, succumbed to temptation in every known port in the world until he dropped anchor in his own haven of Ithaca; he succumbed, yes, but unlike his men, whom he left behind in various stages of beastlihood, he was alive to what he was doing, he kept an eye upon himself — the cunning man, the crafty one — and came home as a hero.

David, spying Bathsheba from the housetops, arranged to have her husband Uriah the Hittite set in the forefront of the battle so that he might marry her himself after Uriah's death; and we are surprised (but the myth is not) that the outcome of this distasteful deed was Solomon the Wise. Generations later the lineal descendant of David's tree will say to the man who loved him and betrayed him thrice: 'Thou art Peter, and on this rock shall I build my church.' This rock, this matrix of gross earth and crystal, is the essential hero stuff. For it is through his human failings and his human triumphs that the hero serves his purpose, which is to make himself a channel for the gods to come down to men. In the process of discovering his own identity, he becomes for us, mythologically, the mediating or reconciling element and indeed the pattern. And, also mythologically, in an antique way, we comfort and sustain ourselves with what in us corresponds to the hero.

But is this enough? Perhaps if we could really listen to what the myths are telling us we would hear what I heard myself saying not so long ago: 'Everybody has to be the hero of one story: his own.' I said it lightly; or rather something said it in me, for we know more than we know we know, more than we understand. And if it is true, what an awesome undertaking! All those dragons — give them whatever name you like; those journeys to our own dark underworld, all those imprisoned princesses to be rescued. One would shrink from such an obligation if the alternative was not also so awesome. *Not* to be the hero of one's own story — could one agree to that? Could I fail to be some sort of Demeter, searching the world for my child, myself, my lost Persephone? It is not a question to be answered but responded to, stood under, as it were, with a kind of fear and trembling. Because, to attempt it, I have to be in the same situation as the hero in the Russian story called 'Go I know not whither; bring back I know not what.' It is with this unknowing that I have to set out to find the homeland of myth, that homeland so well described in 'Rumpelstiltzkin' where it is called 'the country where the fox and the hare say goodnight to each other'. This phrase embodies all we need to know. For in effect, this is the country, the conditions where the opposites are reconciled, the place where one goes beyond them. Goodnight, fox, goodnight, hare! I wonder where we can find it, where in ourselves can we look for it?

And yet, is it not always there, and are we ever really out of this East of the Sun, West of the Moon land of myth? Can we escape from it, even if we wish? If you feel that in what I have said about myth (whose garment I have hardly touched), I have drawn too long a bow, you must remember that the long bow itself comes out of a myth, the myth of Philoctetes. And if, as I said at the beginning, you wish to take anything I have said with a grain of salt, do so, always remembering that salt also is an essential mythological ingredient.

First published in 'Parabola' on the theme of The Hero, New York, 1976.

Two Pairs of Shoes

ABU KASSEM'S SLIPPERS

LISTEN to the story of Abu Kassem, the merchant, who was known throughout Baghdad not only for his riches and his parsimony but also for his slippers which were the outward and visible sign of his miserliness. They were so old, so dirty, so patched and tattered that they were the bane of every cobbler in the city and a byword among the citizens.

Clad in this deplorable footwear and a shabby kaftan Abu Kassem would go shuffling through the bazaar sniffing around for bargains. One day he happened on a collection of little crystal bottles which, after much haggling, he managed to buy quite cheaply. And then, with typical miser's luck, he came upon, at cut-price, a large supply of attar of roses with which to fill the bottles. The bazaar was agog at this double stroke and Abu Kassem, congratulating himself on his sagacity, decided to celebrate the occasion by paying a visit to the public bath.

There, in the dressing room, he met his old friend Hassan who took him to task in the matter of his slippers. 'Look at them, Abu Kassem! Any beggar would throw them away. But thou with all thy stored-up riches dost refuse to part with the dreadful things!'

'Waste not, want not,' said Abu Dassem. 'There is still a lot of wear in them.' And he took off the offending slippers and hurried into the bath.

But Fate had caught him in her grip, as we shall presently see. It so happened that the Cadi of Baghdad had also decided to bathe that day. Abu Kassem finished before him, put on his outer clothes and turban and felt about for his slippers. Where were they? They had disappeared. But in their place was another pair, shiny and bright and new. 'Ah,' said Abu Kassem. 'This is Hassan's work. He has gone out into the marketplace and bought me another pair of slippers.' He drew on the resplendent footwear and went home thoroughly pleased with himself.

But what did the Cadi say, I wonder, when his servants, searching the dressing-room for their master's slippers, brought him a tattered pair of objects that everybody recognized as belonging to Abu Kassem? The story is silent on this point. All we know is that he sent immediately for the culprit, fined him an enormous sum and restored to him his slippers.

Abu Kassem was sad at heart, as he looked at the ragged objects. To have had to pay so much for so little! Well, at least they would give him no more trouble. He would get rid of the wretched things. So, with a gesture of farewell he flung them into the River Tigris. 'That,' he thought, 'is the end of them!' Alas and alack! Poor foolish man! Little did he know.

A few days later some fishermen discovered in their net two bundles of tattered leather. 'Abu Kassem's slippers!' they said, and angrily hurled the offending footwear through Abu Kassem's window.

Down went the row of crystal bottles and up rose the scent of attar of roses as Abu Kassem's splendid bargains went crashing to the floor.

The miser was beside himself. He swept up the scattered glassy fragments and seized upon his slippers. 'Wretches!' he cried. 'This is enough! Ye shall do me no more harm.' Thereupon, he took a shovel, dug a hole in his tulip garden and buried his once-prized possessions.

'What can he be doing?' a neighbour asked, as he watched the labouring figure. 'A rich man with so many servants to be digging in his own garden! He must be looking for hidden treasure. I will go and tell the Caliph!'

And since it is a law that hidden treasure belongs to the state, Abu Kassem soon found himself in court, standing before the governor. Where, he was asked, had he put the treasure? And when he protested that there was no treasure, that he had merely been burying a pair of old slippers, the statement was received with laughter and general disbelief. The more he protested the more unlikely the story seemed, even to himself. Inevitably, he paid the fine and went home to unearth his slippers.

'The cursed things!' he cried, in despair. 'Shall I never rid myself of them?' He decided, then, to take the slippers out of the city, far from the sight of men. This he did. He hied him out into the country, dropped the offenders into a pond and breathed a sigh of relief. At last, he had seen the last of them!

But Fate had not finished with Abu Kassem. When he returned he discovered that the pond had been no pond but a reservoir, that the slippers had fouled the water-pipes, that the workmen had recognized the slippers — how, indeed, could they help it? — and that he himself was to go to jail for stopping the city's water supply. So once again he paid a fine and once again he carried home his old unwanted possessions.

What was to be done? How could he free himself from his slippers and all their devil's tricks? Earth had refused them, so had water. What remained? Fire, of course! He would burn them to ashes. However, at the moment they were still wet, so he put them out on the rooftop to dry. There they lay, bleaching in the sun, till a dog on a nearby rooftop spied them, leapt the intervening space and snatched up the fatal slippers. He tossed them lightly into the air and down they fell to the street below where a woman was passing by. Now, it so happened that this woman was pregnant and the sudden blow on the top of her head quickly brought on a miscarriage. Her indignant husband, seeing from what the blow had come, ran to the judge and demanded payment. So Abu Kassem, now distraught, had once more to put his hand in his pocket.

But he cried, as he flung the money down and brandished the slippers aloft: 'Lord judge, hear me! Be my witness. These slippers have been the bane of my life. Their tricks have reduced me to penury. Set me free from them, I implore thee! Let the evils that they bring in their train no longer be visited on my head. Of thy mercy, let this be enough!'

And the story relates that the Cadi, being a merciful man, heard the miser's plea. But he counselled Abu Kassem, saying 'Hear, O Merchant, the voice of wisdom. Nothing lasts for ever, it says, and when a thing is no longer useful that thing should be relinquished.'

Retold from the Thamarat Ul-Awrak (Fruit of Leaves) of Ibn Hijjat Al-Hamawi.

THE SANDALS OF AYAZ

Listen now to the story of Ayaz who had risen from a lowly condition to that of Treasurer and trusted friend at the court of the great King Mahmud. From time to time, in the course of his duties, Ayaz would bring his master a tally of all the gold and silver and jewels that were stored in the palace cellars. But of the contents of the modest chamber in the topmost tower he brought no tally at all. Every day he climbed to this little room and remained there for a certain time. And every day as he came out he locked the heavy door securely and kept the key in his pocket. What lay behind that locked door was known to nobody and Ayaz never spoke of it.

Now, it so happened that on a particular occasion the King came into the council chamber carrying a large pearl which he gave to the Vizier. 'Tell me,' he said, 'what this pearl is worth.'

'More than a hundred ass-loads of gold,' the Vizier replied.

'Break it!' commanded King Mahmud.

'But how should I break it?' the Vizier cried. 'How could I waste this priceless thing?'

'Well said!' exclaimed the King, and presented him with a dress of honour.

Then he turned to the palace Chamberlain and handed him the pearl.

'What is this jewel worth?' he asked.

'Half a kingdom, may God preserve it!'

'Break it,' commanded King Mahmud.

'Alas, such a deed would be a great pity. How could I be an enemy to the treasure house of the King?'

'Well said,' the King exclaimed, and he gave the Chamberlain a robe of honour. And turned to the Minister of Justice.

So it went on. Each courtier refused to break the pearl and to each the King gave a costly garment. Unfortunate men! How was it that they could not guess that they were being put to the test?

Last of all came the turn of Ayaz.

'Tell me what this pearl is worth.'

'More,' said Ayaz, 'than I can say.'

'Break it,' commanded King Mahmud.

Now Ayaz had two stones in his sleeve. And without a moment's hesitation he crushed the pearl between the stone and so reduced it to dust.

The courtiers rose up in a clamour. 'Whoever breaks such a radiant thing is an infidel!' they cried.

'O princes,' Ayaz cried to them. 'What is more precious to your hearts — the pearl or the King's command? He is lacking in the true pearl who puts a stone before the King. When I look for radiance, I turn my gaze to him.'

At that the courtiers bowed their heads, realizing that they had been deflected from the path of truth by the grandeur of a worldly bauble. 'Alas,' they cried, 'our fate is sealed.'

'For the sake of a coloured stone,' said the King, 'my command has been held contemptible.' And he made a sign to the Executioner.

But Ayaz, full of boundless love, prostrated himself before the throne. 'O thou from whom comes every fortune, grant them, as a boon, their lives and do not banish them from thy presence. He who ignores thy least command, what should teach him except thy pardon?'

The King heard the words of his faithful servant and for love of him reprieved the rest.

The courtiers breathed a sigh of relief. They had been given back their lives. But as the fox is to the lion, so were they to Ayaz.

Before long they were plotting against him, whispering scandal to each other.

'What has he hidden in the uppermost chamber, of which he keeps the key? Is he not Treasurer to the King? Of a truth, he has hoarded gold and silver and is keeping a secret store for himself. It is right that we tell the King.'

So they did that. And the King wondered. 'What has my servant concealed from me?'

And he gave orders to a certain Amir saying, 'Go at midnight and force the door and whatever you find is yours.'

Now, the King had no evil thoughts of Ayaz. He was putting the courtiers on trial. Nevertheless, his heart misgave him, lest the charge be true and his servant shamed.

'He has not done this thing,' he mused. 'And if he has it is rightly done. Let Ayaz have whatever he will for he is my beloved. I need a mouth as broad as heaven to describe the qualities of one who is envied by the angels.'

Thus he thought within himself while the courtiers went to work. They struck at the door of the uppermost chamber and broke the iron lock. Then they swarmed in, jostling each other, greedily seeking the hidden treasure.

They looked to the right. They looked to the left. Up and down and round they looked. But the little uppermost room was empty, except for a dusty sheepskin jacket and a pair of tattered sandals.

'Bring picks and shovels!' the courtiers cried. Thereupon they began to dig, making holes in the walls and floor. And the very holes cried out against them: 'Behold, O men, we are empty.'

The fact, indeed, could not be denied. No treasure lay in the uppermost chamber and the courtiers returned to the King, palefaced and ashamed.

'Are you heavy-laden?' the King asked, slyly. 'Show me the hoarded gold and jewels and the treasure my faithful friend has stolen.'

'O, King of the world,' they cried. 'Forgive! We have nothing but a sheepskin jacket and a pair of sandal shoon.'

'Nay,' said the King. 'I deal not with punishment or forgiveness. That right belongs to Ayaz.'

'O king,' said Ayaz, 'the command is thine. When the sun is here the star is naughted. Let it be remembered on their behalf that if I had neglected jacket and shoon, I should not have sown the seeds of envy.'

'I shall note it,' answered King Mahmud. 'But, O Ayaz, tell me this. Why these marks of affection to a rustic shoe? Thou hast mingled so much of thy soul's love with two old articles of dress, and kept them both in a chamber. Why in the presence of these things doest thou show so much humility?'

'It is fit that I do so,' said Ayaz. 'I was low on the earth and thou lifted me up. From my tent thou hast brought me to marble halls. I know that all this eminence is but a gift of thine, otherwise I am nothing but this sheepskin jacket and this pair of sandal shoon. The Prophet himself hath propounded this matter when he said "He who knows himself, knows God." The seed from which I came is my shoon, my blood is the sheepskin jacket. I therefore commune with my beginnings. "Do not regard thy present greatness," the sheepskin jacket tells me. "Remember, Ayaz!" say the sandal shoon. So I keep them, O Master, to remind me. That is all my secret.'

Retold from The Mathnawi of Jalalu' ddin Rumi.

First published in 'Parabola' on the theme of Initiation, New York, 1976.

Fear No More
the Heat of the Sun

I WAS walking through the streets of London, inwardly saying No to my life. 'Set me free of things,' I prayed, 'the merciless brute matter of *objects* that bears us down with its tyranny till living is hardly living.' And my prayer, miraculously, was answered. From somewhere — for lack of a better word, call it that — came the voice of W. H. Auden:

> *The glacier knocks in the cupboard,*
> *The desert sighs in the bed*
> *And the crack of the tea cup opens*
> *A lane to the land of the dead.*

Of course! I should have remembered sooner! The lost cap of the blender and the broken chair-leg that had set me searching for replacements, were nothing — if I would let them be — but doors into other dimensions. From lying prone, I stood up in myself, sensing my length and breadth and height, drawing in life from my surroundings and — was it coincidence or fate? — there before me was the Brompton graveyard, forty acres of trees and marble, that lies full fathom five in quiet under the noise of the city.

I have always loved graveyards and here I stood, lifesize, by one of the largest in England and at the same time dwindled — or not yet grown — in another in the Southern Hemisphere. This situation, impossible to the reason, is no great feat mythologically. It can happen at any moment.

In my family when we lived in the wilds of Australia, the children were sent out of church before the sermon, probably to the relief of the congregation, certainly to the consternation of the vicar. For he knew from experience that the churchyard, when he next saw it, would have undergone certain changes. Miss Jebb's profusion of metal roses, glassed in against marauding hands, might be shared with Mr Perse, who had none; or distributed among the Teeth — Isaac Tooth, Sarah Tooth, Simon Tooth, Athene Tooth — Athene and no stone owl! Lucinda Fry, aged three months, and dead for more than twenty years, would be lifted, mythically, from her grave and dandled, intangible but real to us, from one pair of arms to another. (Do not cry at being dead, Lucinda! you'll become a star like Castor and Pollux.) Deeply steeped in *Robin Hood,* we robbed the rich and gave to the poor. From graves that still had friends to tend them, we took cut flowers from the pannikins and doled them out, just rather than merciful, to those that had been forgotten. And if the sermon were long enough we would visit Amos Tupper, whose grave with its simple marble curb was a convenient spot for lying down in, arms folded, feet together. 'Here lies X,' we informed each other, 'beloved child of Y and Z, gone and deeply regretted.' We took turns at being deeply regretted, tasting for a moment our death-in-life, seriously and with confidence. For Amos, we knew, would never haunt us. With his gravemould sprinkled on our backs, we still had no fear of Amos. He was so far away and so long ago that we felt him as a beneficient presence, near and neighbourly.

But the new graves with their fading flowers — violets whitening, lilies darkening — we passed with eyes averted. Down there beneath the mounded earth were persons we had seen and known, looking so beautiful, the grown-ups said, which was something we did not believe. They were palpable, ugly and frightening, too close to the huge fact of death, not yet gone into the Dreaming. They faced us with the unfaceable and forced us to live, if but for a moment, with the fearful contradiction — This will happen to me some day /No, no, I shall live forever.

But now, myself on the way to Amos, I know that the word contradiction is not really exact; that between all pairs of opposites there is a point — could we but find it — of reconciliation. From the first breath, when we choke on air to the last when air forsakes us, dying is happening to us. Occasionally, for a waking moment, such as I found in the Brompton graveyard, we ourselves happen to it, as the reconciling factor. Here, in this forest of trees and marble, to know oneself pregnant with one's death — an organic, growing shape within — is to experience a surge of energy, life so much at its apogee, that one feels one has the strength to leave it. The readiness, after all, is all.

Look! There at the edge of the crowding headstones is a small rectangle of empty earth, large enough, I would have said, for one more parcel of flesh and bones to become, in time, its essential grass. In principle, the graveyard is closed but in England, land of compromise, it is always possible to find someone who has a string to pull. Snobbishly speaking, it's a good address, mostly Carrara, a little limestone, and in the democracy of death one would soon be on terms with the neighbours; the stone children, boy and girl, dutifully guarding their father's grave with, clearly, no relish for the task; the 'Darling sister' whose brother, in a paroxysm of grief — 'Thou hast ravished my heart, my sister, my spouse' — raised up upon her a marble mound almost as high as the tallest trees and on top of that, a Virgin; Major Arbuthnot under his broken pillar — 'Oh, withered is the garland of the war/The soldier's pole is fallen' —; the life-sized angel with a child-size trumpet, too small even to wake the living, let alone Mr and Mrs Cooper who died in 1903; Albert Henry Glossop Harris who, 'Looking for the face I had/Before the world was made' has a finely carved bust of himself on the top of an obelisk; Lot Brass, aged sixteen, wordlessly reminding passers-by that 'Golden lads and girls all must/Like chimney-sweepers come to dust'; and all the thousand others.

In the west of Ireland there is a tradition that the last corpse into the graveyard must sweep and keep it tidy. If it should happen that two funerals occur at the same time, the cart-drivers whip up their willing horses and race the last lap of the journey in order to get their man in first. I would not mind sweeping leaves in the Brompton — provided, of course, they let me in — for, like the monk in the Zen story, I would shake the trees before I began so as not to do it more than once. And tidying up would be merely child's play for the place is so orderly, so shipshape, that the last one in must have been a sailor or a very meticulous housewife.

A pair of lovers, neither in their first youth, stroll past me hand in hand. They are in heaven, not a graveyard, in spite of the surrounding headstones with their elegies of love and loss. Two small boys, in school caps, clearly on a bird-nesting trip, are craning up at the ilex trees, like Johnny-head-in-air. A mother, pushing a child in a stroller, bustles domestically by, using the graveyard, I assume, as a short cut between supermarkets. But no, I am wrong. She lifts the child out of his harness and settles him on a marble anchor inscribed with the motto *God is Love.* He straddles it regally, king of the world, eating a chocolate biscuit. It pleases me that he and the nesting boys are here, weaving their own mythology around the fact of life-and-death. We cannot begin too early, I feel, to make our truce with it. I have seen children playing in little family plots in Maine, set in the midst of fir trees; in Père Lachaise with its mausoleums; in the cemetery for Soviet heroes in the Grounds of the Alexander Nevsky Monastery — stone propellers above the airmen, cement machine-guns for the soldiers. And I think of a child in an English graveyard, eagerly searching among the headstones, with the eye of a connoisseur. 'I'm choosing my grave,' he said to me. 'And this,' he pointed, 'is the one I want. Promise me that when I'm dead you'll give me one just like it.'

I promised. Why burden him with time and statistics? Or the fact that when he was ready for his Celtic cross I would be weaving rain with the Pleiads or hunting with Orion? Now he is a grown man, preparing himself for fatherhood in a house whose one-apple-tree garden abuts upon this graveyard wall. Its windows look out on the marble forest and when the children are old enough they, too, will come to hunt for birds' nests, in and out among angels.

The mother gathers up her child but not before he has offered his biscuit to a tall leonine grey-haired man who has wandered into the graveyard. 'Take it!' I beg him, wordlessly, and to my delight the gift is accepted, courteously and with relish. He is still eating as he makes a gesture asking me if he may share my bench. It is as if the Balzac in the Louvre, grown milder, with all passion spent, had suddenly come to life. He sits there, like a brooding bird, gathered into himself. Indeed, we are like two brooding birds. Silence and sunlight wrap us round and in it we seem to commune together, taking upon us 'the mystery of things/As if we were God's spies.' Has he, too, found the crack in the tea-cup? Does he, too, swing between the poles of confidence and fear—'I will not cease from mental fight' and *Timor mortis conturbat me?* Is he, too, collaborating with Necessity? It cannot be otherwise, I feel. We are both pared down to essentials. Why am I here? What is the meaning of this inconstant aggregate I glibly call myself? Who walks the world under my name? Whatever the answers, one has to admit that life, at best, is a tragic business, but — and here is the paradox, and paradox relates not only to earth, it is a cosmic phenomenon, as Einstein was to discover — once one freely makes the admission and casts off the heavy burden of hope, the situation changes. Something new has entered the field. The last word is by no means said. To give this new dimension a name would bring things to a conclusion. It can only be approached from the standpoint of myth — which is itself a way of thinking — and let the fecund questions rise. Of what is man the metaphor? Of what Eucharistic feast are we the sacrificial bread? Is it possible that in time beyond time I shall know as I am known? How can earth do the will of heaven?

A song-burst comes from the tree above us. 'A wren!' exclaims Balzac, looking astonished. 'In October!' I say, with equal wonder. He waits until the bird is silent, then he readies himself to depart. *'Au revoir!'* he says, and bows. The phrase, for a moment, startles me. How, when, where would we meet again? And then I remember the old song. 'You'll take the high road/and I'll take the low road.' Why should the low road reach Scotland first? Ask any Highlander and he'll tell you. The low road is the road of the dead. And so, untrammelled by space and time, they will always outpace the living. Was Balzac thinking of *Loch Lomond?* If so, he and I will meet in Scotland, or perhaps in Brompton, it doesn't matter. Here and there, by that time, will be the same for us 'Thou thy worldly task hath done/Home art gone and ta'en thy wages.'

The wren again shatters the silence and swoops towards the homes of the living, perhaps to the one with the apple tree where a child awaits its life-and-death. I send it a silent message:

You there, setting out on your journey, you newly risen from the Void, remembering still your original face and knowing all there is to be known — that all so soon forgotten — you, still swinging in your veiny hammock, spirit moving on the face of the waters, pray for me now and at the hour of my birth. I will do the same for you.

First published in 'Parabola' on the theme of Death, New York, 1977.

The Legacy
of the Ancestors

In the Nothingness Yhi stirred in her dream, waiting for Baiame,
The Great Spirit. He came and woke the world. 'No, no!' cried all
the evil spirits. 'Sleep, sleep, sleep!' But Baiame had already spoken
the word and animals and insects and birds awoke and began to
creep out of their caves; death came to life in the lakes and rivers;
fish swam up to the surface. Yhi began her pilgrimage to North,
South, East, and West, and trees, grasses, stones, and mountains
sprang up in her footsteps. Then Baiame said: 'My thought needs
form. I will give it my own.' So it was that man was made.

THIS is a pretty enough aboriginal story — each tribe has its own
version — but perhaps a little too coherent, too obviously worked
upon by missionaries in order to fit the thought of a paleolithic
race into their own schemata. There are tales of devout clerics in
the Australian bush robing naked bodies in Christian garments,
crowning fish-oiled heads with flowers and performing marriage
and baptismal services over persons already — by fact of birth and
benefit of totem — religiously dedicated to the spirits of iguana,
emu or wattle, and who, after the ceremony, promptly returned
to their familiar allegiances.

Anthropologists are constantly on the lookout for evidence of
where the original Australians came from, but so far have not
found a single folk tale that gives a clue to their migration. Are
they survivors of some primitive race that could have inhabited
a vast Antarctic continent of which South America, South Africa
and Australia may once have formed a part? Do they derive from
a Dravidian people driven from the Indian Deccan, who drifted
in bark boats to the Northern Territory and eventually overran
the continent? These questions are for experts, men of science.
What we are pursuing here is organic and essential stuff — how
they lived, what they believed, the substance of the folk. If one

thinks of the Caduceus of Mercury, it is possible — all symbols being multisided, giving off light in every direction — to equate the central winged rod with names, dates, and carbon tests, and the two intertwining serpents with what the legend-making mind has done with historical material. Scientific fact and intimate personal experience together converge upon the truth.

Fortunately we have a great body of intimate matter relating to the Northwest, Western and Southern tribes, in the writings of Daisy Bates who, like her near-contemporary, Mary Kingsley, in West Africa, went to live among the natives in a state of what can only be called communion. Anthropology is the study of man, and all true women, even without benefit of scientific training — and Daisy Bates was a journalist, not a scientist — are natural anthropologists. For thirty-five years, from the turn of the century onward, she shared the life of the aborigines, living amid their nakedness clad in neatly tailored Edwardian garments, veiled toque, high-heeled shoes and clean white cotton gloves. Mary Kingsley, equally fastidious sartorially, in Victorian cape, bonnet and elastic-sided boots, once pursued into the African jungle a member of the Fang tribe who had shot at her with a musket, crying with anthropological fervor — and, clearly, some feminine curiosity — 'But why? Just tell me why!'

There was no 'why' in Daisy Bates. She simply 'sat down' — an aboriginal word for camping — and listened to what the aborigines had to tell, never imposing her own intelligence and beliefs upon them but waiting patiently for separate pieces of information to form themselves into a coherent whole. The stories sometimes took years to emerge. And since 'whites' were originally held to be the returned spirits of aboriginal ancestors, it was not difficult for her to persuade them that she was *mirroojandu*, or magic woman, and one of the twenty-two wives of Leberr, an ancestor who lived in the Dreamtime. This idea of the Dreamtime (or Dreaming), called variously *Yamminga, Nyetting, Dhoogoor, Ungud,* is central to the thought of all the Australian tribes. Any relative farther back than a grandfather or farther forward than a grandson was held to be in the Dreamtime — which was not, in fact, time at all, but rather timelessness; space, too, and spacelessness; matter, spirit, life and death, everything and always.

It was against this backdrop of the Dreamtime, the ever-germinating myth, that the drama of aboriginal life was played out for Daisy Bates. Tribe after tribe converged on the eight-foot tent that was her home — never to enter it, etiquette on both sides would forbid that — but to pour out their hearts. She became for them Kabbarli, the grandmother, to whom it was safe to tell tribal laws and disclose the secrets of dance and ritual that their own women must neither see nor know on pain of instant death.

She, too, tells a story of Baiame, but a Baiame shorn of Biblical overtones, an old gigantic ancestor lying asleep with his head on his arm who was one day to wake and gobble up everything that lives. This Baiame did not create the world. It was, quite simply, *there* — the tale goes no farther back than that — a flat, featureless, naked land on which the ancestors, by crossing and re-crossing it, raised up hills, rivers, stones and trees. Moreover, it ended at the horizon. A person coming to the perilous edge might lose his footing and be lost, descending, like Hopkins, the frightful gulf, the 'Cliffs of fall, no-man-fathomed.'

It was data such as these that Kabbarli, tucking Galileo away in a pocket, had to appear to accept. She was to look in vain for a father figure up in the sky. In *her* tribes, as she called them — allowing for the possibility that other tribes might have different beliefs — the only deity was a serpent god, or *woggal,* who dominated earth and heaven and punished evildoers. She kept her own counsel, treated the serpent with respect and watched the effect of its rule upon the people. Foreknowing, perhaps, the yet unwritten words of her countryman, W. B. Yeats, 'For ceremony is name of the rich horn/And custom of the spreading laurel tree,' she very early understood that for the aborigine, custom creates law and that to follow the patterns of behaviour prescribed by the ancestors and to live as the heroes did in the Dreamtime sustain both man and the earth. 'Within his own tribal laws,' she wrote, 'the aboriginal is bound hand and foot by tradition; beyond them he knows no ethics.' Everywhere, however, she found the basic doctrine of pre-existing souls, or life-germs, which referred to everything in nature — man, wombat, wild cherry, eagle. All was one, and one flesh. Kangaroo could be mother or brother, curlew or acacia a true-born sister. And Daisy Bates accepted all, not in any sense 'going native' but, while keeping the winged rod in mind, letting the two entwining serpents do their work within her.

The story of Kabbarli is an anthropological elegy. She knew that her *boggarli* (grandsons) were a dying race — if not into oblivion, at any rate into the sepulchre of white government. 'The aboriginal,' she wrote, 'can withstand all reverses of nature, except civilization.' So she spent her life birthing them peacefully into their death and preparing their memorial. She nursed the sick, fed the hungry from her meager store, encouraged the efforts of the old to get back to the place of their birth, lest their spirit trespass on strange country and the way be lost, at the moment of death, to the land of Kur'an'up — an island in the Western sea, not so far, one notes philologically, from the Irish Tir na n'Og. She learned by heart the songs of one group and taught them to another and handed on the *bamburu*, the crudely marked letter-sticks that were their only attempt at written language — a type, perhaps, of the Celtic ogham. She gathered and hid from the female members of the tribes the freely-given totems, the cult images she had seen raised on high by the elders before the prostrate warriors, primitive wafers at a primitive mass. Alone among women she became a spectator at the bloodletting, blood-drinking initiations of the young men and stood her ground, when mothers and sisters fled, at the dread voice of Nalga, the Bull-roarer, to look upon whose spirit means death. She was present at ritual corroborees and learned by heart the Dreamtime chants of which the aborigines no longer knew the meaning. She sat by, containing her abhorrence, when they killed and ate their newborn infants, while noting at the same time that cannibalism was sometimes performed as a funeral observance in honour of a deceased adult. Eater and eaten, all was one and Daisy Bates looked on without weighing, without imposing shame or guilt on a race that knew of neither.

And when at last she had to leave them — even Kabbarli, to their surprise, could not last for ever — with the totems, her notes and her set of Dickens packed into kerosene cases, she stood among them at a railway siding distributing, for the first time, money, calling each one by his native name and, to save them from 'heart crying,' singing *Now the Day is Over*. Her simplicity, as it had always been, was a reflection of their own.

So the train would have carried her away, not in their minds, to a distant city, but simply into the Dreamtime. They would go back to their tribal lands and pursue for a time their antique ways, settling nowhere, neither sowing nor reaping, subsisting on what the earth provided — opossum, mallee-leaf, wichetty grub. But before long they would find themselves strangers in their pristine world, their honey-groves trampled by the white man's herds, their ritual places desecrated. How would the earth fare, they must have wondered, with no one to propitiate the spirits in caves and lakes and hills? In the course of time, they would find themselves in reservations and eventually in tailored suits and parliamentary lobbies. A handful of the invading race, belatedly consulting its conscience, would demand for them a place in society — even encourage them to want it — collect the totem boards for museums and display the sacred grounds to tourists.

Lacking the old life-giving ritual, the antique images slept. The stories lost their sacred meaning. What Platypus said to Bandicoott and the exploits of the sugar-glider became amusements for white children. A race unchronicled for millenniums had stepped from timelessness into time and is now in the history books. And to be enshrined in the history books is to be, though numerically alive, mythologically dead. What was passing has passed.

But nothing is ultimately lost, as the aborigines themselves would once have known. Death on one plane may be life on another. In dying into law and order they have left a legacy behind for anyone who will take it — could it perhaps be modern man? — a gift from the ancestors, the concept of the Dreamtime. We need it. Dare we make the claim and shoulder the consequences? Faced with, or rather sustained by, the Dreamtime we could live in our existential world of fact, explanation and certainty, our darkened-by-brightness kingdom of knowing, in contact with our Unknowing. It could place us in the context of myth and remind us of what we like to forget — that life does not open and close like a book but is open-ended, mysterious, incapable of solutions. The dates on tombstones tell us little. They are segments of one unknown whole. The 'original face' of the Zen koan takes no account of birth or death; if once, it must be always. Before and after are subjective concepts, they relate to serial time. The Dreaming is objective Now, the everlasting nonexistence from which existence rises. If the aborigine's service to it was to live in *participation mystique* with stones and trees and ancestors, an entity only in so far as he was a member of a tribe, our service, perhaps, is to become aware of our separate, detribalized, individual selves. 'He who knows himself knows God,' said Jalal al-din Rumi, making the further unspoken assumption that God himself, knowing all, also needs to be known. To pursue this requires a dimension of myth, and for myth to exist it is necessary that between one second and another time must have a stop. It is in this nonmoment of wakefulness that man is on terms with paradox. The past, irreparable and gone, can be repaired by the present; harlot alone is the true virgin; Nirvana and Samsara are one; from the point of view of the farther side, *this* is the Other Shore.

Given this legacy of the Dreamtime it is we who must waken the images, absorb their ambivalent power and explore them in ourselves — cannibal, totem and taboo, the wild man and the sage. We have to become our own ancestors — no great feat in terms of myth — and receive from ourselves the Dreamtime teachings. They will tell us, again mythologically, that what is irreconcilable is at the same time reconciled; that our profane, desacralized life — a lawful process in linear time — is the seeding ground of the sacred; that if I forget thee, Jerusalem, Jerusalem nevertheless is there; that rock is gold that does not know itself; and that in the darkness of Kali Yuga fallen light is renewed.

First published in 'Parabola' on the theme of Creation, New York, 1977.

If She's Not Gone, She Lives There Still

A CONVERSATION BETWEEN
MICHAEL DAMES AND P L TRAVERS

PLT: I have always been deeply interested in stone circles, and I've just come back from Rollright, from a modern Druid ceremony for All Soul's day, which of course is the Druids' ancient New Year. The ceremony itself was hilarious: the Druids, male and female, dressed up like Scott of the Antarctic (it was bitterly cold) with their Druid cloaks over their furs, cavorting about among the stones and handing each other hard-boiled eggs. But the stones themselves! They were marvellous, magic, charged with power, ancient and serene, taking no notice of anybody. I longed to be left alone with them, to stay with them till sunset when, so the local people say, they go down to the river to bathe. Once, at Chartres, left alone by a party of friends who wanted to look at the crypt, I just sat there in the great silence feeling something — I still can't give it a name — gathering about me and the top of my head slowly rising. Something is going to be told me, I thought. And then the group came rushing back and my moment was gone for ever. When I told an archaeologist friend about this he said, 'No wonder. Don't you know of the old legend that under the cathedral is a Neolithic stone circle? That's why they built it there.' And I remember seeing Stonehenge, misty in the moonlight, and having something of the same feeling. A thirteen-year-old boy whom I was driving to his new public school stood beside me, and I wondered if it seemed to him, too, that the stones were lifting into the air, dancing, one could almost say. He was silent, but as we turned back to the car, he said, 'After that, I could stand anything. That circle makes one feel protected.' Now does all this, in your mind, refer to Avebury and Silbury? I feel quite sure it must.

MD: Yes; and I think your remarks about the slightly unsatisfactory quality of the Druid takeover of the Rollrights refer to what was for me the starting point.

The digging into the largest prehistoric man-made mountain in Europe, which is Silbury Hill in North Wiltshire, was begun on the basis that it contained a patriarchal burial of a prince, a ruler from the Bronze or Iron Age; and it wasn't until 1968, the last of many such digs, that conclusive proof came that in fact the monument was Stone Age or Neolithic, and so for that matter, as had been proved slightly earlier, was the adjacent stone circle, perhaps the greatest in the world, of Avebury. So what we're dealing with there is a group of monuments, within sight of each other, which by common consent formed the metropolis of Neolithic Britain. The first, and I would say possibly the greatest, British civilization was unquestionably based on the cult of the Great Goddess. Now, once the date was known, archaeologists asserted they would be able to link those tremendous physical remains to an accepted body of belief and a culture; but conspicuously this hasn't been done yet. I would say a conspiracy of silence has descended; so that about 1970, living in the area, I was overwhelmed by this sense of discontinuity, really, between the archaeologists' avowed intent to make cultural sense of what they'd found and what actually happened — which was *nothing*, in the way of interpretation. So I began to try to find out as much as I could about Neolithic culture, having had an archaeological training in the first place, but being vastly ignorant, as most students of archaeology are, about comparative religion, folklore, and ethnographic Stone Age communities. We just never come across the material in a conventional archaeological course.

PLT: That's what one misses in all archaeology. It demands the proof, but it doesn't care about the meaning.

MD: Well, I'm not against careful collection of data, but ultimately one has to have the modesty to carry that data to a point of view, a way of looking at it that is different from the narrowly rational — a point of view where symbolism in all its richness becomes rational. Now one of the things that struck me about Silbury was that all the effort had gone into concentrating on this vast conical mount with the flat top, and no effort at all had been directed toward the surrounding moat, which is 1100 feet long and curiously curved in a way that doesn't make any kind of engineering sense. But this great 'quarry', if you like, fills up with water, (even though there's 15 feet of silt in the ditch now) regularly once a year. It occurred to me that what one was looking at there was a monument which was also an image, an image of the Great Mother whose body was defined by this lake, and whose belly, or full womb, was the mound; so that the Harvest Mother, pregnant, was there lying on the ground as a picture. And not only a picture, but a picture that *moved*, with the help of sunlight and moonlight; the reflected strength of the two eyes in the sky comes to the Mother and helps her completion. By saying that I wish to indicate two things: first of all, the long axis of her reclining body is bang on an east-west line, that marvelous spindle of equilibrium between the seasons where night and day are of equal duration. And then if you go there at the quarter day, Lammas, the traditional start of harvest in Britain, you'll see the moon coming up over an adjacent spring and striking its first light on her water thigh at exactly the place where you expect a child's head to emerge. Then as the night goes on, this flicker of moonlight moves around the Mother, onto her knee, and crosses a narrow natural causeway of undisturbed chalk before filling up progressively a 'child' moat, a little disconnected piece of moat which is hugged tight against the belly mound of the hill itself; and the moon goes on through the night and eventually sets on the breast, so that the last moonlight you see is a flicker of white on the breast. I regard this as an intentional, *kinetic* representation of the harvest birth. The child isn't born to starve, but to drink; and simultaneously on the 100 feet of flat summit there's a little cornfield with room for the first fruits festival to take place.

PLT: Doesn't that refer to the old idea that 'she' — (I call her *she* because I feel very strongly with you that whatever this is, it is a maternal symbol) — that the mound was constructed 'while a posset of milk was seething?'

MD: Yes, that's fascinating. The folklore fragment which you quote was recorded by John Aubrey in the mid-seventeenth century, and seems completely random and meaningless — that a hill was built while a posset was seething; but it really fits in precisely. What is the posset? It is the underworld, if you like, the world beneath the lake, the world trapped in the rock; and at harvest, with the coming of the right moment, the milk swirls up and creates a mound of joyful food, a sacred liquid. And of course the cult of the corn dolly, which now fills our gift shops, once filled the reality of farming with imagery which went on from the harvest back into the farmhouse and the barn in winter, and then was returned to the field to be ploughed in the following spring, creating a great cycle, which I think the adjacent monuments helped to celebrate.

But you were asking me, before we started taping, about the name Silbury, weren't you?

PLT: Yes. You say in your book that first of all they thought that there was buried there some mythological figure called King Sil.

MD: Yes, that's right. There are two ways of looking at the King Sil fragment. One can think of it as a later patriarchal injection which developed as time went on, because King Sil was transformed in the eighteenth century into a golden monarch on a horse, full-sized.

PLT: Transformed, in the mind of the folk, you mean.

MD: Yes, but I think there's also a possibility, at least, of an original theme there, insofar as the goddess worldwide always has a male consort, and if he's a consort of corn, he's golden. So I haven't quite made my mind up about which of those to choose!

PLT: I would accept that; it's a good mythological analogy, and perhaps that was in the folk. When I say 'the folk', you know, I mean naturally the people of that time, who lived in fields and hills; but, for that matter, we're all 'folk' — the people who walk in the streets. We forget it; we despise the term. But really we ourselves are the folk and quite capable of absorbing this mythological material when given to us.

MD: I think that's very important indeed. We're not really dealing with history, something chronologically remote, but with that eternal present that real myth deals with. Certainly my working on Silbury has helped me to endure living in the city, rather than the opposite; because all forms of earthly bounty are basically holy whether they come in cans or carts. But one of the things that interests me particularly about the Wiltshire monuments around Silbury is their unique relationship to the natural land forms. In central Wiltshire the downs undulate in a marvellously anthropomorphic manner, and it does rather seem like an extended body going on mile after mile. Indeed, the Wiltshire place-names emphasize that that was how the 'folk' viewed their countryside. Now when we're asked why did they choose the particular locality of Avebury to make this supreme effort, I think the answer lies in two springs which are very close by: Swallowhead and the adjacent Waden Spring. These two springs happen by a stupendous geographical fluke to line up with the Lammas quarter day sunrise, 70° east and north in one direction, and the Lammas moonset at 250° east and north in the other. So that presented with this 'cue' by the goddess landscape, they responded with the supreme statement of this architectural image very close by. It is an interesting fact that water from Swallowhead Spring was taken to the top of Silbury and drunk on Mothering Sunday* as late as 1850.

PLT: You know, that brings us right back to a study I recently made of the nursery rhyme, 'Jack and Jill.' Pondering upon this, I thought, why would they go *up* the hill? Water notoriously flows down to the lowest place. Then I discovered a clue in Sweden. Jack and Jill were supposed to have been seen by Mani, the moon, going up the hill to take water from the sacred well of Brigir. So they were taken up and put in the moon, and the Swedes think that, where we see a man in the moon, they see Jack and Jill carrying the water. And you say in your book that even quite lately, perhaps a hundred years ago, people were carrying fresh spring water up to the top of Silbury to drink it there ceremonially and religiously. Don't you think it refers?

MD: Absolutely. Isn't that amazing? Yes, I think there's a strong possibility of that.

How to get on into the next season I suppose is the problem that farmers worry about; although it happens inevitably. I don't know whether you would agree that the basic myth of the world seems to be to bring people to the next threshold with a sense of its rightness and its appropriateness in time, rather than to have any kind of jerkiness or trauma about the change. It's very interesting to me, having spent so long working on Silbury, that from the top you can see this marvellous long barrow, which is 330 feet long, on the adjoining down — the West Kennet long barrow; and if one accepts the credibility of architecture-as-image (and certainly people like Philip Rawson and Vincent Scully and Joseph Campbell would seem to accept that), then what is this long thing? Well, I suggest in my latest book, *The Avebury Cycle*, that we're looking there at the 'Hag' — or I think your word was 'Crone' — and the crone with its long spine of sandstone boulders, covered with chalk, has a hollow end to it; in this case, the funeral chambers of West Kennet long barrow. The chambers are five-lobed; and they are a dreadful place. They were visited well over a thousand years, as archaeologists have proved, and the population wandered amongst the rotting remains of jumbled-up corpses; a terrible, terrible spectacle. And yet isn't this just the way to wisdom that

---

* The fourth Sunday in Lent when motherhood and the Mother of the Gods were especially honoured.

in certain Tantric traditions is known to be both necessary and, in the end, loving?

PLT: Indeed, in the Tantric scripture the Great Mother represents this, too. And when you talk about the long barrows, aren't you telling also of those you can find in Ireland? I have been in the Brugh of Angus, which is now called New Grange. They have made it a place fit for tourists now, with electric light, and enlarged the opening so that people can stand up and walk through into the sacred inner chamber. But in the old days, I remember having to crawl through that narrow birth-passage, on my hands and knees, with a candle. And in the central chamber — I don't know whether you've seen it; it's all carved and marked with the most mysterious hieroglyphs. I was alone in there with the man who had persuaded me to this awful adventure. And I was overcome with the vibrations and the sense of power that was in this place. I could hardly stand it. It was very like, but much greater than, what I felt at Chartres. One was overcome by these tremendous — oh, sensations isn't the right word! One's whole body was vivified; it was almost unbearable.

MD: That's interesting: the comparison you bring up with New Grange as it's now called, in that the long tunnel there, landing up in this cruciform chamber, seems as you say like being born in reverse — being born to the underworld. And that's why I find the shape of the West Kennet long barrow funeral chambers absolutely fascinating, because they seem to be an enlarged version of the squatting goddess image, which is usually connected with birth — many authorities regard the Neolithic figurines as portrayals of the act of parturition — only now in her deathly aspect, hidden within this long barrow mound. Here is the squatting goddess as receiver into the world of chaos, into the world of the collapse of vegetable form, into the world of ploughing and winter. Round the chambers runs a river of dry stone wallings, which have been carried there from 30 miles away, which I think simulate the dry river which the Old Hag of Scottish folklore is said to have created at the winter quarter day, at Martinmas; with her skinny arm and thin wand she touched the rivers and they turned to stone. And here one sees such a river as part of the architecture.

I suppose at this time of year — here we are sitting in the darkest part of the year — one always longs for spring. One of the big questions about the Avebury Cycle is how did they effect this wonderful miracle of springtime? My scrutiny of the evidence seems to suggest that it was effected with great difficulty and concentrated effort. Many primitive communities divide their adolescents, boys from girls, and the boys and girls both and separately die to childhood and are born as adults.

PLT: I'd like to know this — did they have, in your thinking, a rite of passage by which they made the transit from childhood to adolescence, to maturity? Have we any evidence of this?

MD: Well, I think the archaeological hardware is there. In the case of the female incarceration at the onset of puberty, there is a temple called the Sanctuary ideally suited to such a function. It was a conical hut built of wood, 65 feet in diameter — that incidentally is the distance from Swallowhead Spring to the main river, and it's also the diameter of a wattle ring buried in the very core of Silbury. So standing in the doorway of the Sanctuary hut, an adolescent girl was standing in the hollow form of the kernel of Silbury in a hut which archaeologists reconstruct in exactly the same shape as Silbury itself, only of course much smaller; and she could see her maternal future silhouetted against the skyline in the shape of the chalk mound which overlaid the wattle bands at the core of Silbury.

PLT: Would you say (I know we only speak mythologically) that Avebury with its long avenues and its great circle of stones and its inner sanctuaries of sun and moon, stands in relation to Silbury as maiden stands to mother?

MD: I think that is quite likely, with the slight qualification that it is Maiden and her Bridegroom in relation to Mother. If we got as far as the Sanctuary for the girls, the stone avenue called the West Kennet avenue leads from there to the Avebury Henge, and an equivalent avenue called the Beckhampton leads to the same Avebury Henge: this massive ditch and ring of standing stones, some of them over 14 feet high, within which there are two circles. Now I think of the Avebury Henge as a wedding ring, both in the human sense and also the marriage of cattle, and also the wedding of the binary opposites of yin and yang coming together to make the start of a new generation of happenings. In saying that I hope to establish what is well known in every other part of the world where Neolithic culture has been studied: namely, that the synchronization of the farming year — the activity of ploughing the soil and seeding it and watching the crop rise and eventually harvesting it — is synchronized, I believe, in imagery, with stages in the human life cycle. When we get to the Henge, we get to coitus, to the lovematch; and the shape of the outer bank, which again, like Silbury, is water-filled — that's why they dug down so far; it's now silt-filled — the shape I believe is based on that U-shape that you can see on the goddess's apron in Minoan Crete; you can see it in India and certainly you can see it in Swallowhead Spring. That design is equivalent to the human female vulva from which all waters flow. Now the male avenue, Beckhampton Avenue, is extended into that female containing-shape in a feature known as the D feature: a setting of stones within one of the two internal circles. So that architecturally again, the marriage, the serpentine energy of spring — in the Celtic tradition, the maiden was the serpent — these serpentine energies meet and coalesce at Avebury. And from Avebury, if you stand at the centre of that great temple, you can just see the summit of Silbury hill over the horizon.

PLT: You see what's in store for you, in fact! You see what's waiting.

MD: Exactly. That's right. Before literacy, you may manifest that which you desired in art and architecture. And architecture is the mother of the arts; it contains the smaller icons; it is the platform for human performance. And it is an astounding grief to me that we've deprived ourselves of this knowledge of architecture as a symbolic imagery and are content with mere building. What a deprivation to inflict upon oneself willingly! I don't understand it. About two years after I had begun my exploration into the meaning of the monuments, I had the great good fortune to come across Cassirer's great book, *The Philosophy of Symbolic Forms*, and with delight I realized that the principles of mythic space awareness which he elucidated there completely confirmed my gradually accumulating convictions concerning the nature of sacred space in and between the Wiltshire monuments. In particular, his statement that 'the development of the mythical feeling of space always starts from the opposition of day and night, light and darkness', fitted exactly my feelings about the primary natural symbol in the area, the Swallowhead Spring. There, the black hole in the white chalk rock is the unforgettable doorway between two worlds, inviting movement in both directions. In fact, the annual fluctuation in the water table yearly enacts this interplay — the stream sinking back into the ground in autumn, and spouting forth anew in early spring. In the Silbury and Avebury monuments, the movement between dark and light also has an aquatic aspect. Flights of Neolithic steps carved out with antler tines lead from below the water level in the deeply quarried moats at the Silbury water breast, and at the marriage henge. Walking through the surface of the magic water mirror, the population could enter the dark liquid body of the Lady of the Lake, and emerge with an intuitive and factually correct understanding of the source of all life. Equally, one is led to realize that far from being an arbitrary choice, the preference for an east-west axis in monument planning is another consequence of the light-dark structure of the year at the gateway between winter and summer, marking sunrise and sunset positions at the equinoxes, the perfect equilibrium. Similarly, the light climax of each day and of every full-moon night registers due south when those bodies are highest in the sky. Is it no more than an accident that the bridegroom's door to the Avebury Henge, and the vulva of the Silbury birth goddess, *and* the sacred Swallowhead Spring, *and* sun and moon at zenith, are in alignment, due north-south?

PLT: All you're saying leads me to think of the extraordinarily natural order in the way of life of these Neolithic people. They followed the laws of sun and moon and seasons and in that way they must have served their goddess, served her faithfully — because wasn't she their mother? And faithfully she gave them increase. Now look what's happened to us: the goddess has become the state. Nobody shows it any duty or service; everybody says 'I want, I want', and expects to be freely given to, as once the Mother gave — but in return for service.

MD: Yes. I think one thing that follows from what you've just said is the way we tend nowadays to separate the cerebral from the physical, which I suppose is the legacy of Christianity, that activity of division; whereas in what one can discover of the pattern of life in Neolithic communities, there's no such separation. What confirmation can we find of this merging of physical and intellectual at the Avebury monuments? I think one can see them as double images, quite legitimately. I've spoken of the Avebury horseshoe as a vulva with phallus incorporated into it. But it is equally possible to see it as 'skull' with two inner circles as eye sockets or eyes. Similarly if you look at Silbury itself from the east, it's the squatting Mother with the moat. If you look at it from the west, it's a huge eyeball in a water head, so that the division between spirit and body which we've suffered from for the last two thousand years seems never to have been an issue there at all. And the iconography supports this total fusion of those two aspects of human existence.

PLT: The sense of sacredness must have been within them, not only in the shape of the earth, their tellurian temple. This reminds me of something that was written in the early seventeenth century by a writer named Samuel Purchas, in his book *Microcosmos*. He says, 'Why then, O man, know thyself and know all things. Thou hast thy body, a book of nature, and carriest a little model of the greater world continually about thee.' Wasn't this what Avebury and Silbury were telling us, that in a sense, we're in the Great Mother; and alternately, the Great Mother is in us. We can't escape. **MD:** Yes; and I'm convinced (with Lévi-Strauss and Cassirer) that the Neolithic peoples knew that, and brought the physical reality of the body into their architecture as a mode of measurement. In Avebury parish I find that they sought to construct their buildings using a linear module derived from a fusion of the two aspects of physical reality uppermost in their experience — namely the human body, and the external environment understood as a superhuman body. I believe that this fusion was effected by that most physical of measuring devices, the human stride. Plainly they strode everywhere, but in seeking a sacred module as the basis of an architecture whose function was to heighten the sacredness of the local natural endowment, they might be expected to turn to the landscape at its most potently active — that is, to the two springs of Swallowhead and Waden, and to pace out the trickle of waters from chalk source to the river Kennet. These tributaries, the life-ways of the Goddess-landscape running so memorably from the underworld, were regarded as sacred till the eighteenth century. Today these tributaries, measured in abstract (yet sensuously derived) feet, are 65 feet and 400 feet respectively. Is it just coincidence that both these modules occur over and over again in the major dimensions of all the Avebury monuments? For example, 65 feet is the diameter of Silbury core fence, the diameter of the Sanctuary hut, the width of the West Kennet long barrow facade, and the distance between the Avebury circles. The Silbury mound height is 65' ×2, and dozens of examples of simple multiples appear to be present throughout the ensemble.

The validity of turning to the springs for measuring rods would have been greatly enhanced for them by reason of their alignment on the sunrise-moonset quarter day axis, 70°-250° east of north; and the local building module would have received some of its authority from the celestial hemisphere and some from the underworld, at critical moments in the annual cycle of each. Since the buildings themselves were each designed to engage in a dialogue between Above and Below, balanced about the soil line (the farmers' equator), the rationale of a measured loyalty to the *genius loci* becomes strong. In particular contrast to our own abstract numerology, the plotting of Neolithic sacred space depends, I believe, on populating the landscape with figures, *human* figures, prepared to walk the superhuman geography, and to extend what was found into an architecture loyal to the place of its foundation. The awareness of space, and measured space as *active* rather than static, is also brought into focus by the two lengths of running water, whose vitality was subsequently embodied in, and reflected by, the kinetic, living architecture, as a genetic inheritance.

Around the four great monuments we've been discussing, there is an even larger image of the Great Mother, I believe, composed of 26 long barrows and certain other circles and causeway camps, which occupies a 25 square mile tract of downland, and all these are Neolithic sites. They have their arms, or horns if you like, along the crests of the downs, overlooking the Vale of Pewsey, and from there the whole majestic figure can be seen stretching away into the distance. In their very core, in their gut, are the monuments: Silbury, West Kennet long barrow, the avenues of the Avebury Henge, as almost internal tracts to this larger image — although each of the internal monuments operates as an image in its own right. So as you say, it goes from the very smallest individual to the very largest thing imaginable, the universe. And all intermediate stages were accessible to these people, because they had this basic micro-macro view of things, which we talk about rather glibly perhaps nowadays without allowing for the physical outcome of that idea in the view of primitive society: namely, that that whole territory, that whole country was a figure, a body. One can hear the peoples in the Sudan today speaking of the marsh areas of their lands as the Mother's groin and the upland mountains as her breasts. The key to primitive geography of the world can be seen in such a group of monuments as we have there.

The other thing is in the sense of space: all of these things laid out in space; I think it's wrong to isolate space from time. Sacred space, I believe, is a marriage of space with time. And the space becomes sacred at certain prescribed times, and then becomes prosaic again until the next bringing together of space and time. The word 'Silbury' itself comes from the Old English 'blessed time', 'harvest time' — so the Silbury moat lights up for the birth moment at that blessed time.

I think that's what I feel about sacred space in that particular area.

PLT: The poet and sage A. E. used to say to me when I was very young, 'The earth is a living being.' You're actually saying that this is what the people of the Neolithic times thought, not only of their temples, but of their planet.

MD: Exactly. Yes, they needed the temples to confirm and bring into sharper focus that which they believed already about the world in general. For that reason, people came from all over the British Isles to the Avebury Cycle of monuments, as has been shown by archaeological finds. It was truly a national focus for eternity, the year rolling on as a great circle of interlocking events. Indeed it was still being used in Saxon and medieval times, so that it had an enormously long life-span, as is right for a farming cycle attached to the Great Goddess who seems able to skip with ease across racial divisions and political upheavals.

PLT: Oh, she does! She is mentioned in Taoists texts as the Mountain Mother. There's your Silbury again. In Japan, she's a peach tree. The oldest fairy tale in Japan is called 'Peach Boy' and he's born of this peach tree. In China, the symbol for the Great Mother is jade. It's the symbol at once of death and immortality. You find her everywhere. You can't take a step without her! In my field, which I think of as the fairy tale, you can always tell the antiquity of a tale when it has, as its chief character, a woman. She always refers to the Great Mother. For instance, in 'Snow White', 'Cinderella', 'Allerleirauh', and above all 'The Sleeping Beauty.'

MD: This is marvellous, because the fragments of the tattered remains of the English folk tradition are really little episodes in this great story, the only central story from which all other stories derive — that of the seasonal metamorphosis of the central divine being and her male consort.

PLT: We see it in one of the oldest English anonymous poems:

> *I sing of a maiden who is mateless,*
> *King of all kings, her son she chose.*

She chose — which means, in essence, she accepted — accepted in every sense. He's clearly lover as well as son.

MD: Yes. Even in post-medieval times there has been, up until the Puritan revolution, a capacity for the Great Mother to survive in amongst, and infuse a certain kind of life into, Christianity on the one hand and the most uninformed folk appetites on the other. There is a wonderful value there.

I think if one looks for a folk image to set alongside the two stone avenues going to the Avebury Wedding Ring, one can't do better than go to a village in Staffordshire called Abbots Bromley, where dancers including Maid Marian and Dirty Bet go around and beat

the bounds of the parish and form two snaky dances which lead
into a circle — two serpents coalescing in a circle. It seems to be
a very important theme in folk dancing. It's certainly true there,
and the horned aspect of the goddess is also part of that rite because
most of the dancers carry huge stag horns or reindeer horns.

PLT: Isn't it so that these dances — I've seen them myself — are
all performed with the utmost gravity, as though they were a
service to something that perhaps the dancers have forgotten?

MD: Yes, there's a stateliness about them.

PLT: Wouldn't you say that perhaps all dance, however profane,
is even if unconsciously, done before the Lord? Remember in the
Apocryphal Book of St John, in the Hymn of Jesus where he makes
the disciples stand about him in a ring. They dance and sing —
strophe and antistrophe.

MD: Yes, because what is dance? It is the kinetic involvement of
the individuals in a thing greater than themselves, a pattern which
can turn from solar orb into serpentine riverflow with an ordered
measure to it, the bringing of order into the random chaos of
overwhelming experience. I know from having camped in a
thunderstorm near Silbury that one can be scared out of one's wits
by the alarming power of natural forces even in the mild and
melodious southern English countryside.

At all times the community has sought to order this in an
affirmative way and to face the terrors of existence, and to come
to terms with them.

PLT: Do you think that these ideas that have grown up in you
around Silbury and Avebury are still available to the folk? Are there
any legends connected with Avebury and Silbury, such as there
are with the Rollright stones who go down to the river to bathe
and to drink? What do the people round about think? Is she still
the holy place?

MD: No, in the organized sense of Mother Goddess worship —
I don't think there's any such activity; but in the broader sense,
the Neolithic realities, what were they? Moving clouds, rain,
sunshine — things coming out of the ground, things dying into
the ground. Those are our realities. We still eat food from the
ground — it comes from nowhere else.

PLT: Though for us, it comes from the supermarket.

MD: Ah, but the supermarket *is* the ground, except its moved
sideways slightly! Similarly, the movements of the population to
the coasts at Lammas, the great July-August rush. I can't bring
myself to despise the seaside paraphernalia because if we despise

our sun at our seaside, then we have no right to speak joyfully of the Neolithic, because the physical realities still potentially contain as much sacredness as they ever did.

PLT: Well — perhaps it's not so much that she is lost to us, but (aside from the sense in which you're speaking) we are in a way lost to her, except insofar as a handful of us remember our service to her. There is said to be the remnants of a Celtic tribe still living in the wilds of Derbyshire where life is lived according to the laws of the Great Mother. She's worshipped there. I heard about it and I promised I wouldn't try to track them down, though I would very much like to talk to them. Perhaps it's true that like the seasons, all things come around again; I think it *is* true. There's an old nursery rhyme that you yourself quoted in *The Silbury Treasure:*

> *There was an old woman lived under a hill,*
> *And if she's not gone, she lives there still.*

MD: Yes. And I think that for everyone born of woman, the relationship between the individual and the containing maternal shape is so fundamental during our first nine months of pre-life that it is impossible to eradicate it from any group of adults in a complete and decisive and final way. It represents, even in its submerged state, a form of reality which attaches us both to our literal mothers and to the earth in general.

PLT: So, at Silbury, she lives there still.

MD: Right!

First published in 'Parabola' on the theme of Sacred Space, New York, 1978.

Letter to a
Learned Astrologer

RUPERT, do you remember the wine and the candles and you poring over the charts and saying, 'Something is wrong. The hour, the month, the year, the place. You are simply not a Leo.'

'Do you mean that I was left on a doorstep? But there are records. You have seen them.'

'Yes, yes, I know all that. But where is the swing of the tasselled tail, the roar in the jungle, the proud mane?'

'You are right,' said Hilary, not at all as an astrologer but as a man convinced of the truth of his own instinct. 'She could never, ever, be a lion. That defenseless smile!'

'Yes,' you went on. 'And when Helen and I went to Greece and asked her what we should bring back — "Something that costs a penny," she said. And the job we had finding it! Leo would have wanted something grander.' It was clear that the Lion was not your favourite sign.

So, together, you tried to remake the past, while Helen and I, mute as caryatids, and no wiser — but perhaps no more foolish, either — looked on as you juggled with times and planets; ripped me untimely from the womb to birth me, according to your joint assumptions, into a more appropriate sign.

And the planets would not budge.

You sighed and set to work on the soufflé. 'Sun in mid-heaven, all that largesse in the zenith, but you don't really live your sign. No swanning around. No king of the beasts. It may, of course, be due to your Saturn. But Saturn is the great Teacher and the signs say you are willing to learn. It's as if — and I'm not now being scientific — as if you felt there was something missing.'

'Well, what's in the mid-hell?' I asked.

'Nadir,' you corrected me. 'Nothing. It's quite empty.'

Something stirred. Not a flash of light. I have never been to

Damascus. It was more as if an inward glass had very gently cracked. A thought went blowing through me that was wiser than my own. Quick to come and quick to go among the wine and candles.

Afterwards, you cast the Tarot and took down the lines, as you always did, whenever I threw the *I Ching*. I was shy of doing either by myself, a feeling of insufficiency that left me when you were part of the process.

'Ah, that,' you said, 'is your Mars trine Venus. The black fish with white eye, white fish with black. You will always want the two of them together in the circle. But you know that. Chart or no chart.'

We all laughed. Vive la différence!

And again that conceptual cracking of glass.

It took me years to learn what it meant. And I could not talk to you about it. You had gone away among wandering stars whose courses only Helen could chart. And, in any case, would I have told you? To speak of anything till it is ripe — that is dangerous. Maybe, indeed, it's dangerous ever to speak at all.

So I let things go on fermenting in me till gradually I came to understand that the two fish function on many levels. It did not occur to you that night, when we laughed at Mars and Venus, that, as well as those planetary lovers, the South would naturally long for the North and the zenith not be satisfied until it was aligned with the nadir, nor the sun content without the dark.

Ever since I can remember, that full mid-heaven had for me been empty. As a child I used to dread the sunset because of the longing that came with it. 'There must be something else,' I would say, not at all knowing what it was, but knowing, too, that as far as the wind blows and the sky is blue I would go and find it.

I seized upon any opportunity that would set me on my way. One came when a special issue of the *Children's Encyclopedia* — sent by some relative from England — slipped from the postman's saddlebags and disgorged a letter addressed to me. 'Dear child,' it began sweetly, in a manly human hand; and went on to outline the delectable subjects the editor was preparing, inviting me to explore with him the worlds that were opening up before me and earnestly wishing for my future happiness. It was signed 'Affectionately, Arthur Mee.' I had received my first love letter.

In vain did the grown-ups rudely assure me that it wasn't written to me. Thousands of children would receive the same letter which, moreover, was not written by hand but by some sort of machine. I did not believe them. To do so would be to accept betrayal. Here was a man who understood exactly what I needed. So I wrote to this Arthur Mee, explaining my situation — as far as I then understood it — and asked him to send me the fare to England. (How else could I go exploring with him?) He would not have to provide for me, I assured him, for I planned to sweep crossings, like Little Joe.

The answer was long in coming — and when it came, unsatisfactory. He had no real wish, apparently, to go with me anywhere, he had no continuing concern for my welfare; there was no sign of cheque or postal order; merely an injunction — a great-aunt's rather than a lover's — to be a good girl and help my mother. Signed Somebody Something, Secretary. And not even by hand.

Naturally, I was reprimanded. Not for Soliciting Strange Men but for Bothering That Dear Mr Mee.

Years later, I was to learn that Dear Mr Mee had detested children but, according to someone who had worked with him, had delighted in Mary Poppins. I wonder what course my life would have followed — Robert Frost's 'road not taken'! — if he had delighted in me.

It was a setback. But children take such things in their stride. They are familiar with the word No from the time they are in the womb. Another door, I knew, would open. And, to my mind, it did.

Walking on the hillside one day, I came upon a group of gypsies. Now, gypsies, I knew, were apt to steal children. They also travelled the world. The juxtaposition of two such facts seemed to me auspicious. But these were not tinker gypsies. They were creatures such as I had never seen — tall, stately men in blue gowns and women veiled in black. Looking back, I see that they must have been Mohammedans, with their peaked tents and a camel browsing. Any child stolen by such people would be taking part in a pilgrimage — or perhaps a circus, I wasn't sure which — that would, without doubt, end up in England. So I stationed myself on the edge of the camp, waiting, like something on a bargain counter, to be speedily snapped up. Nothing happened. The noble people went about their chores, quietly, taking no notice of me and addressing each other in some strange tongue. Shocked at this lack of enterprise, I took the affair into my own hands, marched towards the tallest man and — prompted by an atavistic impulse very far from childish — unlatched my sandals and offered them to him. If he took those — obscurely, I was sure of it — he would certainly take me. A veiled woman gave me a kindly smile as he turned the sandals in his hands to see how they were made. Then he bent down, deftly buckled them on my feet and gently but determinedly directed me to the road. It was impossible to misunderstand. They were not going to take me across the world. I was there for the plucking and the gypsies did not want me.

'Not surprisingly,' was the dry comment, when I reached home.

Families, perhaps luckily, have a unique facility for minimizing capacities and aspirations simply by disbelieving in them, making them butts for witticisms. The wise child quickly learns to dissemble and keep its dream safe and intact.

Never for a moment was my intention shaken. But gradually I came to see that 'Ask and ye shall receive' is no penny-in-the-slot affair, request at one end, gift-package at the other. No one would take me bodily to where I wanted to go — which was not merely, I came to sense, a geographical locality but as well an inward country. I would have to do more growing up, begin to put away childish things and find the money myself. Time, not always maleficent, helped. It is, by its nature, on the side of Necessity. And when, at last, pullet still rather than full-grown fowl, I stood in London with ten pounds in hand — five of which I promptly lost — the ancestors dwelling in my blood who, all my life, had summoned me with insistent eldritch voices, murmured together, like contented cats. In my person, the Antipodes had come to their own Antipodes. So, rejecting the fairy-tale injunction to sip no sup in the Underworld, I drank deep of the sunless North and was ready to take the consequences. Persephone, reft from her sunny field, taken below by her dark bridegroom — from corn in the ear to corn at the root — did not eat of the pomegranate more readily. If, later, at Eleusis, she was to be co-equal with her mother at the elevation of the grain, this was the thing she had to do. And also take the consequences.

It had not been easy. But then I had never expected ease. Was it that old guru, Saturn, who coined the phrase, later pilfered by Yeats, 'The fascination of what's difficult' and taught it to those 'afflicted' by him, to show them how to live their own sign? I throve on what was difficult, the difficult man, the difficult child; the arduous exploring of the Empty Quarter, your nadir, where no planets were — where, perhaps, (dear Brutus!) it was necessary that I should become my own planet; the discovery that in lack lies treasure if you are willing to find it; and that by confronting the Unknown — not as though it were knowable but as an absolute

—one receives, oh, intimations; the hard-won realization that life, like Coyote, is a trickster, conning one into expectations that have no basis in reality; that there is nothing to expect, nothing to be gained, and nobody to blame; that there are no rights of any kind but only a purpose to be served — was that my 'something else'? I had to learn that to be vulnerable, naked and defenseless is the only way to safety; that the sieve knows a lot about water, emptiness of plenitude, the Erynnes of kindliness. This is easy to say, less so to accept. But one can grow ripe on difficulty as a plum grows ripe on sunlight.

Your charts were not wrong. I am a Leo. And your instinct was right. I am not a lion. I carry no golden shawl on my shoulders. I have never felt I was king of the beasts. But the lion, remember, keeps a hand-maiden — not consort, she's no queen of the jungle — the nakedest of all creatures, kin to him only in one aspect, the tassel on the tail. But it is she who does the work, kills the zebra, gives the cubs what they need and him his fabled share. She also — my zoologist affirms what I inwardly know — reserves a fair portion for herself. Servant she may be, but not slave. Naked, she has her pride. Do not offer her less than her due. She will not accept it.

And so, I owe you a debt. That night, all unconsciously, you revealed to me — though I did not realize it till much later — the dual nature of the signs. But for your doubts about times and places I might have gone through life tossing a non-existent mane and chafing at the burden of it. As it is, I travel light and keep Delos in my mind.

There, in that island, where nobody may be born or die (nor presumably — though I have not heard this explicitly stated — participate in that third process that reconciles birth and death) stands the avenue of lions. But *are* they lions, or *solely* lions, stripped as they are down to the bone of the regal vestments, their manes — if they *are* manes — simply tokens, mere metaphors of the chisel? Have we not here a twofold symbol of the island's twofold lord — neither lion nor lioness, but sacerdotally both — priest-and-priestess of Apollo and Artemis, son-and-daughter in each marble shape of the son and daughter of the sun?

Perhaps you think this irrelevant. I have no right to be right, remember — nor wrong, either, for that matter. But, knowing the charts, you will also know that I cannot evade the two fish. Therefore, I have a need to question something I cannot help but call the monolordship of the zodiac. All right — we have Pisces and Gemini, both pairs astrologically always assumed to be males. But can there be any place, process, activity, concept where the two fish, complementary opposites, have not, by the very nature of things, each their own particular sphere? Is not every sign lawfully partnered by its counterpart, its mute spouse, leman, affinity?

On a fishmonger's slab, a female trout cannot be distinguished from the male; on a dish they taste exactly the same. But in their own watery world, they must surely function differently; and, astrologically, as bearers of portent, if the signs have influence at all, this difference must work upon the souls born under Pisces.

Aries, Taurus, Capricorn, are, like Leo, the grandees, and easily accessible to this concept. They are, let us say, the coverers. One can see their analogues, the covered, in every field and pasture, creatures bearing appellations that the world has turned into epithets. What woman, under the sign of the Ram, would confess to being a sheep; a thing that bleats, stands in queues and obeys even a dog? Yet if you have ever lived near a flock you will know that each sheep speaks with her own voice; attacks your backside if you annoy her; teaches her young to suckle kneeling and knows that Christ did not say to Peter 'Feed my wolverines.'

And who, when asked her zodiacal identity, will say 'I am a cow!' Yet the cow gives milk, of all creatures is the most meditative, thinking things over in mind and stomach without presuming to come to conclusions. If it could be said of me what Robert Louis Stevenson said of her, I would feel I could die happy.

> *And blown by all the winds that pass*
> *And wet with all the showers,*
> *She walks amid the meadow grass*
> *And eats the meadow flowers.*

As for the she-Capricorn, will she admit to Nanny-Goat? Yet Nanny, too, ruminates and is milked; fosters younglings not of her breed; is quick to attack, slow to obey; compared to the billy, smells like a rose and has a digestion that can cope as easily with the lid of a kettle as with a blade of grass. Strong, earthy, dauntless, affectionate — no bad way to live by the sign of the Goat, if you're willing to assume the name.

As to the Twins, traditionally the lily-white boys a-clothed all in green-o, Castor and Pollux, tamers of horses — well, one can but wonder! The abstract symbol, which more often reveals the inner meaning than the figurative version of a sign, shows Gemini

simply as the Roman II. If *Green Grow the Rushes-o* had rather
said 'the lily-white *children*,' it would have come closer to the truth.
The Gemini-she can also tame horses — indeed, it is part of her
role to do so — but her horses will be of a different colour and she
will tame them differently. Indirectly. With hint and suggestion.
Going forward one moment and withdrawing the next. Never let
him see that you want him, and the colt will come sniffing at the
bridle.

With Cancer, we are again in water and, as with Pisces, who am
I, creature of earth, to know how a sea-thing functions? Crabs move
sideways. But this biological fact merely assures me — myself a
lover of indirection as a way to find direction out — that on the
broad beaches and down in the ocean, the sideways-going of the
female would be somehow different from that of the male, sidling,
devious, oblique. Here, again, it is best to stay with the symbol
which, without words, pours its meaning out, to be apprehended
if not understood. Hath the rain a father? Who can know the heart
of a crustacean?

Let us pass Lord Leo by. We have, in a sense, dealt with him. And
he will not notice our neglect. As male — and all but a few females
— he is wholly concerned with his own grandeur, and hedged with
his kingly divinity.

So we come to her, the one sign in the zodiac traditionally
presented in feminine guise. But why? Are there no male virgins?
And what does virginity mean here — the nun, the monk, chords
of *Ave Maria* only, no *Hymen O Hymenae*? Surely not. It is possible
to be profligate and still in a state of Virgo grace. The clue lies —
again! — in the abstract sign, so like — one cannot but feel it was
by intention — that of Scorpio; the M with the tail turned inwards,
to screen, protect, preserve untouched; and the M with the tail
turned outwards, to touch, to sting, to remind. Does not that
inverted tail suggest that in both male and female some part should
be kept intact, unravished, his or her idiosyncratic own, the secret
seed of the self? The woman who gives — or inflicts? — her All will
feel betrayed by and revile the man who will not part with his. If
All is given, what is left? An emptiness that nothing will fill, not
even resentment. On the other hand, the man who is lost and
drowns in her will never satisfy the woman, who is looking for a
rock. 'Where are *you*?' she will say. 'Where is that in you that is
not for me and is, for that reason, precious?' In fact, she is asking
him to be Libra, with male in one scale, female the other; holding
the balance; not overthrown. And if he cannot manage this, she

will be well within her rights if she hops into the next sign and gives him a scorpion sting.

Both Scorpios — again my zoologist! — have poison in their tails. 'But would not the sexes,' I inquired, 'use their weapon in different ways?' 'No, no,' he replied. 'Same tail, same sting!' He is not a man who would have any truck with metaphor or symbol. But stinging is a feminine activity, no matter which sex does it. A female Scorpio, I tend to think, would wilily, before shooting her dart, make sure there was not a dock leaf handy.

I was careful, as you may imagine, not to press the expert about the Centaur. 'A myth!' he would scoff, meaning lie, of course. 'A way of telling savages that man is a twofold composite of intellect and lust. How could there be a female centaur?' And I would merely raise my eyebrows and wonder where he had been all his life. But a woman born under Sagittarius will, if only figuratively, also need to hit — or miss — the mark. And to do it in her own way which is not the way of a man. Watch any archery contest — a man will use his bow and arrow simply as adjuncts, instruments. With a woman, they are part of herself. (It is the same with a tennis racket.) She is the bow-string and the *flèche*. It is she herself who flies to the target. And can we forget the Amazons, daughters of the Great Goddess, formed as vessels for bearing life, who mutilated their mother-part in order more deftly to inflict death? No, for they are ever with us, allegorically breastless, demanding, in spite of their lineage, equality with men. Equality! One does not know whether to laugh or weep at such a declination. A difficult sign to live, the Archer.

And what of Aquarius, whose age, some say, is already here. Others disagree — no matter. If it be not now it is to come. Our readiness is all. Well, we have waited long for it, some two thousand years. In the pictorial zodiac, the one who will lead us to the upper chamber is always shown as a man alone, not a female in sight. But what does he carry in his hand? A pitcher, flagon, or amphora, the ultimate morphology of the feminine! And the abstract sign is that of water, the element of Yin. Black fish with white eye, white fish with black are not more essential to each other than these two, man and watering-pot. The process is one — relationship at every level — but the functions, naturally, are two. 'I will pour out.' 'I will be poured.' Is there not an echo here of St John's Apocrypha? To me this is the epitome of all the zodiacal signs. It tells us, more clearly than any of the others, that where there is one, there will be two; and if two, inevitably three, the blest proceeding third —

life-giving, baptismal, releasing water — or spirit, if you like. That
proceeding third — neither and both — is, to me, the heart of the
matter. If I could choose, I would choose this sign. But, as with
rights, there are no choices. Only that implacable purpose, my
'something else' that awaits the name that, under Aquarius, may
perhaps be spoken.

You may say, for you are a learned man, that all this has always
been implicit in astrological parlance; that Eve, after all, is a rib
of Adam and why extrapolate at length on one of Adam's parts?
Even so, Sir, the doubt remains. Why, on that night of wine and
candles, did you not descry, within the Lion, the lion's naked rib?
Typically, I had to do the work myself, to travel far and dig deep
in order even to come to the question.

I will take this letter to the river bank and ask Charon to row it
over. He surely will not charge me. I know that you will not lightly
dismiss it, if only for friendship's sake. You may even, perhaps,
discuss it with cronies. If Pythagoras, whom I deeply revere, should
happen to be among them, say — even though he smile at my foible
— that if he were not a vegetarian, except, of course, in the matter
of beans, I would gladly kill a springbok for him.

Of course, I shall not look for an answer. My business is with
questions. But when at last I pay my obol, meet me at the ferry!

First published in 'Parabola' on the theme of Androgyny, New York, 1973.

The Youngest Brother

IN ORDER to come to the Youngest Brother we have to go a long way back — retrace our footsteps, as it were, to the world of the Mother Goddess. In matriarchal society, the law of *Jungstens Recht* — the right of the last born — invariably prevailed. The logic of this is obvious. In the nature of things the youngest was likely to live the longest and would therefore be the natural support of aged parents, if alive, and inheritor, eventually, of farm, castle or kingdom. Moreover, in all the versions of *The Three Brothers* — a theme as universal as the universe — the youngest is the stay-at-home, sometimes as the parents' darling, more often as a simpleton, the two elders, presumably, having collared the best of the genes. This, too, sounds logical. But, beware! When did a fairy tale worth its salt have any truck with logic? And isn't this one asking us to look at the concept of Simpleton and see it as the grain of sand round which is to be crystalized the pearl of the story's meaning?

How simple is Simpleton, after all? Are we to think of him as a noodle, sib to the Three Wise men of Gotham? The story refutes the suggestion. Is he related to Simple Simon who went a-fishing for to catch a whale? The story, albeit guilefully, says 'Yes, he is — blood brother!' For what, we must ask, is his mother's pail but the ocean? And where else would a sensible man attempt to catch a whale?

But, first, let us pay our respects to language and grieve for the way it has been degraded. It is we who have turned Simon into a noodle because we have lost the significance of his qualifying adjective. Simple (whose oldest dictionary meaning is *innocent*, not knowing, and yet, oh, it's tricky, not ignorant, either; nor stupid, it has a celestial shrewdness) is kin to the word silly; and silly comes from the Old English *saelig*, meaning blessed and, by extension, holy. In old songs and poems — and not so very old either — the phrase 'my sweet silly' was often used as a love-word to a child; Sir Philip Sidney's Astrophel apostrophises his Stella with 'O heavenly fool!'; Lear, weeping over Cordelia — a feminine aspect of the Youngest Brother — cries, 'My poor fool is hanged!' . Pope, in his *Essay on Man* says:

*Go teach eternal wisdom how to rule
Then drop into thyself and be a fool.*

The cup of legend runneth over with fools who have taken this advice. One finds them, most often, linked to the mighty, as complementary opposites. One, Filipos, according to Xenophon, dared to cross swords with Socrates and, though rebuked, was not deflated. He was fool enough to understand that a steady diet of the verities needs to be salted with flippancy in order to make it digestible. Solomon himself, not biblically, but in legend's book, was out-riddled by Marcolphus who, once wise enough to confound the wise, under Christianity dwindled into a mere Lord of Misrule, by which appellation he is now known. In Europe we have Till Eulenspiegel, a Western cousin of Nassr Eddin, whose name, not for nothing, means owl-mirror — Athene's bird of wisdom reflected in a glass, sagacity and nonsense interacting. And the Teutonic Kasperle, with cap and bells and minimal knapsack, who, like the Fool of the Tarot, serenely passes through the world, here and there alike to him, unaware — or perhaps aware and unafraid — of the crocodile lying in wait.

Shakespeare's fools, designed to throw light on princely follies, accepting to be wronged and mocked so that others may ease themselves in laughter of what, in them, is mocked and wronged — are often more memorable than their masters, for they carry the story's inner meaning. They are the jokers in the pack, becoming a king or a seven at the will of the dealer, always aware that, for all the sunlight, the rain it raineth every day. The early Chaplin, while it was still instinctive in him, had something of this quality. So, too, had Don Quixote; and the Jugo-Slavian Boudala whom the folk assimilated to the Buddha; and so, superlatively, had Ryokan, the fool of Zen, who, when his house was robbed, rejoiced. 'They left the best thing, the moon at the window!' If these were mad, then let us, you and I, not be less. 'The madman,' as Rumi says, 'is he that has not gone mad'; or, as the Bible puts it, has not made himself a fool for Christ's sake; nor yet become one of the children of light, than whom the children of this world are, it is said, so much wiser. We should remember all these, and there are more, as we come to the theme of the Three Brothers.

You know the story — there is no tradition that does not have it. Always it begins with requirement — something has to be sought for and (this is important) brought home — the water of life, the abducted sister, the golden apples, the mother borne away by a whirlwind. And no one but the three brothers can be deputed to perform the task.

So, first the eldest sets out, always spurning, or disregarding, advice from the dwarf, the toad, or Merlin. And, inevitably, since these are the harbingers of fate, he finds himself caught in a ravine, baulked at the foot of unscalable cliffs, pent in the Dark Tower of Elfland — it is all one prison, however named. If one thinks of the adventure in terms of an octave, he has gone as far as the note Mi and, for him, the quest ends there.

Now it is the turn of the second brother. He, too, is accosted by the sibylline figures; he, too, disdains the proffered help; he, too, can go no further. A certain energy is needed to leap the crevasse of the semitone and so arrive at Fa. And neither brother, from lack of wish, understanding, faith — put any word on it you like — is able to acquire it. And so, at home, there is consternation. With the elder sons lost or dead, the quest, it appears, has failed.

But the Youngest Brother now steps forward. Since the story's purpose must be served, who but himself is left to serve it?

'No, no,' the parents cry. 'You are young! You have not the wit.'

'Then, without wit!' says the Youngest Brother. And every fool murmurs assent to the phrase.

So, witlessly, off he goes, harkening to the oracles, following after the way-showers, be it ball, blown feather, beckoning cat. In Grimm's story *The Water of Life* — for me the archetypal version — the guide is a dwarf, quintessential creature of earth and as such privy to earth's secrets and the whereabouts of her vital wellspring.

'You will find it,' he tells the Youngest Brother, 'in the courtyard of an enchanted castle. Strike the door thrice with this wand of iron, throw these loaves of bread to the lions. Take the water ere the clock strikes twelve.' The tale is packed with symbols. And, of course there is an imprisoned princess, the hero's complementary figure, the Yin that enables the Yang to prevail. 'You have set me free,' she tells our lad. 'Fill your cup and take it home and come back in a year's time.'

So far, so good. The Youngest has leapt from Mi to Fa. The octave can continue on its way and we can be content. Or can we? The answer, apparently, is no. Every note in the scale must be sounded. Disregarding the dwarf's warning but answering to the story's need, the last-born rescues his two brothers, shows them the water,

describes the maiden, and thereupon falls asleep. And here, as
between cup and lip, there are slips between note and note. Even
at the last moment, the treasure can be lost. The brothers steal
the elixir, substitute salt water for it, which the innocent Youngest
gives the king who, therefore, unlike God, is mocked. 'Put him
to death!' the father cries. He does not know that one of the Saving
Friends — this time in the form of a huntsman — will come to the
Youngest's aid.

So now he must serve a further term in order to vault across the
abyss, far deeper than that between Mi and Fa, that lies between
the Ti of one octave and the succeeding Do. He hires himself out
to foreign lords who have need of his magic wand and bread.
Anyone not familiar with the theme would think we had heard
the last of him, which is just what the fairy tale intends. With its
ingrained sense of drama — even melodrama — it slyly keeps us
in suspense in order to build up to the well-known recognition
scene which exposes the duplicity of the elder brothers and shows
the Youngest as true hero, alive, and moreover, so rich and famous
that, though relieved, we are also anxious. Can this be Simpleton,
we wonder, the one we have loved since childhood for his lack of
worldly gifts? Is this the earth that the meek inherit? If so, do we
want to be meek?

And then, with a sweeping, theatrical gesture — the fairy tales
are all ham actors — the story points to the heart of the matter,
the fair, the chaste, the unexpressive She who, in various symbolic
guises has been with us from the beginning; the requirement, the
enchanted castle, the water of life, the princess — or woman of
Samaria? — who dwells beside the well. For now the allotted year
is over, and the last great task must be undertaken. She issues a
proclamation. He who shall ride straight up the road to her door
is the one who shall have her hand in marriage.

At once the three leap to the saddle. And the first, as he
approaches it, perceives that the road is made of gold. What! Sully
such a highway? Never! So, prudently, he rides to the right, and
is refused admission. The second brother rides to the left and he,
too, is denied. But the third doesn't even notice the road, be it gold,
macadam, or Orion's Belt. With his heart set solely upon that She,
he gallops along it — oh, he gallops! Yes, he is Simpleton, indeed,
given back to us with his witlessness, his imprudence, his lack of
self. And we can be sure, though the tale is not on this point explicit
— that when the question 'Who is there?' is asked, the Youngest
Brother will reply, as Majnun to Laila in the Persian story, not 'It
is I!' but 'Thou!'

The stories grow as we ourselves grow. They are trees that are meant to put forth fruit, the ripened fruit of question. That being so, I have for a long time asked myself whether those three brothers are really three, or a threefold composite of one man, three stages in a single life? And whether the story is not a pattern, at once ancient and familiar, of how — if we could! — to live our own lives?

Here he is, that man, as eldest brother, setting out upon the quest — an essential element in any life whether in or out of a book. He has, or believes he has, everything — youth, beauty, capacity. And, above all, he *knows!* What does he need with the hoi polloi, be it dwarf, toad, little old woman, who presume to offer him advice as though he — he! — were in a tight corner? But very soon he finds out that that is exactly where he is and the helpers seem to have disappeared.

Well, then, there is nothing else for it, he has to become the second brother; older and perhaps, now, not so strong and handsome. Ah, but he's clever, he's a man of the world and he knows his way about it. So he, too, dismisses the counsellors and, having learnt nothing from experience, lands up in the same old place.

And in this place — I have to assume it, since I've asked the question — he begins to take stock of the situation and consider how to get out of it. Worldly wisdom, worldly possessions, will never help him here. But can he throw overboard his having, and what is harder, his knowing? Make a friend of Necessity? Cease to live by bread alone and cast himself on the waters as bread? Become the Youngest Brother?

The story, wordlessly, says Yes! At the same time it mutely points a finger at what has not yet been explored — the dual nature of the quest, the mutuality of its contraries, its inherent paradox. 'I do not seek, I find,' said Picasso, almost, but not quite hitting the mark. 'I am found' would be nearer to the truth.

In his earlier phases, this one man we are contemplating is concerned only with seeking. All that he needs for the quest, he believes, is contained within himself. Having no conception of what is 'other', he thinks of the way as a mere object, inanimate, passive, there to be used; of the treasure as a commodity that merely awaits the taking.

But once he is in the tight place, he is forced, for the quest's sake — or the life's — to confront the dualities. Perhaps he begins to understand that the tight place itself is by no means all it appears to be; that the way could actively *carry* him onward and the treasure come hurrying to meet him — upon a single condition.

'If I seek,' he comes to realize, 'then I am also sought. It does not all depend on me. And yet, to the extent that I am able to be found, it all depends on me.'

So, he lets go — not his possessions but his possessing, uses the tight place as a springboard and marches forward against the thorn — empty and capable of being filled, helpless and able to be helped; unknowing and knowing that only unknowing can bring him to his knowing. It is thus that the man becomes the child, the last the first, the wise, the fool, grown — not created — pure in heart. Only such a one, says the story, can put out a hand for the treasure. And even so, properly to have it, he must first be ready to lose it. What he was must steal it from what he is, while he sleeps, or forgets what he is. A further novitiate must be served before he can truly claim as his own, the water, that She, or his soul.

One task remains. In every version of the story, the Youngest either forgives his brothers or sees that they are fitted out with princesses of their own. You could say that he was re-enacting Plato's myth of the Cave, where those who have risen to the light go down again to rescue others who still live with the shadows. Or, as an alternative — which is more properly a similitude — this one man, by taking pity on himself (which has nothing to do with self-pity) repairs his past and redeems his world. And if *his* past, then all the past; if *his* world, then all the world. You cannot purify one stretch of the river without affecting the whole. If sweet Thames runs, for a moment, softly, so, too, do Ganges, Mississippi, Neva. 'To repair the past,' a wise Teacher said, 'is to prepare the future.' What then would this man's future be? I hazard a suggestion. 'It's all yours,' he would say to eternal wisdom and drop into himself. Or to put it into fairy tale words, he would live happily ever after — a hackneyed phrase, I admit, but one of significance. What does it mean? Nirvana? The kingdom of heaven? The void? Only a fool would know, I think, and he would be fool enough not to tell.

Now, this is all hint and surmise, a fallible finger thrust at the moon. You will know far more of *The Water of Life* by reading it yourselves. Like the loaves that the dwarf gave the Youngest Brother, it is a barrel of meal that does not waste, a never-failing wellspring.

And so, as the Russian storytellers say, the wind blows and the rain rains, put a log on the fire and give me to drink. For the tale has now come to its end. And if you don't like it, don't listen.

First published in 'Parabola' on the theme of The Trickster, New York, 1979.

The Primary World

I WAS brought up in Ancient Greece, a country I have never seen, even in its modern aspect. That this was so was made clear to me when I came to read *The Republic*. Plato somewhere makes the point that the most profound truths can be elicited from children when, simply, stealthily, logically, they are asked the right questions at the right moment and in the right order. At the same time, he holds no brief for formal education — ethical, philosophical, mathematical. The early needs of his ideal citizens will be amply filled, as were his own, by traditional myths and stories. And Aristotle echoes him, in this if not in other foibles, by asserting that 'The lover of myths, compact of wonders, is by the same token a lover of wisdom.'

This is not to suggest, far from it, a background of erudition, but rather one of lore and legend. What had been good enough for my parents — the lively, articulate, hotchpotch stuff bequeathed by remote ancestors and added to miscellaneously by each new generation — was good enough, they thought, for children. Questions they did, unwittingly, ask and were often appalled by the replies; and as often brought to the brink of madness by the questions their questions evoked.

These, as was inevitable, became part of the general folklore; the stories, ballads, old wives' tales shared among widely scattered neighbours, that made our antipodean world — archaic, antique, for all its newness — intimate and coherent. Heaven was merely a celestial suburb, bright with its close and bending stars, inhabited by a circle of friends, familiar however patrician — the Two Bold Pointers of the Southern Cross, Orion with his studded belt, Venus, early to bed and to rise. And among these dwelt, apparently, the well-wisher who was nightly reminded to pity mice implicitly, bless our nearest relatives and, as a personal addendum, teach Father not to cheat at Ludo.

The smallest event, in that huge landscape, became, of necessity, an occasion. To take a trip to the nearest town, no town in any modern sense, was to ride in triumph through Persepolis; the loss of a milk tooth no less an omen than the dropping of Cinderella's slipper; the gift of a pig's head or a batch of papers arriving from England, the excuse for a celebration. So, to horse, far and wide, with invitations. Come tonight to a dance! And presently, to banjo and fiddle, the house would be turning in a gyre — Bacchic for all its rusticity — with 'Strip the Willow,' 'Six-Hand Duke,' 'Lochiel,' 'Waltzing Matilda.'

Waltzing Matilda, I then thought, was none other than our washerwoman, the third person in a trinity known as Father, Mother and Mat. Notoriously inadequate as a laundress, she was also notorious, for miles around, for her masterly telling of grims. This was a word much bandied about, and in my crooked understanding, got from essentially grimmish parents, I took it as a generic term for narrative, tarradiddle, story. Matilda's grims — so much more important to her, and to us, than having clean sheets and underwear — were centred round a vagrant gypsy, 'unsighted and yet seeing all', whom she called familiarly Ould Raff. I had to grow taller and cross the world before I knew him for Raftery, the Homer of the Irish hedgerows, whom A. E. and Yeats so deeply revered.

But Matilda was not the only teller. In a certain sense, everyone had a grim. The grim was social currency. Rumour and gossip were founded upon it, so was the Sunday sermon. 'There was a man went forth to sow' and 'Leda lay under the wing of the swan,' inevitably, were grims. Only when the alphabet had revealed itself through stencils on tea-chests, letters stamped on bags of flour, labels on boxes of Beecham's Pills, 'Jumble Today' on the church board — only then did I understand that grims were, in fact, Grimms! 'Sweetheart Roland,' 'The Goose Girl' and the rest had been corralled, like a herd of wild horses, and stabled in a book — or, two books to be precise; squat, red, sturdy volumes, coarse of paper, close of print, discovered in my father's bookcase along with *Twelve Deathbed Scenes* and someone called William Shakespeare. Did *he* know a grim or two, I wondered.

They are faded now, those two old friends, their red weathered to pink; but in spite of time and rough usage, however loving, well able to cope with more of the same from future generations.

There have, of course, been next-of-kin or, at any rate, successors. One of these is here to my hand, in Ralph Mannheim's translation.

And the mere thought that I am not only permitted, but required by the editor to read a new Grimms, fills me with intimate joy. My blood runs as softly as Sweet Thames. And then, at the outset, it encounters a weir.

'I thought the time had come,' says the Introduction, 'to attempt a new translation that would be faithful to the Grimm brothers' faithfulness.' Indeed, a noble ambition. But has no one, hitherto, been faithful? It is true that the red books went out of print and that *Household Tales* no longer flourished. Was it after the First World War that people who had been children themselves and would therefore have known the brute facts of life, decided that Grimms were too grim? It would have been about that time that childhood qua childhood assumed importance. A passing phase — 10 seconds out of a total of 60 — became, as it were, a thing in itself; something static, with boundaries, and capable of being mapped as one charts a geographical unit. 'Inspect it, dissect it, and protect it!' said psychologists, teachers, social workers. So, children became, for the first time, childish. And, to keep them from knowing what they knew — and, sorrowfully, have always known — they were told about the fairies in flowers, boys who didn't want to grow up, Mr and Mrs Mickey Mouse; but not of 'The Devil's Sooty Brother,' 'The Blue Light,' 'Pif-Paf-Poultrie.' The only Grimms available, until about 35 years ago, were carefully bowdlerized selections, or the occasional single story, used as a sort of lay figure for an illustrator's creations. And even these were suspect. Librarians in the New York Public Library, proudly showing a guest around, put fingers to their lips when asked: 'But where are the *Household Tales*?' Oh, they were there, along with the myths, but kept in an inner secret chamber. Parents were anxious, it was said, that their young be shielded from anything that could lead to wishful thinking.

Wishful thinking! If there are latitudes less accessible to wishful thinking than the fairy tales, I would like them pointed out to me. To enter such dangerous terrain, you need a stout heart, a will well-tempered and a bulletproof digestion. But, perhaps, after all, those parents were right. The strong drink brewed by Grimms and the myths produces, in those who can stomach it, the stuff of which heroes are made. And heroes, in the long run, may be far more difficult to live with than any wishful thinker.

But time, as time must, came round again. And the door of that inner chamber opened. An article appeared in the *Herald Tribune* suggesting that the tales had meaning, lamenting the loss of their ancient lore and praying that someone with a seeing eye would cast it on the Complete Grimms and publish it, along with the Notes, in Margaret Hunt's (1894) translation.

That night, at a party, W. H. Auden came striding in, brandishing the paper aloft. 'This is what we want!' he cried. And that was what we got — or almost. The Pantheon Press, thinking wishfully, borrowed the two red books and acted. James Stern, short story writer, master of German as well as English, was brought in to remove — as delicately as one playing spillikins — the Victorian squeamishnesses; Padraic Colum, himself a man of the Irish hedgerows, to reintroduce the stories; and Joseph Campbell, addict and scholar, to collate the material of the Afterword. But, alas, no Notes. That word is poison to publishers. They believe that when it comes in at the door the buyer flies out of the window. But who, young or old, wouldn't want to know of the Story-Wife of Niederzwehren, de Alte Marie, and the Old Soldier, all of whom, time upon time with the same details, told the stories to the brothers? Or the fact, enormous and wonderful, that giants take out their hearts when they sleep?

Never mind. Grimms were back. The world, unprecedentedly, had noted and long remembered. And, as if the Pantheon edition were not enough — a book fit for a grandee — the Southern Illinois University Press published a new translation (1960) — simple, colloquial, unadorned — by Francis Magoun and Alexander Krappe — again without notes but, and let them be blessed for this, with German as well as English titles.

So, remembering the Fifth Commandment, it has to be said that the Mannheim version, with its assumption that no one has, until now, been faithful, may perhaps be the bird of loudest lay but not by any stretch of fancy the sole Arabian tree.

It is a competent, lively text — 'As spry as a fish in water' — delicious! But allowing for the fact that we tend to stick to older versions as barnacles to a keel, we must, sometimes, in honour, cry 'No!' to the new.

Take, for instance, 'The Juniper Tree,' most fearful and beautiful of stories, where the father, unknowing, eats his son in a stew. Both Hunt and Magoun have him exclaim: 'Give me more! I feel it is all mine!' — as, indeed, alas, it is. But Mannheim has 'It belongs to me.' More faithful this may be, linguistically, but it has lost faith with truth and terror. Taste, feel, sense and difference in levels prove it, as Keats said, upon the pulse. From that 'All mine!' we fall like stones to where the son is a mere belonging, a trinket or a walking stick, not the father's substantive soul.

And again no! In 'Harsichenbraut,' which means The Little Hare's Bride, Hunt and Magoun — rejecting leveret as recondite — settle, acceptably, for Hare. But Mannheim, flinging his faithfulness to the wind, takes Harsichen for Kaninchen and panders to the populace with 'Bunny Rabbit's Bride.' Now, hare has never been bunny rabbit; it belongs, biologically, to a different genus; is born, unlike rabbit, furred and waking; lives in the overland, not in warrens; and even asleep — cousin german to Ould Raff, perhaps! — has an ever open eye. In every culture, every tradition, the hare is a divinatory spirit with dimensions both mythological and symbolic that a rabbit could never aspire to. But who, in a degraded world, can measure up to the fabulous? It has to be domesticated. But a hare will die if kept in a hutch. So, the primrose path being easier, we descend to bunnies.

The great success of *Watership Down,* a portentous modern allegory with rather less portent than *Peter Rabbit,* was due to the fact that its goodies and baddies were dear familiar furry bobtails; Bunny St George, after various rabbity tribulations, outburrowing Bunny Hitler (or Trotsky?) and then at last disappearing — not into a pie, as one might have hoped — but into a sort of Bunny Nirvana! Mrs MacGregor, where are you?

There are no rabbits in Hans Andersen. But, for all that, unlike the Grimms, he has never been in eclipse. His tales were among my early grims and I loved, and still love, his retellings of what he was told in childhood — tough, shrewd, ironic, witty — and his own folksy, miniscule fables, 'Five Peas in the Same Pod,' 'The Darning Needle,' 'Soup on a Sausage Pin,' 'Auntie Toothache,' as well as that subtle story, 'The Shadow,' wherein he showed himself, for once, to be wiser than he knew. But the great reverberant set-pieces, so admired, wept over, doted upon — 'Mermaid,' 'Snow Queen,' 'Red Shoes,' etc. filled me, in childhood, with unease and a feeling that I was being got at. Oh, I wept and, I suppose, doted — but felt no better for it. Grimms belonged to the sunlight, asked nothing, never apologized, curdled the blood with delight and horror, dispensed justice, fortified the spirit. Andersen, moon-man, asked for mercy, was always sorry, curdled the feelings with bane-and-honey and undermined the vitality by his endless appeal for pity. When the millstone was dropped on the wicked stepmother, I did not miss a breath. That was how it should be. But for Karen who had her feet cut off because she preferred red shoes to God, I had to break my heart; suffer for Kay and his monstrous word — 'the artifice of Eternity,' as Yeats put it — when 'now', as it seemed to me then, and does still, would have been a better, if more demanding word; and try, ever failing, to be a good child in order to shorten, by 300 years, the term of the mermaid's waiting time.

That story has much to answer for. It is in the last three paragraphs — so sad, so romantic, the devotees say — that Andersen, with his wanton sweetness, his too-much rubbing of Aladdin's lamp, stands most in need of forgiveness. All right, let the creature have her wish — though it breaks all cosmic laws — but you may not let its consummation, a barren, adult illusion anyway, depend upon the chivalry of those not yet adulterated. She has given up her tail — good. She has graduated to air — better, at any rate from *her* point of view. Let her now discover patience. The soul will happen in its own time. But — a year taken off when a child behaves well; a tear shed and a day added whenever a child is naughty? Andersen, this is blackmail. And the children know it, and say nothing. There's magnanimity for you.

The Secondary World — Tolkien's phrase — fashioned as it is by fallible man, is full of such moral pitfalls. In this regard, one needs to read Tolkien's wonderful essay 'On Fairy Tales' many times over, taking note of its intricate warp and woof, its air of being a palimpsest, before one arrives at what he means by Primary and Secondary. And even then, one cannot be sure that one has indeed arrived.

> It is not [he says] difficult to imagine the peculiar excitement and joy that one would feel, if any specially beautiful fairy story were found to be *'primarily' true, its narrative to be history,* without thereby necessarily losing the mythical or allegorical significance that it has possessed.

This suggests that, for him, the 'true' is that which can be documented, an element of history. For me, remembering D. H. Lawrence's axiom — 'There is the truth of truth as well as the truth of fact', for which he should be canonized — the opposite holds good. For me, the Primary World is that which has never been invented but came into being, along with the blood stream, as a legacy from the Authors who, according to Blake, — that word again! — are in Eternity. All the rest is manmade, or as Tolkien has it, 'subcreated'; the Secondary World. He himself is a subcreator; Ursula Le Guin is also one; so, too, is Sweetheart Hans in his own imagined tales — though his is not a tangible subworld, like Middle Earth or Earthsea, but rather an inner idioverse where the annals are all of Andersen and Andersen makes the laws.

Tolkien and Le Guin, suckled on the Ancient Code, pay filial duty to their wet-nurse, except for one moment when Tolkien lapses. Or was it not a lapse at all but rather prevision and intention that made Bilbo acquire the ring by unheroic means? That would make all the difference and give to what, in essence, is a grandiose adventure story, a much larger dimension. It may be — and I'm giving it the benefit of a very doubtful doubt — that this was a foreshadowing of the ambivalent outcome.

In *The Silmarillion* — and if you've read that you don't need Purgatory — Frodo restores the ring to the fire, as in the Niebelungenlied it is restored to the water, with the self-effacement one expects from any well-brought up hero. In *The Lord of the Rings,* infringing all the laws of lore, the great deed happens by accident. Fallible hero, and villain who proves at last redemptive — the one who would keep and the one who would get — grapple together at the edge of the chasm; and Gollum, with the ring in his hand, loses his footing and falls. You can't lose footing intentionally; it's a happening, not a deliberate act. So, after all the oracular pother, the ring is not restored, but lost, a very different matter. Did Tolkien realize that with such an equivocal beginning, the story, for all its mythical content, would inevitably have an ambiguous ending? The question will not be acceptable to those who chalk up 'Frodo lives!' on any convenient wall. Even so, it needs to be aired. 'Is it possible,' asks John Davy, in his essay "The Education of Children," 'that, in turning to drugs and Tolkien, teenagers may in part be attempting to make good the lack of fairy tales in infant school?' I think it may well be so. The lack has to be made up somehow. And all those seemingly endless volumes may serve a significant purpose.

For Tolkien is one of the signs of the times. Those who emigrate to the space colonies of the future will certainly take him with them. All subcreations will be needed there to give the inhabitants — I had almost said inmates — an inner psychic plenitude to balance the outer emptiness.

But the Primary World — in all its aspects subsumed for me under the generic terms of 'Grimms' — could never become acclimatized to a climate made by man. It needs, in order to go on living, the things man cannot create — the earth with all its composted dead, the rain that raineth every day, the seasons, nightfall, silence — and an ear free of all pulsation but that of its own blood.

Only in such a well-found steading could Apollo, resting at dusk from his day's herding, tell the stories to Admetus, the yeoman monarch who, in time, would pass them on to his children.

But who told Apollo? Tom o' Bedlam?

I know more than Apollo
For oft when he lies sleeping
I hear the stars at mortal wars
And the wounded welkin weeping.

Very well, then. But who told Tom? Unnecessary question. What matters is that *we* be told, ourselves wounded as the welkin is, and so in need of solace. And that we, in turn, become Tom — for this generation and those to come — and tell the ever-spreading circumference which, never doubt it, will also be wounded, the news of its navel centre.

I owe it to you, old ancestors, quick and still vocal in my blood, that I have been, however ineptly, a gladiator in this ring and kept, under one collective name, its unfallen day about me.

So, hail! I who am about to die — one year, twenty years, a hundred — salute you, faithful brothers!

Waltz with me, Jakob and Wilhelm. Tell me a grim, Matilda.

First published in 'Parabola' on the theme of The Child, New York, 1979.

Five Women

AMONG THE PHAEACIANS — MAIDEN

So, kirtling up their robes, the young girls trod the clothes in the stream, and spread them out on the shore of the sea, playing at ball till the sun should dry them.

But when the ball, flung too far, was lost into the eddying current, they set up such a treble clamour that the sleeping man awoke.

And again they cried and chastely fled as he came and stood before them naked, holding the decorous bough as a shield, the gold of head and chest and loins silvered by salt from the sea.

Only one, the King's daughter, stood her ground, sensing the lordliness of his essence and finding him comely withal.

It was she who clothed him in new-washed raiment, telling him in whose meadows he stood, bidding him follow in the wake of her wagon as far as her father's palace.

It was she, standing behind a pillar, who watched him assume, as custom required, the supplicant's place among the ashes; saw him beckoned to a higher place by her father; and, for a moment, caught his glance as he passed to his bed beneath the rafters.

For the length of his sojourn on the island, I think it would have been always thus: she, virgin and circumspect, watching at the rim of events for his moving shape among them; he, a man well-known to woman and, in his own way, circumspect, Argus-eyed for a glimpse of her amid the congregation.

When, jeered at by the younger men — 'Are you not merchant rather than gamesman?' — he hurled the stone so far afield that the earth rushed away beneath it, it was to her, anonymous in the crowd of women, that he raised his hand in salute; from her when the minstrel sang of the Wooden Horse, the siege of Troy and its grievous outcome, that he hid his tears in his sleeve; for her that

— when asked for news of Odysseus — he acknowledged his name.

Thereafter, from some hidden vantage point, she would have listened to his story, the litany of a man's adventures on the way to his meridian — Calypso, Circe, the Lotus Eaters, Cyclops, Aeolus, the Laestrygons, the descent into Hades, the song of the Sirens, the thrust between Scylla and Charybdis, the cattle of the Sun slaughtered.

And at last when, with the feasting over, libations poured and gifts given, the princes gathered upon the sea-banks to escort him to his hollow ship, she would have taken her place among them and he, as surely, have sought her there.

This was farewell. And with farewell one can speak one's heart, and freely, since it is but once.

'Sir, when you come to your wife and heartland, bethink thee of me upon a moment, for that to me first thou owest the ransom of life.'

'I will remember thee all my days and pray to the gods to requite thee.'

One can pack a lifetime into a sentence.

'We should leave life,' said Nietszche, 'as Odysseus left Nausicaa, not enamoured, but blessing.'

Ah, if we could! And even go further — love it and leave it and also bless. For were they not enamoured? Literature, to say nothing of life, is full of such affinities — the noon-day man and the morning girl, signalling each to other as they go their separate ways. But Homer, though never chary of words, left a later poet to say it.

> *She loved him for the dangers he had passed*
> *And he loved her that she did pity them.*

And is it not most probable that she, sandal-footed upon the strand, and he in the stern of the well-found ship, would stand and keep their mutual vigil, eye unto eye as the distance lengthened, till ship and island both disappeared — one to the East, one to the West, down the curve of the rounded sea?

For she was the last glimpse of his heyday and he her first glimpse of hers.

UNDER THE NYSIAN PLAIN — DAUGHTER

I hear your footsteps, they vibrate above me, crossing, re-crossing the Nysian plain. And the lilies fall, the grass fades and the grain does not lift its head.

Mother, mother, do not grieve! All brides are ravished. When morning comes, we are not what we were. I am already more than daughter. I have eaten what Aidoneus gave. The single seed of pomegranate was rosy and sweet upon the tongue. Now we together, all the dark weather, dead to the world keep house unknown.

It was meet that, having plucked the flower, I should go down to the root, as once from the root-place under your breasts I came forth to pluck the flower. This twofold journey, from dark to light and from light to dark makes me more yours than ever, your seed beneath the earth.

So, Mother, dry your falling tears. When the Spring comes, I, twice-born, will come with it. Let the lilies blow, the grass grow green and the grain be white to the harvest. Look for your child at Eleusis!

BY THE RIVER EUROTUS — PARAMOUR

Mother, may I go out to swim?
Yes, my darling daughter!
Hang your clothes on the mulberry bush
But don't go near the water.

So, having swum — you don't do all that your mother tells you — the girl lay naked beside the water, lazily eating ripe mulberries, thinking and hardly thinking the thoughts that run in the blood.

It has been said that when on earth great beauty goes exempt from danger, it will be endangered by a source on High. She was alone. There was nobody in sight. How could she know, untaught by her beauty, that she had been seen and noted?

But suddenly she was aware of stillness — no stir of wind, no leaf bending, no lapping of the tide. All time was gathered into a second, the universe holding its breath.

And in herself, too, there was stillness, as of a pitcher filled to the brim, sufficient with the sufficiency that waits to be poured out.

Then, as if from nowhere, there he was, white and majestic upon the waters that lifted him forward, himself not moving.

A maiden impudence rose within her. Who did he think he was, then, lording it in her father's demesne, moor hens dipping, rushes bowing as he passed on his processional way, motionless as a painted swan upon a painted river?

She stepped into the stream to accost him, mulberry in her outstretched palm.

'Goosey,' she mocked him. 'Goosey Gander?' For what was he doing in a lady's chamber?

In the round black unblinking eye a light quickened and flashed. He became a moving hieroglyph, a great white arc from tail to beak that seized the fruit — and her.

So, in a cumulus of feather, clipped by the steel of pinion and breastbone, she was fathomed from the height to the depth, lifted and whirled through world upon world, the still pitcher spilled and refilled before the indifferent beak would let her drop and turn to pluck at the sedge.

Of the tales that daughters
Tell their poor old mothers
Which by all accounts are
Often very odd;
Leda's was a story
Stranger than all others —
What was there to say but
Glory be to God.

Even so, her mother said more.

'A dark eye with a light in the centre? Musha, my girl, that was no bird, no bird at all for all the feather. Why would you not be harkening to me, with Tyndareus, the fine boy-o — a steady, decent mortal lad — already with his foot in the door and a wedding ring in his hand? Ochone, Ochone, what will come of it?'

Well, what came of it, at the ninth month midnight, was two hyacinthine eggs, Troy fallen, Agamemnon murdered, Helen magicked away to Egypt, horseboys turned into stars!

The tale has been told since Word was spoken and never once has it warned one soul to look before he leaps — if, indeed, the looking could serve a purpose! What is in it, is in it. What will be, will be. Shed no tear for milk that is spilt. Cause is seldom a match for effect.

A morning dip, a forbidden peep at a sleeping lover, a little finger pricked by a spindle — who knows how anything will end?

IN THE UNDERWORLD — WIFE

Speak, Poet, of him who with his lute made trees
and the mountain tops that freeze
Bow their heads when he did sing!

But of me, his constant muse, you will be silent. Dead wives tell no tales. Give them no obituaries, Sir, lest haply their immaculate hero be shown as fallible man.

Oh, yes. When the innocent serpent struck, he clamoured of love at the gates of Heaven. 'Gods, restore my bride, I pray you! Let me go down to Hell to fetch her!' Give him his due. He did what he could.

So, with sanction and proviso, he came, singing and strumming to the rescue. But he was all sound and here was silence. He was all light and here was the dark. In the chthonic corridors there is neither taper nor echo.

Could you not trust yourself, Orpheus, or, if not yourself, the me in you, and know my footfall to be your heartbeat, a mute and mutual tattoo played to restore us to the sun? Did your blood not tell you that I would follow?

It did. But you dared not believe it. Disregarding that dread proviso, you faltered and turned your head!

Well, go your ways, my second serpent. Sing, wallowing in the world's pity — alas, to have twice lost a bride to Hades! But of what that lost bride has lost, the world will take no note.

Sing, for, indeed, you cannot help it. The gods are tricksters, their beneficence equivocal. The gift of song is but half a gift if the singer cannot refrain from singing. And even when that turned head is severed — O Maenads, avenge Eurydice! — it still will babble upon the waters, its oracles envied by Apollo, honoured in earth and sky.

O head, if I lived, I would gather you to me, rock you upon my faithful arm, silence with mine your bleating mouth.

But the dead have no compassion. They lack the heart and bowels for it. What is love? 'Tis not hereafter. Anger alone crosses all borders and forever vibrates in the lifeless shades.

So, my curse on you and your lute!

ON A SWISS MOUNTAIN — MOTHER

At the highest point the cross stands, thick-set, rough-hewn, still almost forest. Its broad vertical, solid and warm, mediates the sun to my back. Above me its freight hangs from the crosstrees, sensed rather than seen. For I dare not look up. The sky is too deep. I would drown in the bottomless blue. But the burden is known by the shadow it throws, the curve of a bent leg against the straight and the patch of sunlight between.

Ah, shadows! They tell us more than it ever can, the substantial thing that throws them. The intangible shape upon the grass, that at any moment a cloud may rub out, opens towards me maternal arms. Welcome, my everlasting child! For the first time I understand that the cross is life as well as death, a wide world-mothering symbol. Oh, my head knew it, but head-knowing is hardly knowing. The body must make it its own.

I glance across valleys to the other mountains. In every high alpine meadow stands another homely mother-rood, holding its son to its breast. And I think of those who set up the trees and carved the suspended figures. Old men they would inevitably be, seasoned by all the living and dying that the young have yet to do — Andreas, Rudi or Beat, ankle-deep among the shavings, hands apt to chisel and awl, cutting, curving, smoothing, sanding, evoking from mindless wood a man. Whoever you are, alive or dead, that shaped the unseen one above me, be blessed, old carpenter!

On my last day, however — for who knows if I will come again? — I confront my vertigo and look up. A dizzying glimpse of head and crown and then I must cravenly look away. But, at least, eyes closed, I can reach up a hand to the sun-warmed wooden foot.

It is cold. My fingers discern a blistered smoothness — cracks and wens and pimples of paint over something harder than wood. It is iron! He has not been carved, but poured from a mould; not a man-made man, a machine-made thing, supported on a block, also moulded, that bears the corporative name, *Larrieux et Cie.*

Where can it be, near or far, the workshop that pours forth a spate of Christs? A lucrative proceeding, surely. There are many mountains in the world and each needs its mute Reminder.

I imagine a moving assembly belt, bearing along the recumbent figures and, as they pass, artisans affixing to them the details of nail and crown. The scene is cheerful — talking and laughter, the humming of well-oiled machines, a foreman urging on his mates to complete the quota for the day. *'Dépeche-toi, Louis! Francois! Marc! Et toi, dépeche! Toi, je dis!'*

My God, he is looking at *me!* And why not? Am I not liberated? Lifted up to equality with any Marc or Louis? I, who had thought it my part to bear him, heavy and lively in my shoaling net; and, later, after thirty-three years, heavy and lifeless across my knees — am at liberty, required even, to give him the nail and the thorn.

Stabat Mater seeking the child in the temple, Stabat Mater when water is turned into wine, Stabat Mater amid the palms and shouting, Stabat Mater in the field of Golgotha — I now have the right to forswear all this. Sisters, you have set me free!

He comes towards me, acquiescent, one hole — sound economy! — gouged through the two crossed feet. I seize the bolt and ram it home. The five o'clock whistle blows and the moving line comes to a halt.

'Alors, mes amis, c'est terminé. Let us have a *fine* at the corner bistro. What shall it be? Hyssop and gall? A sponge dipped in vinegar? Wormwood? *Santé, tout le monde. A demain!'*

A demain? No. There is no tomorrow. Rather, *à Dieu. Ite missa est.*

Farewell, Andreas, Rudi, Beat! You were once, but you are no more.

So, to you, *Larrieux et Cie*, for doing what nobody else would do, for doing what had to be done — *merci!*

And to you, Necessity, that it had to be done at all — mercy!

First published in 'Parabola', under the original title 'Four Women' (less Under the Nysian Plain — Daughter), on the theme of Woman, New York, 1980.

What the
Bee Knows

'MYTH, Symbol, and Tradition' was the phrase I originally wrote
at the top of the page, for editors like large, cloudy titles. Then I
looked at what I had written and, wordlessly, the words reproached
me. I hope I had the grace to blush at my own presumption, and
their portentousness. How could I, if I lived for a thousand years,
attempt to cover more than a hectare of that enormous landscape?

So, I let out the air, in a manner of speaking, dwindled to my
appropriate size and gave myself over to that process for which,
for lack of a more erudite term, I have coined the phrase 'Thinking
is linking.' I thought of Kerenyi — 'Mythology occupies a higher
position in the *bios*, the existence, of a people in which it is still
more alive than poetry, storytelling or any other art.' And of
Malinowski — 'Myth is not merely a story but a reality lived.' And,
along with these, the word 'pollen', the most pervasive substance
in the world, kept knocking at my ear. Or rather, not knocking,
but humming. What hums? What buzzes? What travels the world?
Suddenly, I found what I sought. *What the bee knows*, I told
myself, that is what I'm after.

But even as I patted my back, I found myself cursing, and not
for the first time, the artful trickiness of words, their capriciousness,
their lack of conscience. Betray them and they will betray you. Be
true to them and, without compunction, they will also betray you,
foxily turning all the tables, thumbing syntactical noses. For —
nota bene! — if you speak or write about *what the bee knows*, what
the listener, or the reader, will get — indeed, cannot help but get
— is Myth, Symbol, and Tradition! You see the paradox? The
words, by their very perfidy — which is also their honourable
intention — have brought us to where we need to be. For, to stand
in the presence of paradox, to be spiked on the horns of dilemma,
between what is small and what is great, microcosm and

macrocosm, or, if you like, the two ends of the stick, is the only posture we can assume in front of this ancient knowledge — one could even say everlasting knowledge.

For the Bee has at all times and places been the symbol of life — life as immortality. In the Celtic languages, the Cornish 'beu', the Irish 'beo', the Welsh 'byw', can all be translated as 'alive' or 'living'; the Greek 'bios' has been mentioned above and is the French 'abeille' not akin to these? So, the Bee stands for — or is a manifestation of — the fundamental verb 'to be'. 'I am, thou art, he is,' it declares, as it goes humming past.

No wonder, then, that mythologically the Bee is the ritual creature of a host of lordly ones — symbol of Vishnu, Indra, and Krishna who are known in India as the 'Three Nectar-Born.' The bow of Kama, the Hindu god of erotic love, whose arrow is tipped with bane and honey, is strung — how aptly! — with bees. In Greek mythology, the bee hovers over the head of Artemis and its Greek name, Melissa, is a title borne by the priestesses of Demeter, Persephone, and Rhea. Among the ancient Egyptians it was believed that bees sprang from the tears of the Sun god; in Christianity it is Christ who weeps them. Gaia, the earth, the Great Goddess of the Sumerians, and the Virgin Mary are all apostrophized as the Mother Bee.

And as the myth descends into Time and becomes the tales that old wives tell, we hear of the 'Wisdom of the Bees,' and the 'Secret Knowledge of the Bees,' and are counselled, in Scottish Highland stories, to 'ask the Wild Bee what the Druids knew'.

To anyone capable of suspending for a moment the cavortings of the rational mind, of accepting myth for what it is — not lie but the very veritable truth — it needs no great inward effort to act upon such advice. It's a matter, merely, of listening.

If the Buddha could unfold his teaching to the Nagas, why would not a Druid whisper his to an attentive bee? Perhaps we are being told here that wisdom is too strong a draught for man to take, as it were, neat; that it needs to be mediated to him, the words wordlessly disclosed by creatures, bee and snake.

But this apprising of the bees, telling them, for all one knows, what they already know, is not the business merely of great ones. The bees are constantly being told. No beekeeper would fail to do it. For if they are not courteously kept informed of everything that happens, they will take umbrage, swarm, and fly away, or die of grief or resentment. In the British Isles and all over Europe, the folk continually keep the bees abreast of the news, at national as well as local level; decking the hives with crêpe or ribbon, whichever fits the case. On one occasion, an ancient great-aunt of mine, hieratically assuming a head-dress of feather and globules of jet, required me to accompany her to the beehives. 'But you surely don't need a hat, Aunt Jane! They're only at the end of the garden.' 'It is the custom,' she said, grandly. 'Put a scarf over your head.' Arrived, she stood in silence for a moment. Then — 'I have to tell you,' she said, formally, 'that King George V is dead. You may be sorry, but I am not. He was not an interesting man. Besides,' she added — as though the bees needed the telling! — 'everyone has to die'.

Again, at a wedding reception in an Irish garden, I found the gardener, a family retainer, morosely surveying the scene. 'All this colloguing and gallivanting, and never a word to the bees!' he grumbled. 'Why not tell them yourself?' I asked him. 'Is it me to be doing such a thing? It needs to be one of the kin.' 'Well,' I told him, 'the bride and the groom are my godchildren. Would I be near enough?' 'Ah, you would!' he said, with a brightening eye. 'Yer a bit of a bee yerself.' So, puffed up with this piece of flattery, I went and told the hive and it hummed. The news would be spread abroad and doubtless commented upon.

How does one get to be a bit of a bee? I've always remembered that phrase and have come to believe that the way to it is to recognize that in spite of one's knowing — all the stuff that has been picked up, or poured in along the way — one is always in some very deep sense in front of the Unknown; and I mean the Unknown as absolute and unknowable, that which unremittingly evokes the question without ever guaranteeing the answer. I think that it is only by taking this far from comfortable stance that one becomes able to receive the intimations that the Unknown is continually sending back to us, as a river at its sea-mouth sends back news of the sea to its source.

These intimations are essentially bee-stuff — not, or not only, the ritual dance upon the petal, the pollen brought home on proboscis or leg, the honey generated and fermented by what the bee finds within and without — but bee-stuff, nevertheless. For we, too, have been and are always being told those things that are known to the bees — whether we hear it is another matter. There is a fund of ancient knowledge in man's very bloodstream, if he but knew it. The secrets of the runes, the megalithic stones, the mysterious process we call language — our ancient forefathers understood them — are there in the flowing blood, witnessed to, equivocally but veraciously, by such oracles as myth, symbol, tradition, parable, fairy tale, ritual, legend.

I am not talking here of what is known as the supernatural or of extra-sensory perception. For me such words are like Prospero's insubstantial pageant faded. The natural is enough. Nature, if it is nature at all, has supernature up its sleeve; sensory perception has the extra under its belt. No, I speak of the substantial bloodstream and the body that contains it, microcosm of the macrocosmic planet and all its running rivers. In every tradition, every religion, the body is the essential alchemical vessel in which everything happens. An old Tibetan scripture says 'This little body holdeth all.' And a verse from the Pali Canon reads — 'My friend, in this very body, six feet of it with its senses, thoughts, and feelings, is the world, the origin of the world, the ceasing of the world and the way of its cessation.' In Egypt it was known as 'the Net,' a device for catching what can be caught — herring or leviathan, the drowned wreck with its salty gold, papyrus hidden in sealed amphora, the songs the Sirens sang. Was it by chance, I wonder, that the disciples in the Gospels were, largely, fishermen, dredging with nets for the things of the deep, for fish and more than fish? And is not all this telling us — as a bee might tell if it could speak — that nothing is truly known until it is known organically? My mind, by rote, is aware of the concept that 'Full fathom five my father lies' and the words, though lovely, are merely words. But when I learn that a fathom is not merely a five foot abstraction but the wide stretch of a man's arms — that palpable, tangible, bodily gesture! — I understand with the whole of me how deep I have to dive for him; and to know that nothing of him doth fade but doth suffer a sea-change into something rich and strange.

Shakespeare, being Shakespeare, must have realized when he wrote that song that it was a shining indication of the way the bloodstream worked. It takes my father — or the primal stuff, whichever you like — deep down into its meandering fluid and, lawfully, pays it no mind. By law — again the paradox — he, or it, has to be forgotten.

Who is there who does not have the fleeting sense — here for a moment and gone again — that once, long ago, we were told a story that now forever eludes us? What was it? Who told it? Why is something known and then not known? Where shall I look for what I have lost?

There is a clue to this phenomenon in a piece of Hebrew folklore. When a child is born, it says, an angel recites the Torah to it and tells it all and everything. That done, he puts his finger on the infant lip, leaving a cleft that is there for ever and says one word 'Forget!'

Later, the Hasidists elaborated the legend, introducing an absent-minded angel who, to a child significantly nicknamed Green, told all, but overlooked the injunction. The result was that Green knew everything — at least in his head — and rattled off names and dates and places, driving those about him to the brink of murder. So they smuggled him away to the desert, where he could tell what he knew to the stones, and at last prevailed on another angel to touch him and say the imperative word. After that, Green was silent. Perhaps he came to realize that if a thing is to be remembered, it has first to be forgotten. His mind had to lose its knowing to the bloodstream in order that there it could be digested, simmered as in a crucible, suffer the sea-change and be given back. So, my father's bones become coral. I can wear him as a necklace.

It is by this process of distillation, a world within a grain of sand, that what the bees know is divulged to us — always unsparingly, never with punches pulled. Take, for instance, the nursery rhymes, those miniscule Greek dramas. From our first breath they are quick to assure us of the sorrowful fact that when the bough breaks the cradle will fall. No question of 'if', you notice. There never was a bough that did not break. We are rocked to sleep, contentedly, by a story that is in no sense a bedtime story. As for king's horses and king's men, anyone who puts his faith in them is quickly disabused of his dream. Humpty Dumpty can never be put together — that is one of the facts of life. And yet — the cunning logic of the bee-stuff — unless Humpty Dumpty falls, you will never get a chicken!

'Are you sleeping?' we ask of Frère Jacques. And, no bones about it, yes he is, the monk whose monkish vow was to wake! Ding, dang, dong. The bell is rung. But does he hear it? We are never told. The bees are cagey, temperamental — mum when you want them to hum and, another time, before we have even learned to spell, imposing upon us in full-throated chorus precepts most difficult to follow. 'Leave them alone and they'll come home.' In other words — 'Sit still. Do nothing. All will be well.' If I had the courage — and it needs daring — I would take Bo-Peep as my patron saint. Nothing lost, think of it, not even their tails!

Carl Gustav Jung who, clearly, must often have hearkened to the bees, once wrote, 'One could almost say that if all the world's traditions were cut off at a single blow the whole of culture and the whole history of religion would start all over again with the next generation.' A marvellous statement to have 'almost' made. Indeed, why not have gone the whole hog and quite made it? For it is true. And worthy to be stated along with Nietzsche's formulation. 'It is not,' he said, 'that there is some hidden thought or theory at the bottom of myth but that myth itself is a kind or style of thinking; it imports an idea of the universe in its sequence of events, actions, and sufferings.'

Inevitably, in each generation, there will be passionate spirits who listen to the bees with an attentive ear, go hunting for that which has been lost and remake what has been unmade; who know that London Bridge, forever falling down, must forever be built up. Here again we have, masquerading as a nursery game, a symbol of great antiquity, the bridge as threshold — that which at the same time separates and conjoins two worlds, a reconciler of opposites. The bridge, too, outwits the devil — who is known to abhor whatever unites, and whose arch-enemy is running water — by providing a means for the soul's crossing from one stage to another. It is the Sword Across the Abyss of the Grail Legend: it corresponds to the Buddhist raft by which one arrives — given 'Great faith. Great doubt. Great perseverance!' — at that fabled other shore.

They will remind us, those passionate spirits, of all the ritualistic bee-stuff that we have *unlawfully* forgotten. For instance, that Christmas, for all its rejoicing and gallimaufry, is a re-enacting of Christ's Mass — when gold was given for the king, frankincense for the high-priest, and myrrh to anoint the corpse; a reminder, not wholly festive, that with our exchanges of tinselled packets we are bringing to a child and to each other gifts of life and of death. No coin — or myth — is without its obverse.

We kiss under the mistletoe. But do we know, if the bees have not told us, that this rite, too, has one foot in the grave? The golden bough, by means of which Aeneas was able to pass through the Underworld and return unhurt to the light of day was a branch of mistletoe. Baldur the Beautiful, Apollo's Hyperborean brother, was slain by a sprig of mistletoe, the one thing in all the world that had not promised not to hurt him. So, that kiss, for all the pleasure of it, is a gesture of placation. 'Carry us safely through the dark! Mistletoe, do not hurt us!'

And again, at New Year, when the twelve strokes sound and we make our resolutions — 'I will be good; turn over a leaf; be unmade and made anew' — we are embodying, even if we do not know it, or perhaps being embodied by, the myth of eternal return; the periodic destruction and recreation of the cosmos, common to all religions, when world, time, and man himself are, after a ritual pause, ritually renewed. I happened on this primordial theme when I took down, at the bees' dictation, a story that reflects it.

'When does the old year end?' asks a child. 'On the first stroke of midnight,' he is told. 'And the new year — when does it begin?' 'On the last stroke of midnight.' 'Well, then, what happens in between?' The question, once asked, required an answer from those who know what the Druids knew. Long after I had written down this story, I listened to a radio reporter who was describing the ceremonies of an African tribe at the end of their lunar — or solar? — year. At a given moment, it appeared, the chanting and the drumming ceased as the gods invisibly withdrew. For a few seconds — twelve perhaps! — absolute silence reigned. Then the drums broke out again in triumph as the gods invisibly returned with the new year in their arms. 'And,' the reporter added, 'though I do not ask you to believe it, I can vouch for the fact that my tape recorder, for those few moments of sacred silence, without a touch of my hand, stopped spinning.'

Well, a bee could believe it and so could I. Anyone used to yoga practice experiences the ritual pause between the outgoing and the indrawn breath. Between one breathtime and the next, between one lifetime and the next, something waits for a moment.

Our profane life is full of these hidden meanings, of clues that we are at pains to find but pass by, not knowing what to look for — or, more exactly, how to let meaning discover *us*. For this to happen we need to become aware, as our forefathers were well aware, that by the fact of having a body, the very fact of being born, each of us has assumed a place in the cosmos and is part of all that is. But not only that.

Myth, by design, makes it clear that we are meant to be something more than our own personal history. It places us — and it is not a comfortable position — squarely between the opposing forces that keep us, and the world, in balance — the two Earth Shapers, benign and malignant, checking and disciplining each other to produce a viable whole. One has only to think of Prometheus, forethought, and Epimetheus, his unfortunate brother; of Ahura Mazdao and Angra Mainyu, the light and the dark of Zoroastrianism; of the Hindu Vishnu and Shiva, preserver and destroyer; of the Navajo Water-Child, son of the rivers, and Monster-Slayer, born of fire — the cool, flowing sap of one and the solar heat of the other; the angels and devils of Christianity.

How pleasant it would be, and easeful, to be able to choose between them; to fall to one side or the other and so escape the conflict. But the myth allows us no soft option, at any time in our lives. A child of three once said to me, 'I am two boys, Goodly and Badly.' Alas, too young for this! I thought, but at the same time realized that truth requires us to be young, no matter what our age. And then came the faltering, anxious question — 'Which do you like best?' I knew the answer, and all the breadth and depth of it, but I had to appear to pay it mind. If I chose Goodly, then Badly would be in the wilderness, alone with his badliness and lost. If Badly, then Goodly would be in the same plight, alone with his goodliness. 'Joy and woe are woven fine/A clothing for the soul divine.' 'To tell you the truth,' I said gravely, 'I like them both the same.' The look of anxiety turned to relief and a trustful hand met mine.

A passing moment? Maybe. A lifetime is a passing moment. Rilke was in the same plight — who is not? — when he said, I suppose to a psychiatrist, 'Have a care! Do not take away my devils. Without them, how shall I find my angels?' But he was a poet and hearkened to bees. From them, if in no other way, he would have known of the Chinese Symbol of the Great Ultimate that Zen purloined and made its own — the two fish, black and white conjoined, white with black eye, black with white. With that before us, do we need words?

Nor do we need to be in a special state or a special place — in a temple or on top of a steeple — to approach the things the bees know. Myth, symbol, ritual, tradition, albeit in degraded forms, cry out to us from the street corners. You cannot open a newspaper without finding them crowding there with all their splendour and violence. Every comic strip acclaims them — Superman, Dick Tracy, the Incredible Hulk, all have their prototypes in myths which were never, at any time, pretty stories about the fairies in flowers.

Even our obsession with sport — which makes people smash up trains and stab each other because some man has, or has not, done something to a ball — even this, though ghastly and desacralized, has a taste of the ancient rites, when games were played to honour the illustrious dead or to dedicate man's sweat, his life-stuff, to the rejuvenation of the earth. Not long ago I read of a baseball team whose members, after the death of one of them, wore the dead man's number on their sleeves. And whoever achieved a home run flung up his hand to the sky in salute. The mind had no part in that dedication. It was a wholly instinctive gesture and done by myth itself.

For if man does not, of intention, enact it, keep alive its rituals, preserve unbroken the chain of its being, myth will enact itself through man. It is doing this now, all over the world, with ambivalent intensity — the tidal wave of births and deaths; the devil invoked in the name of God; instant heroes and instant villains; gods masquerading — myth has its wit and irony — as chairman, president, or mullah; Persephone abducted to the Underworld, eating the symbolic pomegranate and her mother searching for her child through the Californian fields; the Great Goddess rising in wrath, dressing up as female priest or terrorist; she who *is* terror as well as beauty — the Hindu Kāli, the Celtic Morrigan, La Belle Dame Sans Merci — and by her very nature priestess with no need of dog-collar to proclaim it, is calling herself, not such honourifics of nobility as Gaia, Isis, Hecate, Hera, but Woman's Liberation. All these show myth in action. For good or ill? That is not the question. It is always good *and* ill.

For, true to its multisidedness, what myth takes with one hand it will give with the other. Anyone able to sit and listen to the bees will constantly find himself reminded of the turbulent groundswell of ancient lore; of what, as St Augustine said, 'Was, is and will ever be.' Ever, yes, and everywhere. The rivers of the world, the planet's bloodstream, commune with each other underground for, in fact, they are all one river — Ganges that flows out of Shiva's hair, Shenandoah and the wide Missouri, the trickle of liquid history with London on its banks — all have the same story to tell. For myth and tradition, no matter what their place of origin, if indeed they ever had an origin — 'the Authors,' as Blake said, 'are in Eternity' — are an inseparable unity; and the symbols, differ in form though they do, act as spindles round which is wound the one essential thread. Any one of them will serve, as Robert Frost put it, 'To stay our minds on and be stayed,' and bring us to our centre.

The Omphalos, for instance, the world navel, where the energy of eternity pours itself into time — Mount Meru, Mount Olympus, the Rock of Jerusalem, the Kaaba, Borobodur, the Kiva; the field of Golgotha mythologically homologized to the Garden of Eden in order that, on the same spot, the second Adam could offer up the life that came down to the first; the temple, the church, the body of man.

The world navel stands, as it were, at the mid-point of another symbol, the cosmic axis, the pole that pierces the three worlds and has as its prototypes pillars, obelisks, minarets, spires, and ziggurats. The Milky Way is held to be a pillar. And also a path to be taken. In old British maps one finds Watling Street, still one of the thoroughfares of London, continuing all the way through Europe and ending up in the sky. No break, in fact, between earth and heaven. Step off a pavement in the city and you're en route for Orion. Whether you get there is another matter.

And the cosmic axis can be assimilated to the World Tree, for me the most central of all. Think of the Norse Yggdrasil, on which, having parted with his right eye in exchange for the gifts of memory and premonition, the god Odin hung suspended, making himself its fruit. 'Nine days I hung on the windy tree, offering myself to myself.' With such a phrase humming within us, can we say that the gods are dead?

In our own tradition, the Cross is par excellence the World Tree, its wood hewn, myth assures us, out of the branch from which Eve plucked the apple. One sees the two-sided logic of this and the depth of the phrase in the Latin liturgy — *O felix culpa!* O happy fault! If the apple had not first been plucked what need would there be of redemption? For man to be ransomed, bought at a price, he has first to be made captive. To remember, one must first forget. To be lifted up, one must first have fallen. If honey, then also sting.

The Buddha sat under the World Tree to receive enlightenment; the tree of the Kabbala, where the vital forces move up and down, is sib to Jacob's ladder with its ascending and descending angels; and in the world of fairy tale there is Jack's miraculous Beanstalk.

A less well known but, for me, the most powerful aspect of the symbol is the Inverted Tree. 'Hast heard,' says the Scandinavian Edda, 'where the tree grows whose crown is on earth and its roots in heaven?' The Rig Veda calls it the Aswattha Tree. Plato speaks of man as 'an inverted tree, of which the roots tend heavenward and the branches down to earth.' The Hanged Man of the Tarot cards is another aspect of that tree as is also Gurdjieff's Ray of Creation, rooted above in the Absolute and descending in a series of octaves through ever denser states of being from one Do to another.

Is not this symbol, in all its aspects, telling us, once again, the old, old story of the Prodigal Son? 'I will arise and go to my Father,' he said when he 'came to himself'. But could he do that, could he turn again home, unless he had first left his father? To be found you have to be lost.

So, we are left in question, which is where the myth is designed to leave us. Time, space, matter are mutable realities. The Sphinx, the Pyramids, the stone temples are, all of them, ultimately, as flimsy as London Bridge; our cities but tents set up in the cosmos. We pass. But what the bee knows, the wisdom that sustains our passing life — however much we deny or ignore it — that for ever remains. Begotten, not made, it is here to declare to us, in the words of the old Greek poet Aratus, that 'Full of Zeus are all the ways of men.' That word 'full' means what it says, and therefore, with the ambiguity of myth, reminds us, too, that the sky is always falling, that the bough inevitably will break and the rain it raineth every day.

What does one do with these trifles, not unconsidered, that are snapped up from the bloodstream? Throw them back, as the fisherman does the tiddler, to let them grow and breed! So — I toss them into a tributary of that whole planetary vein, that flows just around the corner; from which, long wandering beside it, I have learned so much. And also thrown into it so much — lamentation, doubt, question, gratitude, and joy. Let it all go, river, to the sea to be made over, absolved and dissolved, suffer the sea-change and return as bee-stuff.

Sweet Thames, run softly till I end my song!

First published in 'Parabola' on the theme of Earth & Spirit, New York, 1981.

The Seventh Day

'WELL, to begin with, 'twas a courteous thing to do — better still, it was a loving thing. And moreover a thing that had to be.'

'What? Creating Sunday?'

'Ay, begob. Hadn't He said He'd be making man in His own image and here He was, making Himself in man's image — or what, when the time came, would be his image.'

'You mean that He knew it was necessary, that man would need a time to sleep, a day to rest from his labours?'

'I do that. Is it Him that would need to take forty winks, Him with the ever-open eye that noteth the fall of the sparrow? Never a blink did He take at all even after those six days colloguing with the draughtboard.'

'Drawing board?' I hazarded, uncertain as yet of his drift.

Thade, I must tell you, is a Teller, as well as a hedger and ditcher: a story as you watch him turn his spade, the time by a quick glance at the sun, a lie — always superlative — when he thinks the circumstances warrant it.

All untutored, illiterate when it comes to reading the papers, super-literate in the matter of ancient lore, he would not hesitate to take on Socrates if philosophical disputation was required.

'Ay, drawing board. There's not much difference, the way He'd be making the plan and its laws before He set the contrivance going. Like yourself, and you writing a book, that would be the length of it. First, the little glint of a notion and then you'd write it down.'

'So — you're really talking of principles!'

'I am. You're the great one for putting your hand on a word. You should have been a school teacher.' He eyed me impishly, or as impishly as his tortured Irish face would allow, over a pipe of reeking herbs.

'So what you're telling me is this, Thade — that the first six days were simply ideas?'

'Simply, is it? Isn't that the hardest part, the way you'd grind it out of yourself, like the mill-wheel grinding meal; making the flower before it was in the field and the herb before it grew? This is the whip the atheists use to beat you out of the ring. "Arrah," they say. Are ye asking us to believe in a God that knows so little about what is what, that He makes the light on the first day ere ever the sun shows up? As if the one could exist without the other!"'

He shook out his pipe at the edge of the ditch and tamped in coltsfoot and peat.

'In a way,' I said, 'you can hardly blame them.'

'Sure, you can blame them. The sun and the moon and the stars are just lanterns, the like you'd be putting by a hole in the road and blowing them out in the morning. The fourth day was good enough for them. But the light that's companion to the dark, the eternal' — he paused to let the word rise in him — 'the eternal and supernal light, that would have to come first. Inside yourself or outside yourself, that light is the beginning.'

Puff, puff, went the coltsfoot, as I pondered his theme.

'And after the principles — six whole days of them — there had, you see, to be a stop, though it's not an ending I'm meaning. It's the way when I play a scale on my whistle' — a penny pipe dangled from his belt — 'there's a pause before I go on to the next, a sort of gap between the notes where I can take a breath. It's a law. And who but Himself was the one to make it? So, on the seventh day He rested and created the space that had to be between the thought and the act. A gate, you might say, open wide, for anything to enter. And what entered? The Devil himself, without a doubt, and sorrow, too, I'm thinking.'

'So — that was how everything began?'

'It was. The clay, quick as you'd spit, was on the wheel and it spinning the great whales and the winged fowl and the cattle and creeping things. And each after its kind producing and increasing like the multiplication table, the fish slithering through the sea, the herb bearing the promised seed and the trees putting on fruit. What's the digging of a ditch to that? Sure, He'd be sweating with the labour of it, if He'd been like the man He made.'

'Yes. And the man, of course, was the crux of it.'

'He was, then. For without him, where was the why of it all? Can a crustacean be beguiled or a weasel grieve for the grief of the world

or a frog on a lily leaf inquire — Why am I here — and the leaf, too?'
'And those things had to be done?'

'Ay, weren't they on the drawing board? "It's Myself that'll make the laws," He said, "and the Devil will slip in and see they're broken. That will be the way of it and then we'll see what will happen." '

'It doesn't say so in the Bible.'

" 'Tis there, hidden, snug as an egg under a hen. And' — he threw me a dark, ambiguous glance — 'that's where yourself comes in.'

'Me?' It seemed an unlikely statement.

'Who else? Yourself, along with the Serpent. For would Adam hearken to such a one? He'd be too busy naming the beasts. But yourself, with nothing to do at all, would be glad of a little titbit of gossip and the slinking, wheedling, artfulness of having a secret whispered.'

Thade's voice, full of storyteller's guile, was almost serpentine.

'And after that,' he went on, softly, 'how could you help, you being you — and I mean woman — but share the secret with the man and you just out of the warmth of his ribs?'

'But could I, could she, do otherwise? How else —?'

'Increase and multiply? She could not, she had to tell him. Ha! Sin, is it? Well, tell me where would *He* have been, the one that was at last to come, born between the ox and the ass, if it hadn't been for the apple?'

'*O felix culpa!*' I remembered my Latin.

'Ah, the monkish tongue — lissom and glib. I would hear it when I was a lad. Ay, *felix culpa.* They'll send you to Purgatory for that and never note the rest.'

'What rest? Didn't they eat the whole of the apple?'

'They did. And along with the turning to one another, as by law they had to do, they also got the full of the knowing. *There* was the sin and the grief of it, that they would know and not use what they knew to render back the world. But they used the knowledge for themselves and it's them and their kin that now walk in the Garden, swollen with arrogance in their sagacity, and Him that's outside, knocking.'

'That would not have been on the drawing board.'

'Well, it's difficult to believe that it would be.' Thade turned to me a tormented face. 'But who's to know? He's wise and subtle. Arrah, it's a mystery. It's glad I'd be to tell a tale that would knit the ravellings together and give myself ease and comfort. But I'll not do it. It's a mystery and all we can do is to stand before it.'

Unwittingly, near enough as makes no matter, Thade the Teller, hedger and ditcher, was quoting the words of Lear:

> *And take upon us the mystery of things*
> *As if we were God's spies.*

Should I tell him? No. Enough had been told.

He glanced upwards. 'She's there!' he said, nodding at Venus, low in the sky — the evening star always takes him home and, with a shrug that seemed to take on rather than shake off a burden, he left me.

I felt proud of him, the great Thade, for not making a happy ending for either himself or me.

My way lay in the opposite direction. And I thought, as I went, that when we went to sleep tonight, we would expect — if Azrael did not take us — to wake in the morning's sunlight. But as for supernal, eternal light, that, I think Thade would have said, would have to wake in us.

First published in 'Parabola' on the theme of Sleep, New York, 1982.

Where Will All The Stories Go?

A CONVERSATION BETWEEN
LAURENS VAN DER POST AND P L TRAVERS

PLT: Laurens, let us go back to the beginning of things. I have long carried this question — where, having come so far, will all the stories go? Naturally, since it is your country, I am thinking specially of Africa. And I wonder, when everyone there has a gun and a television set, what will happen to the ancient lore? Only today I was reading of the increasing number of suicides among those who leave the wild for the cities. Lacking the extended family, separated from the tribe, and therefore from the stories, what have they to lean upon? Already the stories are becoming unavailable to those who need them most. Well, you know more about this than anyone, almost, in the world. Let us share it together.

vdP: Ah, I do not believe that I know more about stories than you do, but I couldn't love them more. And I love them because it seems to me that without the stories, human beings wouldn't be here. Couldn't be. Human beings *are* a story; they are living a story and anyone open to this story is living a part — perhaps all — of themselves.

PLT: So there is no need to invent myths, which is what — feeling a lack in themselves — people are nowadays trying to do?

vdP: Well, I think that that is an impossibility. It is one of the great illusions of the literature and the art and the life of our time that people like Tolkien are supposed to have 'invented' myths. They have done nothing of the sort. They have substituted a sort of intellectual effort, a conscious determination — which they, quite wrongly, call myth — for this very profound process which cannot come from anywhere but out of life itself. It is something that falls into us. I have been very much concerned about this because, only recently, I was asked to say something about Descartes' famous statement — 'I think, therefore I am.' *There*, it seems to me, is the beginning of the fatal hubris of our time. Of course, there is an area in which we think — who could deny it? — but, really, all the most important aspects of thought come from that which is thinking through us. And this process is the myth, one of the most profound things of life; it is creation itself, which becomes accessible and, in part, energizes and gives, of its own accord, a sense of direction to the human creature. It is something with which — if we use our brains and imagination — we are in partnership. And the story is one of the roots of this area, this area from which the myth arises, which sustains and feeds the human spirit and enables man, and life on earth, to be greater than it could otherwise have been.

PLT: And that's what men are now hunting for — for life's sake, one could say — and they think they can get it by inventing the kind of thing that brought *Roots* to all the television screens in America.

vdP: I thought it was appalling, phony and untrue to myth and even historically untrue. And what makes it so sad is that it comes out of the genuine longing of millions of people for roots, those millions who do not realize that in the most profound sense, we carry our roots within ourselves. They need not be physical roots, which is what this man has tried to provide, a phony kind of physical source for what, in a sense, is the super-physical, a hunger for roots in the myth.

PLT: I would say that really we don't even need that 'super'. It exists. It courses in our blood, carried along from one generation to the next — wouldn't you agree?

vdP: I would. I only use the word 'super' as a substitute for the whole process which moves and works within us.

PLT: It's the same with the word 'supernatural'. For me, the natural includes the 'super'. And this brings us to what you wrote in, I think, *The Heart of the Hunter*, where you say — or, rather, the Bushmen say — 'We are dreamed by a dream.'

vdP: Ah, I was very moved by that because, being in the company of a very ancient form of man, a Stone Age hunter in the Kalahari Desert, I was pressing him to tell me about the Beginning, *his* idea of the Beginning and the beginning of those stories you were speaking of. He looked at me in astonishment and said, 'Well, that's a very difficult thing because, you must know, there's a dream dreaming us.' And this seemed to me to sum it up, to arrive, for instance, at the point where all the explorers of the human spirit have begun — and also ended. It leads us to Shakespeare's famous conclusion in *The Tempest*, one of the last plays he wrote, where he comes face to face with the fact that he has exhausted all his own powers, come to the frontiers of himself, where something other than what has brought him to this point must now carry him on. You remember the epilogue —

And my ending is despair
Unless I be relieved by prayer . . .

But even before that he has come to the conclusion that

We are such stuff
As dreams are made on.

And what is the distance between him and that little Stone Age man who had never before seen a white man and never heard of Shakespeare? For his own myth inside him tells him: 'Look out! Watch! Listen! A dream is dreaming through you.' And this enriches him. It seems to me that this man, whom everybody else thought of as poor, despised, rejected, was rich in a way that we, with our technological abundance, are destitute.

PLT: We have nothing, we are poverty-stricken. This, in a way, is like the Australian concept of the Dreaming, of which I know a little, having been brought up there. Everything that is not at this very instant — when we're chopping wood or finding witchetty grubs — is in the Dreaming. I can go into the Dreaming and you can go into the Dreaming at any moment and be refreshed. The anthropologists call it the Dreamtime but that word 'time' immediately makes things move serially, puts them into place and locality. The Aborigines speak of it as the Dreaming — in their tribal tongues, *Tamminga* or *Dooghoor* — and for them everything is there. It is similar to what the Celtic peoples mythically call the Cauldron. They cannot go further back in their thought than a great-grandfather, nor further forward than a great-grandson. Beyond these, all is in the Dreaming — the making of the world, the great days, the great heroes. I was reminded of all this when reading — oh, it comes in several of your books — of what you — or the Bushmen, rather — call 'tapping'. 'There is a tapping in me'. Perhaps if Tolkien and the makers of *Roots* and all the other inventors of what cannot be invented could hear that tapping, listen for it as your Bushmen do, it could be in them as well, don't you think?

vdP: Yes. It is very interesting that we have both instinctively picked on Tolkien, because — though few realize it — Tolkien himself was born in Bushman country — at a place I know very well. And his own journey, his particular inward journey, began when, as a boy of eight, he had a vision of the evening star in the sky over Africa, that part of Africa which was ancient Bushman country. And to that extent he was sustained. It was those first eight African years that impelled him on his journey and aroused in him a sense of the importance of myth; but not sufficiently strongly for him to approach the myth in a spirit of humility, in the sense that he could have laid himself down and said: 'Take over. Tell me what you're about.' Instead, he began telling the myth what *it* was about and so, of course, it's no longer mythology. It doesn't work.

PLT: It remains invention. It comes out of his own enthusiasm and not from the myth's requirement.

vdP: It is the same process which has made modern man speak of this organic, dynamic force in the human spirit as unreal. They use myth as a synonym of that which is not.

PLT: As synonymous with lie. I am constantly protesting against that. What would Mantis say, I wonder, Mantis who is one of the great embodiments of myth that you write of so often and that I remember, too, from childhood. For me she was simply a praying mantis, I did not know her as a mythical creature. But she filled me with a sense of wonder — the long narrow-waisted insect praying. I would stand for hours watching her, wondering when the prayer would end. But it never did. The saints must envy such energy! And then, when I grew up, I found Mantis in your books and knew her — or him? — for one of the Lordly Ones. Tell a little about that.

vdP: Well, it's almost impossible for me to see Mantis as apart from my own beginning because of my early experience. One of the great influences in my life was a Stone Age nurse, far more important to me than my own parents. I remember, as a very little boy, hearing her talking with Mantis. She was asking, in the Bushman tongue, 'How high is the water?' And the mantis would put down its tiny hands.

PLT: You actually saw the mantis doing this? It is so completely a ritual.

vdP: I saw the mantis doing this. And I protested to my nurse, 'But, look, we're not near any water. We're a thousand miles from the sea. Why do you talk to Mantis about water? Does water come out of the desert?' 'Well,' she said, 'in the beginning, water was everywhere and Mantis was nearly drowned. And a bee came and rescued him and flew and flew all day long till the sun began to go down. Then the bee looked desperately round for a place where it could put Mantis and, suddenly, there it was! A wonderful flower above the water, a flower we no longer see on this earth, and the bee put Mantis inside it. So Mantis was safe, for from there, under the power of his own wings, he could find a dry rock to sit on.'

PLT: Ah, the bee! It had to be in the story, the sacred creature that everywhere brings and symbolizes life. Do you remember how the bees stung you and tried to send you away from the place of the sacred tree, so that your presence should not profane it? You first saw it in the swamp, remember, then in your dream, and again among those mysterious rocks that would not have their photographs taken. The bee was there, in that place of magic, where the paintings refused to go into the camera.

vdP: This is one of the strangest things that ever happened to me and it continues to haunt me. It's as though there's a parable in it, for, at that moment, not only myself, but the people for whom I was responsible, were in very grave danger. We were in a great treacherous swamp and one of my paddlers — we were using dugouts — was Samutchoso, a name meaning 'That which is left after reaping' — I didn't know that he was the so-called witch-doctor of my dug-out people, the Makoros — and he said to me: 'There's something I ought to tell you. Out there in the desert there are some hills and in these hills, right inside them, there are many rooms, and in these rooms live the master spirits of all created life. And on top of these hills, there's a pool of water that has never yet dried up; and beside this pool there is a tree whose name we not only do not know, but are not allowed to try to know, a tree that has fruit on it and this fruit is the fruit of knowledge.' 'Why are you telling me this?' I asked. 'Ah,' he said, 'that is for *you* to say.' 'Well, if we get out of this alive,' I said, 'will you take me there?' 'Yes, I will,' he said, 'but on one condition — that on the way to the hills there is no shooting, no killing. It's a law of their spirits — they are called the Slippery Hills, the Tsoudilo Hills — that no one may come to them with blood on his hands.'

I solemnly agreed.

Well, it so happened that I had a great deal of trouble getting out of the swamp and after that many difficulties to face. But when, many months later, I was free to go back, I myself remembered my pledge but, alas, I forgot to share it with the people who were travelling with me. So, on the way to the hills, with Samutchoso guiding us — I, as always, in the rear, for in the desert that is where trouble starts — one of those in front sighted a buck and, knowing that we needed food, shot it. I went cold when I heard those shots ring out and, seeing the expression on Samutchoso's face, I said to myself, 'Pray God, they've missed!' and to Samutchoso, 'Forgive me. Don't blame them. I forgot to tell them.' 'It's not for me to forgive,' he said. 'Only the spirits can do that.'

When we caught up with the others we found that, unfortunately, they had not missed but had killed two animals. And, when we eventually got to the hills, rising so extraordinarily out of the desert, we were in trouble from the moment we arrived. All night, with our camps pitched at the foot of the hills, hyenas and jackals and carrion crows cried like creatures out of *The Valkyrie*. But when my mechanic, who was also my tape-recordist, tried to record those noises, the machine — we had very primitive equipment but the best that could then be had — simply wouldn't work. It had been all right before, but now we could get nothing from it. And then, at dawn, just as we were waking, we were suddenly attacked by hordes of bees, coming from all directions. One of my guides, on all my Kalahari journeys, a marvellous and blameless man who had been for three years in the desert with me, got forty-three stings and was very ill. Curiously enough, I, alone, was not stung. And the moment the sun rose, all the bees vanished. So, we set out to start filming on the way. Looming above the desert, we came across a large rock and on it a set of rock paintings which no human being — I mean the words in the European sense — had ever seen. 'Film!' I shouted, and the camera started to turn. Then, suddenly, it snapped! It wouldn't work. The photographer inserted another magazine. Again the thing started turning and again it snapped and went out. So it continued all the morning, magazine after magazine not working and, as a last straw, the pivot on which the magazine turned — it was a fine German Araflex camera — disintegrated. Imagine it — a thing of steel! We were now without a camera but I still have in my possession such reels as we could save and its extraordinary how the shots start in frame, then gradually the frame narrows and — then stops.

'Well, at least,' I said to Samutchoso, 'you could, perhaps, take us to that pool that is never without water!'

In silence he led us on, past what must have been an ancient temple of some sort, for all the way to the top of the hills the rocks were embellished with most marvellous paintings — thousands of them, as though the animals they depicted were leading us in procession towards the pool, to keep us company. Thus it was we arrived at the water and beside it the tree with the strange fruit on it and a rock in which could clearly be seen two deep indentations.

'Here,' said Samutchoso, 'is the place where the first spirit knelt when he prayed to the tree to take care of all that had been created. I will show you how he prayed.' And he knelt down in the two marks and was about to raise his hands in prayer, when he fell back, shocked, his face ashen. 'The spirits have tried to kill me,' he cried, and hurried us away, back to the camp, not permitting us to pluck any of the fruit in order that it could be identified. 'No! We are not allowed to take it,' he said. 'The spirits are very angry.'

That night, the recorder again refused to work and the next day we were again assailed by bees. We were all of us in such a state about this that I even began to wonder whether my Landrover could be persuaded to start. For three days we tried to get camera and recorder working — nothing doing, nothing.

PLT: Man's work. Man's work. It failed because something more powerful had taken over.

vdP: Yes. And I was at my wits' end. So I walked out, in the evening, to be on my own, taking my gun — it was dangerous country — simply for protection. I walked for miles round the base of the hills and suddenly, out of them, stepped an enormous Kudu bull, a marvellous animal; it really seemed to me like a god, in the level light of the sun. I looked at it and it looked back at me, absolutely without fear, as though in that look it was trying to tell me something. I was so moved by this that I gave it a military salute; and it turned around and went into the bush and away back up the hill.

As I returned to the camp, something happened in me that made me say to Samutchoso — 'Suppose I wrote a letter to the spirits asking forgiveness and buried it at the foot of the first rock picture — a pair of hands impressed in paint on the rock — do you think that would help?' In reply, he took a needle, asked me for a piece of cotton which he wound round his hand, then, putting the needle in the lifeline of his left hand, he gazed at it in a sort of trance. And suddenly it seemed as though he were seeing millions of beings around him, for he murmured to them 'No, no, not you! Nor you, nor you, but *you over there*, come here to me.' Apparently, whatever it was obeyed, for he communed with it for a long time and then came out of his trance, saying: 'Yes, I think it might work, but the spirits are very angry with you.'

I felt in my bones that this letter would need to be correct in every detail — even with place and time and date and map reference as well. So I wrote, asking forgiveness for any unintentional disrespect we had shown, saying that this letter was an act of contrition not only on our own behalf but on that of others who might come after us. I made everybody sign it and those who could not, made their mark.

'Really, Laurens,' said my hunter — a great friend and terribly English — 'this is too ridiculous! I simply can't do a thing like this! What if they hear of it at my club?' But he signed, nevertheless, and I promised that the club would never know. So we rinsed out an old bottle, put the letter inside, and securely corked it, and Samutchoso and I went out at dawn and buried it at the foot of the hill. A feeling of some kind of catharsis came over me then, and I said to Samutchoso — 'You brought us here. Can you tell me if it will be all right to take us back?' 'It's not for me to say. You must ask the spirits.' And again he went through his motions with the needle. 'The spirits say that all will be well now, but at this place to which you are going — (I did not myself know, at the time, where we were going) — you will meet more trouble. You must realize, however, that it belongs to the past.'

Then, as we walked back he said sadly, even tragically, 'You know, even ten years ago, if you'd offended them like this, you would now, quite surely, be dead. They are not what they were, the spirits.'

PLT: They are not what they were because man is not what he was! Though I can't help feeling a little kindly towards the hunter who was afraid the club might get to hear of it! That spirits could read an English letter and the marks of untutored men — who would believe that? It takes an acquaintance with myth to recognize that what you did was an outward and visible sign of an inward and spiritual intention.

vdP: Yes. And there's a sequel. People now know from my books about this letter and the place where it was buried, and fly aircraft overhead to try to get a glimpse of the paintings. Immediately after my experience a German scientific expedition went to investigate them, and barged in with their trucks which were immediately destroyed by fire. So, it's not just subjective. There is also objective evidence. And yet, knowing all this, and the spirit in which I had done it, they have dug up the bottle and it's now in the museum at Botswana. That's where the myth is, in museums, for most of us.

PLT: Sacrilege. And I asked you where the stories go! I can't ask what we can do to get them back but know only that it has to be done. There must be a few men who understand the need for this. For instance, not long ago, I was told of three or four English doctors who had gone out to live with some African tribe to learn their methods of healing; and how they discovered that this is not a matter of giving a medicine or an antidote to one sick person, but that it is, rather, a communal matter — the whole family, the whole tribe, is concerned with the healing; feasting, dancing, sharing the sickness and the health among all. How could we bring such an activity to our world — such sharedness? But perhaps something has started.

vdP: Well, I think you must just go on telling stories. They, too, are under law and cannot escape from it.

PLT: You mean, perhaps, that, ultimately, the stories themselves can heal?

vdP: Yes, that is probably a more accurate way of saying it. This process cannot be defeated; life itself depends on it. I could tell you so many examples from the primitive world.

PLT: Well, tell me about the one — because I have something to add to it — where the Bushman woman came down on a cord and promised to stay with her Bushman husband as long as he did not look into her basket.

vdP: Yes, that story is much to the point. Stories of the stars play a fantastic role in their lives, if you know how to decode them. You touch the spirit of Greece here. The Bushman's origin of the Milky Way is very like the Greek. I once saw a Bushman woman holding up her child to the sky and asking that it be given the heart of a star.

PLT: I have thought that that's where Haley got his scene where the child is held up to the moon — from your Bushman story.

vdP: Well, you probably know as well as I do the enormous amount of borrowing that goes on in the modern world.

PLT: Ah, but, you know, it has to be, this borrowing. It's not yours or mine. It's there to be taken, a great big cauldron. One man takes something from it, another sees this and says 'That's true, that's what I want.' So he goes and takes it from the first man. I'm not worried about this, it's part of the general heritage.

vdP: Yes. It's only the miserable ego that steps in. In the Bushman story the child was to have the heart of a star because 'the stars', they say, 'are great hunters. You can hear them on their courses up there.' And that hunting, as you know, is a symbol of the search for the story, for meaning. Baudelaire talks about art being the summons on the horn of the hunter. *'Les chasseurs perdus, dans les grands bois.'* Lost in the great forest of life, they blast out the summons which is art, which is story.

PLT: As a child in Australia, the stars seemed so close. I used to think I could hear them humming. I never told anyone, they would have laughed.

vdP: But you do. You do hear them hum. 'Listen,' my Bushmen would say, 'they are hunting.' But to get back to the story of the woman with the basket; it carries an immense mythological charge. The man, after feeling somehow that something was being stolen from him, saw one night a group of beautiful girls coming down from the sky on a cord. Each carried a little tightly woven basket. And one of them he caught. 'Yes,' she said, 'I will live with you, on condition that you never look inside my basket without my permission.' He agreed, but, inevitably, he said 'What the hell!' or the Stone Age equivalent of the phrase. And one day, when he was alone, he opened the basket, peeped inside and roared with laughter. 'You have looked into the basket!' she accused him, when she returned. 'Yes, you silly woman, why make such a secret of it when there is nothing in it? The basket's empty.' 'You saw *nothing?*' She gave him a tragic look, turned her back and disappeared into the sunset. And the Bushman who told me the story said to me, 'It wasn't the looking but the fact that he could not perceive in the basket all the wonders she had brought him from the stars.' And that, for me, in a sense is one of the images that the story is to the human spirit. The basket brings us its star-stuff and the pundits — the intellectuals and the critics — look into it and say it's all rubbish and superstition, and that there's nothing in it.

PLT: Would you accept a carpetbag coming from the stars? I had never read your story, but when Mary Poppins arrived, the children looked into her carpetbag and, like your Bushman, found it empty. And yet out of it came all her mundane daily possessions, including a camp bed! Did all that come from the stars? We do not know. Emptiness is fullness.

vdP: It is, it is. And I think the use of a carpetbag is a wonderful example of what I mean by making a traditional story contemporary. That carpetbag had, in fact, a magic carpet inside it.

PLT: Yes, but disguised. And from where was the magic carpet stolen? Out of the cauldron, of course! For instance, your film on the Kalahari gave me the ostrich egg, which also must have come from there. The ostrich was such a forgetful bird, you said, that she had to put one egg in front of her outside the nest to remind her of what she was doing. Later, when I was listening to the Greek Easter service on the radio, a reporter described the monks filing in, with eyes downcast, all except one, who was gazing round at the congregation. 'Clearly,' said the reporter, 'he had forgotten the ostrich egg hanging over the altar.' But how, I wondered, had the ostrich egg got there? I sensed a myth in the air. Years later, seeing a group of Coptic churches on television, all with ostrich eggs strung across the ceiling, my question arose again. I wrote to the producer, who told me that there were two schools of thought here, one that says the ostrich is a forgetful bird and another that of all the birds she is the most remembering. So, does she remember or does she forget? It almost doesn't matter. The egg, in both cases, is the reminder, and the link between my three experiences.

vdP: Yes, yes, the link. However much we try to deny it, the dream goes dreaming through us. Deep in the spirit of European man there is an ostrich and it lives heraldically. Our Prince of Wales has three ostrich feathers in his crest; in Stone Age mythology, the moon was made out of the feather of an ostrich. So the ostrich, in a sense, is Prometheus, the bird from which man, Mantis and the god-hero stole the fire and brought it to man.

PLT: But there's a sequel to my egg story. Hearing it, a Jungian analyst we both know gave me an ostrich egg to take with me to America. And while I was there it sat on my bookshelf, sometimes but, alas, not always, remembered. And when I was leaving for England, it seemed to me that it said 'Don't take me!' So I gave it to the Dean of the Cathedral Church of St John the Divine in New York who thought it would look well on his mantelpiece. But I knew it wouldn't stay there. The egg would go where it belonged. And it did. The next time I saw it, on another trip, it was hanging in the Cathedral, above the altar of St Saviour's Chapel. There's a story for you!

vdP: And add to it the belief of many primitive people in Africa that the sun is an egg.

PLT: Is it known by whom or what it was laid?

vdP: It hatches great birds! And how it was laid is not to be known. You will find this determination among instinctive people not to try to carry an act of knowing too far. They say, 'This is where we must stop.' And then they let the myth take over and wait till it tells them what else there is.

PLT: That is what I've always found. We must stand in front of the mystery. 'Take upon us,' as Lear said, 'the mystery of things as if we were God's spies.'

vdP: Yes, and if one looks at it that way, one finds the lines of communication between the storyteller of today and the first storyteller; between us and the person who dreams, or is dreamed by the universe, these lines of communication are intact. They can never, never fail.

PLT: We have ancestors.

vdP: We have ancestors. Long ago I sat at the feet of a Japanese storyteller and he began with 'Once Upon a Time.' And years later, in a night of great turmoil, the expression on his face when he said those words came back to me.

PLT: The old phrase! Everywhere!

vdP: And hearing it, a great peace came upon me. I was beyond space and time, everybody was a neighbour — this universal feeling of propinquity which makes the mystics speak of the forever which is now.

PLT: And it will be along these lines, remembering the long genealogical tree, would you say, that we'll preserve them?

vdP: Very good, very good — Yes, through this world of ancestors, this genealogical tree of the spirit and the myth, the material of so-called barbarians. Cafavy, one of the most civilized of modern poets, wrote:

> *And now what will become of us without barbarians?*
> *Those people were some sort of a solution.*

PLT: Let them be blest, the barbarians, and not vanish from the world!

First published in 'Parabola' on the theme of Dreams & Sleeping, New York, 1982.

Speak, Lord

YOU could tell that the Tor, solid upon its ley-line, had once been not only an island but also under the sea. Small, pale shells, half-buried under the thyme, had taken on some of its royal purple. More than once I stubbed my toe on an ammonite that was now almost grass. Here and there, splinters of chank shell were mute reminders of their old forefather, the Giant Chank, that long ago purloined the Vedas so that Vishnu, in his Boar aspect, could dive into the depths to retrieve them, in order to make true the adage that all things come from the sea.

Cone-shaped, a natural pyramid, washed by the invisible ocean, the great hill seemed to be full of magic — or was it my mood that made it so? No matter, I thought. The earth is a living being and I, for a scanted breath of time, am part of it, one with the centuries. Had there been an oak nearby, a Druid would have stepped out from behind it, hieratic, crowned with mistletoe, part of some ancient liturgical process in which I would have shared.

There was no oak tree. Nothing but a twisted thorn-bush, witch-like at the foot of the Tor. And it seemed to me, that from its barbed and craggy branches, a lone female voice was crying, angry in part, in part appealing, 'Let me out! Let me out! Let me out!'

I peered with caution among the boughs. There was nobody there, nothing but air. But the cry went on and on and on, a discordant litany. Clearly, it came from a time not mine, even perhaps, a sphere not mine — a sound remembered by the millennial wind from some old Celtic rite.

I had come to the Tor hoping to be alone with it, no tourists clicking their cameras, getting romantically angled shots of the ruined abbey below, of the water meadows that had once been fenland, of the hawthorn tree that had sprung, so they say, from Joseph of Arimathea's staff when he brought hither the Holy Grail and set in motion its legends.

Luckily there were no tourists, but the Tor was not to be mine alone. Halfway up the hill, a man wrapped in a black cloak and wearing a large-brimmed black hat, flat as a recumbent figure of eight, was leaning against an outcrop of rock.

Black Hat certainly was not a clicker, nor was the Ancient in priestly robes — some foreign cleric, I assumed — who was blindly feeling his way up the slope, a diminutive acolyte beside him. Every now and then, the child would stoop to pick a flower — rest-harrow, trefoil, lady's slipper — add it to the fistful already gathered, and then again offer his shoulder to the trembling, questing hand.

None of these, I thought, would intrude upon my solitude. I would forget them and climb on, not, as I wished, invisible, but at least unremarkable, something not to be noticed.

But it didn't happen like that.

'You're looking for someone!' said Black Hat. It was not a question but an authoritative statement. I was taken aback, off my guard. I had to turn and face him.

He was neither old nor young, I saw, but the epithet 'middle-aged' could not possibly apply. 'Timeless' was rather the word. His face was like a landscape ravaged. Dry riverbeds ran from brow to chin; the cheeks were two eroded hillocks; the nose a promontory. And his eyes! Luminous stones, not green, not blue, but turquoise lit from within. The visage was beautiful, melancholy, grotesque, not of the kind to be smiled at politely nor hurriedly run from. Even so, I would show him I was not in the mood for anything more than a mere exchange of courtesies.

'I'm not exactly looking,' I said, rather less coldly than I intended. 'Planning, rather, to climb up to the top of the Tor and sit there — alone.' I hoped that word had a vicious edge. What business was it of his?

But he was not going to let me be. Somehow I knew it. He would draw out of me — a mere duck to his decoy — what I myself was by no means sure of.

'Not exactly —?' He urged me on.

'Well, not looking, but in a way, pondering. How, for anyone with the faculty, aptitude — what you will — how could he set about summoning up one of those that are — needed?'

It was lamely put. I was suddenly shy. The hugeness of my idea unnerved me. So did his obdurate glance. Characteristically, I had wanted to be alone with the concept, let it elaborate within me, dally with it and see what happened.

'One of those? One of whom?' He was pressing me hard. And

I was no immovable object to meet his irresistible force. However unwilling, I could not but answer and give him the full of my folly.

'Well, the state of the world, so heartless, voilent, profane; sliding, sliding down the slope; everything that belongs to God rendered unto Caesar. And all those Sleepers down the ages who have promised, at its direst need, to return and save the world. How would it be if one — even one — could be awakened and shown the need?'

'Did they promise or was it promised for them, for centuries at the knees of mothers? Or grandmothers, better still?'

I said unwillingly, 'The latter.' That was indeed where I had learned it.

'I thought so! The best of all seminaries.' He smiled at me, indulging a child.

'And you, in your wisdom' — he was now sardonic — 'have decided that the moment has come? The time and the place are right, you think. All you want is the man!'

'Well, don't you?' I demanded. 'Is the idea so improbable?' I was suddenly lost and insecure. I could not argue. He was too much the master.

'Maybe. And maybe not. Time and space — throw in matter, too, if you like — are mutable realities. Not absolutes, as you assume. It is unwise to count upon them. And — forfend! — supposing time and place could be counted upon, whom had you in mind?'

'I was thinking primarily of Arthur and the sword freed from the stone. And if not he, then St George, perhaps. And wasn't Endymion a sleeper? And Charlemagne, King and Emperor, and Frederick Barbarossa? Oh, there are many! You surely know them.' I wanted to add, 'Since you seem to know everything,' but condemned the wish as childish.

'You flatter me.' His smile was kind and condescending.

'But you won't find it easy,' he went on. 'Arthur's tucked up in Avalon — *Inclitus Arthuris insola Avalonia* — under our very feet, so to speak. Attended by the Three Matres — or Fates, if you prefer it that way — and lullabied night and day by their keening. It would need a more potent voice than yours to overtop those ladies.

'As for St George, I hear he's rather down in the mouth. And, indeed, no wonder. To be jockeyed out of the calendar by a bevy of upstart ignorant Romans would discomfort demon, let alone saint. Even his horse, they say, is jaded. And the Dragon, too, is mumpish.

'Then, of course there are the Sans Pareils, Sumerian Ishtar, Peeping Psyche, who — I do not need to tell *you*, lady — was playing a profounder game than *I Spy* or *Hunt the Slipper;* and the Peerless She of the Pricked Finger, all sleeping the chthonic sleep wherein they confront themselves. As Three-in-One, and paired with Eros, it is possible, some elders say, that these are the Sleepers who will save the world. As for me, I hae ma doots. Eros, as soul, is out of favour. 'Not so with me!' do I hear you say? But perhaps you still have a lot to learn.'

'Who has not?' I said curtly, stung within by his assumption, but unwilling to take up cudgels.

'And as for your Frederick and his famous oath — to wake when the Thuringian ravens cease from their endless arguing — I doubt if he'd fill the bill. Think o' that great red mop of beard surging across the table — he fell asleep at dinner, remember. And since beards, unlike sleepers, do not sleep, it must now be half-way across the room, a couch for rats and bats and weasels — a regular beard's nest, forgive the pun! And who is to cut it and set him free when the ravens, if ever, are silent? So — you're in a quandary, aren't you?' he teased.

Then the weather of his face changed. He cupped his chin in his hand, brooding.

'There's always Merlin, of course,' he said, 'Would you settle for him?'

'*Merlin!*' I was taken by surprise and showed it. Merlin was the last person I had in mind.

'But—' I found myself stammering. 'I have never thought of *him* as a Sleeper. I — he — there's something about him, I can't quite name it — ' For indeed, my feelings were ambivalent, my heart aware of its double pulse. I could not hit on the right word and he saw that I could not.

'Too slippery, you think? a bit too much of the Artful Dodger? One of nature's tricksters? Well, maybe, maybe. What else could you expect of one got by a demon on a virgin girl? Half one thing and half the other and even, possibly, something added.' The turquoise eyes were now opaque, blue-green stones under water.

To comment would have been discourteous. So I said only, 'Well, anyway, he doesn't arise. How could he? He has lost his powers, handed them over to the nymph, Nimue, who used them to shut him up in a tower. What use would there be in such a one, a creature of air and darkness?'

'Forgive me, madam, if I suggest that your mythology is a trifle shaky. He did indeed yield up his powers to that plausible, mindless, cozening sweetmeat, for reasons which I leave you to guess — you are, after all, a woman. And she did, indeed, shut him up — in a wall-less tower, most potent of all — one of his minor chicaneries revealed in a careless moment. But — and take note, lady, of that small word — she added a second spell to the first by binding him with a chain of sleep; and that spell not only set him free but gave him back his magic. It is a law — have you not read your *Ramayana*? — that to twice bind is to unbind all. It is she herself who is now in that tower — or its comfortless equivalent — and much plaint does she make of it, except, of course, on those occasions when, feeling the need of a female friend — he's a man, ma'am, after all — he pays her a passing visit.' He grinned. Then his mockery turned to gravity as a faint 'Halloo!' shook the air.

'Have a care, Ancient!' he called through cupped hands. 'Take it slowly. Hold fast to that shoulder!'

The aged man and the young boy were shuffling over the curve of the hill.

'Is it you, friend of ages?' came a watery voice as the incongruous yet concordant pair came slowly into view.

'Ah, that's the question. *Is* it? I have been Ambrosius and Sylvester and also Celedoine. Fish of the sea have I been, too, and a tall tree on a mountain, a stag of five branches with a white forefoot, and herdsman to the sun's cattle, shepherd to the sheep of the Underworld, and many a one beside. It's a braw man anywhere who can answer "This is I!" '

'Have done! Have done! I know your guises. Are you alone? Mine eyes blur. Are you, perhaps, with the — er — dryad?'

'No, no. She is safely locked away. A chance-met, would-be pythoness merely, who thinks to better the fallen world by calling up the Sleepers.'

'Ah, poor thing. And poorer hope. They are, indeed, on the Path of Return but their bourne is not this world. It is an illusion all men have that the Sleepers will come back. They rock themselves to sleep with it and die with the dream upon them.'

'Ay. Sleeping or waking, they dream — *she* dreams. Is it not so?' Black Hat demanded.

I had thought to climb the hill, safe and sure, wrapped in my cloak of romanticism — unwilling to call it that, however, and certainly not to question it. And here were these two pedagogues, one to my right, one to my left, determined to disrobe me of it as a figment, a thing of naught.

'But,' I said, not without resentment. 'Dreaming, surely, is a thing that happens. There is something to learn from it.'

'Happens, indeed! How right you are!' Black Hat gleefully slapped his thigh. But I ignored the interruption.

'Do you not dream, nor he?' I asked, turning from one to the other. 'After all, hasn't it been said that the young men shall see visions and the old men dream dreams?'

The Ancient laughed, a kindly cackle.

'He has no need so to squander himself.' He nodded shakily at Black Hat. 'Nor have any of his kind. As for myself, I have been, indeed, such a young man, Oh, yes, I, Eli, had my vision! And even now, though entitled to dream — as foolish fond old men dream — I abjure the privilege and pray that the vision may not leave me till I pass from the minds of men. The same for him . . .' He touched the boy. 'May he, too, keep it to the end.'

He turned with a quivering smile to Black Hat. 'He is a promised child,' he said. 'Long awaited and vowed at birth. And of late he has been called — three times. So, I brought him to you, as I, too, was brought.'

His bleached eyes sought out my direction.

'A prophet, to be a prophet,' he said, 'for all the summoning from above, must have the good will of the Old Ones, as well. Otherwise the folk will not believe him.'

'Ay, it is so,' Black Hat agreed, hunching himself within his cloak. 'They need to be told what they do not yet know, but also those things they already know and do not know they know.'

He turned and took the boy by the shoulders, gazing at him farsightedly. 'So — you've been called. Three times called. And now, until your moment comes, you will minister to the Ancient.'

He bent his furrowed brow to the smooth one and was silent for a long moment. Then he raised his head.

'What is in me is now in you. And because of it the folk will listen. And, as well, in the tablets of history, you will be a maker of kings. These are high matters,' he told the old man. 'Guard him. He is a link in the chain.' And he thrust the boy towards his master.

But between them the child paused for a moment, gazing at me, reflectively. Then, with a rough urchin gesture, he took a green something from his fistful of flowers, pushed it shyly at me and turned away.

'That jacket's too small for him,' said Black Hat. 'He needs a larger one over the ephod.'

'His mother makes a new one each year. She will bring it to us shortly.'

'Well, you have done for him what you could — and should. Go now, both. Be blessed. And wakeful!'

Black Hat dismissed them with upraised palm, gazing darkly after them as they went.

'And from the seed of the second king . . .' Talking apparently to himself, he absently plucked at the grass. 'Will come a man who indeed will promise — in the spiral of time has already promised — to return and save the world. And you . . .'

He turned upon me savagely, stony eyes dark with their brooding.

'Let you remember what you have seen! You flatter and ease yourself with the myths, with all that has been lived and suffered and gone into the cauldron, like a child playing with gunpowder that may explode and destroy you.'

His eyes assessed me, poring over, apparently, a mixed and unpromising array of elements.

'And yet,' he said slowly, 'you are willing, I think, to pay the price, though you do not know what it is. For the untutored, the way is hard. It is an easy thing to dream — Gramarye, the Matter of Britain, Arthur, Once and Future King returning to fight the present ills so that *you* may have your happy ending and the world dance round a maypole. You know — but you have not faced your knowing — that this is not the meaning. Your seminary must have warned you there is farther than that to go. But have you the courage? Dare you look deeper? Deeper than Avalon? Calvary?'

'No! Not that!' It leapt from me. 'For that to be done again-no, never!'

'Yes! Again! And again! Until man wakes.'

In the wind there sounded far-off echoes — voices coarse with strong emotion, the sound of a lifeless something heavily falling on waiting knees. Does the wind remember everything?

From behind my sleeve, as a child does, I admitted my childishness.

'Yes, I was dreaming,' I confessed. 'Wantoning with the myths, if you like. Laying to my soul, perhaps, the flattering unction of hope. But . . .' I was suddenly aggressive. 'Why should I not dream? Tell me that! What do I — what does anyone — waste?'

'Your life,' said Black Hat, sombrely. 'Oh, for man in general it makes little matter. His nights — and his days — are meant for wasting. But, for an apprentice pythoness . . .'

'You called me by that name — not I!'

'Ay, indeed. Take note of it. By chance you happened on the three of us — the prophet, the boy and — dare I say it? — myself — at a place where sea, air, earth, and sun once met and may meet again. And by chance a Calling was in your mind. But what is chance? Can you answer that? Or, equally, coincidence? Go back far enough and each of them is inevitable, not to be escaped.'

He brooded for a moment over the words, matching one to the other.

'Calling — the double arrow!' he said. ' "That Allah of thine," as Rumi said, "is my 'Here am I!' to thee." Caller and called summon each other. The boy, Samuel, was called. Why should you not be?'

Was he teasing me, I wondered. No. He was waiting for an answer. I gave it in a shake of the head.

'I am empty. I have not the wit.'

'Empty, alas, is what you are not. But a ragbag of scraps of knowing. And a pythoness, anyway, needs no wit. Has she, do you think, stored up in her mind, the wisdom of which she speaks? Not so. A fool could outwit her. It is her business merely to wait — unselfed, quiescent, a vessel only. And out of that vessel, void of all things, the oracle is poured.'

The Water Carrier's Pitcher, I thought. And at that, within me, something quickened. My fullness conceived its emptiness. *Where* was in love with the wine of *Nowhere*. To be known, and to be shown to oneself as a thing of shreds and patches, given back one's original face, was to be restored to Non-entity.

'Of course,' said Black Hat, sardonically, 'I am not suggesting Pharae, nor Delphi, Dordona and the like . . .'

'Of course not!' It was I now mocking him. 'A ragbag of scraps!'

He took no notice.

'But there's many a minor sibyl needed. Augurers of the woods and fields; seers of the village back-streets. Wise Women are not to be despised. Each one, in her way, is a pythoness — a hen-bird pecking the grain.' He grinned.

Oh, clever devil, with his power to touch me twice to the quick! First Calvary, then the woods and by-streets, which also have their Calvaries.

'But you say,' I protested, 'that I must not dream. Can it be learned? How can I be empty?'

'By being full,' he said, gravely. 'And that's no paradox! What is your right hand doing, for instance?'

I glanced down. 'Twisting the rings on my left.'

'And where, at this moment, are you sitting?'

I had to peer over my shoulder.

'On a tuft of purple thyme.'

'A tuft of thyme on the skirts of time. Always the punster — that's me!' he jibed. At himself or me? I could not be sure.

'You're telling me what I should have known. Something within me should have sensed it.'

He nodded.

'I need to know what I know,' I said, putting out a preventive hand. 'No, do not teach me! I can only learn, I cannot be taught. The direction is all I need.'

'I would not, for my life,' he said. 'It is not a lore that can be taught. Absorbed, perhaps, never taught.'

'Every moment of the day lived full and then — I shall be empty?'

'The day is responsible for the night. What is left unlived, or not lived fully, will take its revenge in dreams. Good dreams or bad, they are still dreams, the stuff allowed to be lost from the day making its nightly ferment.'

'And if —?'

'Ah, *If* is ever man's faithful hound, with its slavish, reassuring eyes. But to one who is ready to ignore that gaze — reflection of his own self-love — then the answer to your 'If' is 'Yes.' There will be repose, which is sleep at its purest; the sleep, you could say, that no breath shakes, the sleep the sages aim at.'

We sat in silence, the two of us, confronting this immensity.

Then again the wind rose, and cried, 'Let me out! Let me out!'

'You catch the sound?' Black Hat said, grinning.

'Yes. I heard it when I came to the Tor and it died away when the old man came.'

'It has never died — does that surprise you? It began when I first set foot on the Tor and has since not ceased its plaining. It is you, merely, who have not heard.'

Was it true? Had I let fall into oblivion this particle of life?

I stared at him. *His* step had given rise to the cry? And *who* was it that cried?

Under the eight-shaped black felt hat — the hat that only magicians wear — the lively turquoise eyes met mine, full at once of guile and ruth.

And I knew.

'You are Merlin!' I cried. And, more softly — 'Myrrdin!' The name, in its Celtic guise, was a caress.

'The same! At your service!' He flung his black-bat cloak wide and swung it quickly again about him, the symbols awhirl on the lining.

'And that's no syllogism, ma'am!' He tossed me a blade of grass from his tuffet. 'If you call me by my Old Name, I cannot but be at your service, as you must be at mine. You are now my apprentice.'

He smiled at me equivocally as he turned and called to the calling voice.

'I'm coming, my little hare! I'm coming, my rosebud! *Au revoir*, pythoness. I must away and wake her, for, for all she thinks she's awake, she is not — she only dreams she is. Not that it matters. This is hardly an affair in the realm of Eros. But, the Goatfoot, too, has his province.'

He strode away down the hill, shouting a string of endearments. It is a gift men have that they never look back. When it is finished, it is finished.

This is not so with women. They look for a further chapter. But, resisting my wish to know the ending, I steadfastly turned my face to the hill, not failing, however, to take note that once the incessant voice was silent, the wind murmured and sighed in the thyme as though it were in clover.

Larks were Te Deum-ing over the Tor, their song rising like a fountain from the chalice of the valley. Apples were ripening below — Avalon means the Vale of Apples. There was no sign on the downward road of the sunset man and the morning boy. And if I were to look back at the thorn-bush, I knew I would find it empty.

Had I dreamed all this? If so, it was hardly a good beginning to my apprenticeship. No, it had not been a dream. For, as I sat down at the top of the Tor, cleansed for a moment of myself, with the world turning and I with it round its still and unknown point, I found in my hand three blades of grass. One had been flung at me — gift rather than missile, I dared to think — and the other two must be surely my crumpled share of the fistful of flowers.

I knew I would have to learn what they meant, maybe take many lifetimes learning. But for now I would wait, be still and listen. Like Prince Hui's cook, I had nothing to do. With nothing I would make my way through the world . . .

First published in 'Parabola' on the theme of Dreams & Sleeping, New York, 1982.

Name and
No Name

NAME and no name — we are talking here of a mystery. But when you come to think of it what else but mystery is there to talk about? In a book of mine called *Friend Monkey,* the imaginative child, Edward, suddenly wakes up in the family cabin on the ship that is carrying them from London to the South Seas.

'Where is God?' he demands.

'Here,' answers his mother, automatically. This puts him immediately in a panic.

'But you said he was here when we lived at Putney. He can't be here and there at the same time.'

'God is everywhere,' says his mother, piously. But his father breaks in and saves the situation.

'It's a mystery,' he says. 'Nobody really understands it. You have to take it on trust, Edward. Now, go to sleep, both of you.'

A mystery! What a relief! It was things that were not mysterious that Edward always worried about. Facts. Plain common facts appalled him. But a mystery could take care of itself. He fell asleep at once.

So — the mystery of the name. That has always seemed to me one of the great questions.

Think of the catechism. 'What is your name?' is the first thing it asks, throwing you into the labyrinth at the very outset.

Reading it as a child, long before I was required to study it, I trembled. It was like a mighty trumpet call, a summons to leave the safe place where I was merely an appellation, an infinitesimal particle of one all containing whole — child, grass, linnet, hare.

And the answer it required was equally strange and portentous. 'N, or M' it demanded.

But I was neither N nor M. What, I wondered, would happen to me? And until I became of riper years, I was haunted by the thought that my father, when the time came for my confirmation, would palm me off as one or other of those initials — Norah, perhaps, or Maria — in order to jockey me into heaven, much as the miller in *Rumplestiltzkin*, in order to catch the eye of the king, boasted that his daughter could spin straw into gold — two well-meaning, mendacious parents with, for issue, clearly, a pair of whited sepulchres. For how would I be able to renounce the Devil and all his works when, as far as I knew, I had never met him; or she transform the bedding of beasts or the thatch on the roof into that ineffable substance? What an enigma!

And yet, after all, the thing was done. Everyone knows the story. The king put the girl into a barn that was full of bales of straw and said 'Spin that into gold and I'll marry you!'

And there she sat and there she sat, probably pondering on the iniquity of the dowry system, as she wept her heart out doing nothing because there was nothing she could do.

And the doing nothing did it. Out of nowhere — or everywhere — leapt a little ugly dwarfish man. 'What will you give me, if I spin it for you?' The matter was of little account to him for in the land he came from straw and gold are all one thing, not a pin to choose between them. Divil a mystery was there in it for him.

'The beads round my neck', she told him. And so he spun and took them.

The next day the barn was again full of straw and the creature, quick as you'd spit, turned it into gold and this time she gave him her ring.

But on the third day, for all the gold that was lying there, she could give him nothing for nothing was all she had.

'Well, your first child when you're Queen.' he bargained. And she promised him that. What else could she do? So at once there were three barns full of gold and she with the King at the altar. And at the ninth month — well, more or less — there was the child and there was the little man in her room, agog for his reward.

But now she hadn't the heart for it.

'Anything but the child,' she said. But nothing tempted him. What he wanted, he said, was a living thing. 'Something alive is dearer to me than anything in the world.'

So he made a compact with her.

'If within three days you discover my name, then you shall keep the child.'

So she cudgelled what brains she had and sent out messengers through the land to find out outlandish names. And when the mannikin arrived she rattled off a list of them — Caspar, Melchior, Balthasar. But to each he said 'That is not my name. And there's the first day gone.'

Then she made enquiry of the neighbours, thinking to find something more humble. 'Is it Short-ribs? Is it Sheepshanks? Is it Shake-a-leg?' 'No, it is not, and there's two days gone.'

But on the third day the messenger returned, saying 'Not another name have I found. But in the forest behind the mountains, in the country where the fox and the hare say goodnight to each other, I heard a little old man singing:

Today I brew,
Tomorrow I bake,
The next, the Queen's young child I take,
For little she knows,
That royal dame
That Rumpelstiltzkin is my name.

And as soon as she heard that, she knew. But, womanlike, she pretended.

'Is it Tom?' she asked the next day. 'Is it William? Is it Harry?'
'No!'

'Then is it Rumpelstiltzkin?'

'The Devil has told you!' the creature cried. And he stamped his foot into the earth so deep, so deep, that the earth took him and hid him away in herself.

So goes the story. And the miller's daughter thought 'What luck!'

But luck was nowhere in it. The old man himself was the one who told her for Necessity required that the name be told. There would have been no story without it.

The tale is told everywhere and always the name is known at last. In England it is Tom Tit Tot, in Scotland Whuppety Stoorey, in Russia the creature is Vargaluska, in Spain El Enarno Saltarin, and in Africa he is, of all things, a hippopotamus who goes by the name of Isantim.

Only in the Grimm's version is the name discovered in 'the country where the fox and the hare say goodnight to each other.' Very possibly they invented this but they were steeped enough in lore to realize that the name belongs to another level, a level that can only be activated when the impossible is confronted. Rumpelstiltzkin here is its embodiment. In another story it will take the shape of a frog, a witch, a little old woodsman, for this level is always at work in fairy tales, giving or confiscating gifts.

So — the name discovered, the named one is lost, or at least deprived of his power.

But in the Scottish tale of the Brownie who went haunting the burns, we find the other side of things, the matter of No Name. Splash and paddle he would, in the leaping water and then go with wet feet into the farmhouse. And what was tidy he threw about and what was untidy, he tidied. You wouldn't know where you were with him and no one would follow the road at night lest they meet him face to face. But at last, says the tale, they had him laid. And by what? By a name. A man, merry from the market, greatly daring, took to the road and heard the splashing and slopping. 'Is it yourself, Old Puddlefoot?' he cried, spying the creature. And the Brownie broke in two with despair. 'Oh, I've gotten myself a name!' he cried. And never more was he seen or heard. For such a thing as he, the name was too much. He could not bear the burden. All he wanted was to be one with the wind and the rain. And that's what happened to him.

As to myself, sitting still like the miller's daughter — doing nothing, for what could one do? — I eventually answered the catechism's call and, expecting dissolution, survived. Nobody said 'What? Neither N nor M?' My father, like the miller, was absolved and I was given an identity, made object to some subject that might or might not be someday known. No longer one with the grass and the hare, I was suddenly overwhelmed by the mystery of the name, the obligation, the danger.

For the name, if it binds, also separates. If one asks the question — 'When was it that the lion lay down with the lamb?' the answer inevitably has to be 'Before they were named by Adam.' Once the lion knew what he was and who he was, the King of the Jungle, he had to devour — it was his destiny — the fleecy thing beside him. And she, once she knew that she was a lamb, understood that her part was to put the width of the world between them.

'A power superior to man,' says Plato, 'gave the primordial names to things in such a way that the names are necessarily right and the rightness of the names makes the nature of things visible.'

And the Koran says much the same thing — 'And he taught Adam all the names.'

Thus it was that the children of Adam, having got wind of this law of the name, set themselves — as is done with all laws — to discover means to subvert or evade it. So they invented the euphemism, a placatory process by means of which the lesser word is made to stand in for the greater, the sweet for the bitter, the penknife for the sword, the nickname and the epithet to minimize the fact. To this day you will find farmers who will not speak the name of the fox, for fear he should hear himself called and come forthwith for the chickens. 'Him,' they will say, or 'Prick-Ears', or 'Reynard' with a silent thumb jerked towards the woodland. In the lands that the bear inhabits he is scrupulously referred to as Grandfather, Honey Paw or Little Old Man. Among the Algerian Arabs the lion is spoken of — it is hard to think why — as Mr Johnson, and it is well known that in Africa and Asia a snake is not a snake at all but a coil of rope or a piece of string — neither of which can bite.

In the same way, to keep away the evil spirits, leprosy is known as the Blessed Disease, just as the Erynnes, the avenging deities of Greek mythology, were apostrophized as Eumernides, the Kindly Ones. As for the Devil, he has a thousand nicknames designed, if he is to appear at all, to make him feel like an old family friend and not the Opposing Power — Clootie, Old Hornie, Meister Peter, Old Nick — would such a one harm us, make us pay for our sins? Never!

Thus, on all levels, we mitigate reality in order to be able to face it. By giving the name a sobriquet we think to rob it of its power. But it will not be demythologized. A spade is always a spade, no matter what you call it.

The Name, Ceremony and Tradition have at all times belonged to each other and this relationship necessarily involves Taboo. In myth and folklore Rumpelstiltzkin and the Brownie are humble witnesses to this quarternity, its potencies and its menace.

One thinks of the names that arise out of the high deeds of men or of their physical characteristics, taking from them for ever the one their mothers called them. For instance, Setanta, who destroyed the Hound — in Gaelic, hound is Cu — of the smith Culain, undertook himself to be the hound of the smith and became thereafter Cuculain, one of the great heroes of Ireland; Lugh Ildanach — in Gaelic the All Craftsman — was another and also Dermot who became O'Dyna — in Gaelic the Love Spot or blaze on the brow, whom any woman, and she betrothed to another man, would slip her jesses and follow. On the other hand, among the Grail Knights, it was forbidden to divulge either their names or their origins. The Grail had to be served by Nameless ones. For what name would be worthy of such a task?

In Imperial China, where every ordinary man received throughout his life a succession of names — the birth name, the school name, the marrying name, the fathering name — it was considered a serious crime to mention, even, presumably, to one's pillow, the sacred name of the Emperor. And I was told recently by a traveller to Nepal that when a certain woman was asked her name she gave it, but stoutly refused that of her husband. It was not her part, as a woman, to give away — to who knows what devil — the name of the head of the house. 'Well, tell me the name of the father of your son!' This put her into a quandary. Torn between two taboos, she uneasily whispered her husband's name and presumably heaved a sigh of relief when no dragon materialized to swallow her up.

In all places where life still retains something of ritual, this secrecy of the name is found. I myself, living on the Navaho reservation for a long summer during the war, was ceremoniously given an Indian name and warned not to disclose it to anyone, lest ill-luck follow me and the tribe. I have never told it. Unknown, I felt, it would work within me.

And yet, it was at once known. For next day, having been driven far from the place where I had received it, I rode at twilight up the Canyon de Chelley. Cantering in the silky dust that aeons ago had been river, I came unexpectedly on a group of the People, making their evening meal. Shy to disturb them, I wheeled about, but a man came and held my stirrup and motioned me to the fire. We sat in silence, taking food from the pot, and I sensed somehow that my new name was there. Borne on the wind, on the back of a crow, it lay between us, a tangible thing, the name I could neither assume nor possess but which bound me to the mothering land.

Later, I heard that a woman from that settlement had recently had a nightmare. Someone had called her by the wrong name, an ill-famed name — and she and all the other women had danced the dream to the mouth of the canyon, away and away, out of their world. The simplicity, the wisdom of it — which could be ours if we had the courage and the lack of self-consciousness — to ritualize the fearsome thing and dismiss it as a dance!

It was while I was with the Navaho that I had another experience of the name and its power, not, this time, as a native dance but rather, I suppose, a kind of clodhopping minuet. The Minister for Indian Affairs, an old friend whose guest I was, arranged that I should see as much of the working of the reservation as possible so, since petrol was then so short, I was conveyed to the dances and places of interest in anything that had four wheels — jeeps, trucks, an occasional car. Daily I would wait at a given spot for whoever was told to be my guide and a cowboy called Dan, under whose wing I apparently was, would courteously make the introductions and describe the itinerary. But one morning Dan greeted me with what seemed a kind of savage glee. 'It's free love for you today, ma'am,' he said, with a mocking equivocal look in his eye. I returned the glance coolly, feeling that he did not know me well enough to make that kind of joke.

Then, out from behind the waiting truck came an enormous, bandy-legged cowboy, hewn out rather than fashioned of flesh and cross-eyed into the bargain.

'This,' said Dan, 'is Mr Freelove. He's your guide for today.'

I got into the truck, marvelling at Nature's sense of the ridiculous — to have created such a mis-shapen giant and then allowed him to be saddled with such a name! There had surely to be a redeeming feature — a heart of gold, I told myself, or perhaps the gift of tongues. Neither of these were manifested, however, as we drove out on to the range. He answered all my questions in words of one syllable, grudgingly, as though unwilling to share with me the glories of the desert. I blamed myself merely for existing for he clearly did not want to share with a strange female passenger what for him was merely a work-place.

But it soon appeared that he did not want to share anything with anyone. When we stopped at a wayside range for lunch, where he heaped everything — hamburgers, gravy, salad, lemon-meringue pie on to a single plate — he spoke to nobody and nobody spoke to him. And later, when I was welcomed to an artesian well by a group of men with names such as Tom, Bill, Harry or Dick everyone curtly called him Freelove and left him to work on his own. What inner rift of bitterness was it, I wondered, that made him not only friendless but without, apparently, a friend in himself. I was surprised, therefore when, at the end of the day when the long level sun was gilding the sage brush, he brought the truck to a standstill beside a rock and, motioning me to get out, actually for the first time, vouchsafed some information.

'Dinosaur!' he said gruffly, pointing to some mark on the rock. There were, indeed, indentations but they looked to me like the claw marks of a small and rather under-nourished eagle.

'But, surely,' I said, 'they should be bigger. 'Dinosaurs were enormous.'

He was nettled. 'You ever see a dinosaur?' he demanded.

'Well, no,' I admitted, for of course I hadn't, particularly one scampering across the primal ooze before it set into rock.

'Well, that's a dinosaur's mark, I tell you. Everybody knows it.' So, wishing to stay on the right side of Mr Freelove I accepted the dinosaur and turned to gather an armful of sage brush.

But Mr Freelove had no right side it seemed, for with an ungainly gesture he thrust a few sage branches at me, stuttering and mumbling as he did so, until I became aware that, preposterously, all unwillingly — feeling perhaps that he owed it to his manhood — Mr Freelove was making me a declaration or, rather, a proposition. Unwillingly, without a doubt, for when I said a firm No, I distinctly saw a look of relief leap from one eye to the other. But doubtless having heard of the game from someone, he was determined to play it to the end.

'Well,' he demanded truculently, 'You want to walk home? It's a good twenty miles.'

'Oh,' I said, stepping nimbly into the truck and hoping that I looked as I felt — at once regal and nonchalant — 'I would walk to Salt Lake City.'

Salt Lake City — that set him ablaze. That I would be willing to walk three hundred miles, draggled and footworn, asking only to be shown to my grave, rather than — No, that was too much! He leapt into the driver's seat, turned the truck away from the road and began putting it to every rock as a driver puts a horse to a fence.

'Mr Freelove!' I protested shrilly, not for my sake but for his. For since he was practically twice my size, it was *his* head each time that hit the roof. Up, crack, down, the mad journey went on till, greatly daring, I leaned across and pulled hard on the hand-brake. 'Now,' I said, as we teetered on top of a rock, 'where is your First Aid box?' He gestured blindly, for blood was pouring into his eyes. And presently I had bound up his head, felt the truck pitch on to level land and find its way to the dirt road.

We drove home in silence, the craggy, bitter face beside me made somehow noble by its turban of lint.

Dan met us with astonished eyes. 'What you done to Freelove?' he asked, scenting and hoping for scandal.

'Nothing,' I said and left the scene, knowing that in the community that night there would be speculation of many sorts.

The next time I was due to be driven by Mr Freelove I was careful to take a child along, for protection. His outer wounds had healed but I sensed that the inner one, whatever it was, was still throbbing for to every shrill childish question 'May I honk the horn?', 'May I hold one side of the wheel?' the answer was always a vicious 'Nope!' It was not a sociable journey. But I noticed, when we got to our destination — this time a Navaho settlement — his wordlessness reflected, even harmonized with that of the Indians themselves. The work among them was done in silence, as though its rhythms had no need of words and certainly none of names. Every gesture was a communication.

As I watched this lively interchange, wondering whether, after all, we do not all talk too much, I heard my own voice break the mutual silence.

'Mr Freelove,' I shrieked. For, glancing round, I saw that the child had picked up an Indian playmate, the two had got into the cab of the truck and together had released the brake. Now they were riding down the slope of a hill greeting Eternity with squeals of triumph.

He turned, saw at once what had to be done and twisting himself into a figure of eight, leapt almost gracefully into the truck and jammed on both the brakes. Then he seized the children, thumped them all over mercilessly and threw them, bellowing, at my feet. I burst into tears.

'Ah,' he snarled, 'Ye're soft, ye're sappy. You got to wallop 'em. Makes 'em remember.'

'Oh, its not that, Mr Freelove,' I cried. 'It's the way you were into that cab like a . . . like a lizard. It's because I'm so grateful, Mr Freelove.'

He stared at me, looking as though he could not believe it. His craggy face was amazingly softened and his eyes seemed almost straight.

Grateful! Somebody was grateful to Freelove as they might be to any other human being. He took from his pocket something that might once have been a handkerchief and tentatively dabbed my cheeks.

'Call me Earl!' he entreated.

Earl Freelove! What had his mother been thinking of! But I swallowed and said the name! What else could I have done?

The drive home was companionable and relaxed. The child was allowed to honk the horn at every passing tree. 'Earl,' I said — I was getting used to it, 'do you really believe it was a dinosaur's footprint?' 'Nope!' he said cheerfully. It was enough. We could go for the rest of the way without speaking but in complete community. I was to learn afterwards from an anthropologist that in spite of that Nope and my own doubts, it *was* a dinosaur's footprint, but that did not alter the present situation.

'What you done to Freelove this time?' demanded Dan, as I got down from the truck.

'Nothing,' I again replied. But, in fact I had done everything. I had called him by his name.

'Well something happened,' Dan persisted. 'Can't you hear? He's whistling!'

Now, no man who is not at peace with himself whistles. A man is not a Brownie. He needs a name and that name accepted. He is not a Brownie. He does not dare to be nobody.

Had he lived in ancient Egypt he would have been given two names at birth, a greater and a lesser name. Only the latter was made public. The greater belonged to the Ka or soul and embodied all the individual's magical power. Evil spirits would direct their anger to the lesser name, leaving unharmed the greater, which was thought of as a knot tied in the continuous cord of a particular destiny and determining one of its incarnations or episodes.

In other places there is a special and conformable time to the giving of the name. Among the Igbo people of Nigeria when a child is born it is not considered as being fully part of the world. It still has its true dwelling in wherever its spirit came from. There, the number seven is a magical number. The Igbo week is four days and seven weeks is one month — literally the moon's transit. Only at the end of this portentous time is the child believed to be fully human and entitled to receive a name.

The inner name, the secret name — its equivalent in our world the personal or baptismal name — has immemorially been held to be the vesture or outward form of the soul. And in all teachings that are centred on initiation, the initiate, having reached a certain stage, is given a name appropriate to that state, a name he does not possess but serves. Corbin, in *The Esotericism of the Word,* speaks of the Mystery of the Divine Names — almost Divine hypostases — which from all eternity aspires to be known, that is to say, to be invested in beings who will receive these names and in whom these names will be embodied. Any proper name, therefore, is a theophoric name, a God-bearing name and he who bears it is not its owner but rather, belongs to the Name.'

One thinks of the Bible, the stark absoluteness of the Old Testament where the name of God may be neither known nor spoken. 'Say unto them I AM hath sent me to you' is the nearest the Deity will allow Himself to approach humanity; and then the New with its Christos, whom any man, or indeed child, may salute as Jesus. Has God, perhaps, had a change of heart? Or is it that one of those aspiring Names is, because of the needs of man, allowed to be known and embodied — but known, perhaps only insofar as it is also, in an ultimate sense, unknowable, a mystery. *Revelations* (2.17) hints palpably at this.

> To him that overcometh I will give to eat of the hidden manna and will give him a white stone and in the stone a new name written, which no man knoweth saving him that received it.

Anyone grounded in myth cannot but ask himself whether the 'hidden manna' is not the hypostasis — that which underlies every secret name, from that of the Absolute right down to Rumpelstiltzkin and his kind. And the beautiful Negro spiritual *'Hush! Someone Is Callin' My Name* suggests a similar scale of identity. We know, without needing to be told, who is calling and who is called.

Ah, but that hush is seldom heard. It needs a contained and communal world where, as Yeats put it in *Prayer for my Daughter,*

Ceremony is the name for the rich horn
And custom for the spreading laurel tree.

For in our profane and secular life, where everything is reduced to the least common denominator, we are essentially separate — and lonely. By dispensing with ceremony, with superscription, honorific, patronymic — 'Hi, Steve, meet Joe' — we hopefully imagine that we know one another, and moreover have the right to know, so that, wearing our hearts and all that we are on our sleeves any daw may peck at us.

But, familiarly to wrench from another his personal name before he has had the chance — or, indeed, the wish — to offer it, is to degrade him, to snatch away his dignity, his private innerness. If there is alive in him some of his old ancestral stuff, it will quiver with apprehension — and withdraw. As a woodland creature, part of the speckle of sun and shadow, becomes a fawn and flees, so he will inwardly turn away. Come too near and you have lost him. Only the far can be near. The door has to be knocked at gently if we want to know who is within.

And who is within? There's the whole question. Who are you, stranger, who hears these words and who am I that speak them? When one inwardly puts that question it is not a name that replies. Yet that 'Who am I?' has an answer, I am sure of that. It is known to the blood, but blood has no words.

The great Sufi poet, Rumi, wrote 'Man is like a drop of water that the wind dries up or that sinks into the earth. But if it leaps into the sea, which was its source, the drop is delivered. Its outward form disappears, but its essence is inviolate. So, surrender thy drop', he adjures us, 'and take in exchange the Sea.'

Thus it is all one, name and no name.

As for that child whose name was neither N nor M, my end lies in her beginning. This mystery is the same for us all. And, being a mystery, it is as near as it is far. The snake takes its tail in its mouth and you and I, linnet and hare, parts of one single whole that sometime will reveal all names, are rolled round in our eternal course with rocks and stones and trees.

Sometime, surely, for whether we hear it or not we are continually hailed, continually being summoned.

We need to make a silence for that summons.

Hush! Someone is calling my name.

First published in 'Parabola' on the theme of Ceremonies, New York. 1982.

Leda's Lament

Did she put on his knowledge with his power
Before the indifferent beak would let her drop?
                    W B Yeats, 'Leda and the Swan'

I W A S young then, a mere piece of the world, easy with love, virgin of soul, a thing single and unmixed, for all Tyndareus' tumbling and seed already sown.

Do not upbraid me, maidens, arrogant analogues of my youth, who tell me I should not have walked by the river. Had it been high on the strong hills or among the forests with their scalloped oak-leaves or upon the pavements of the sea, he would have found me. Eternity had me in its eye.

So, go your ways, daughters of Time, swinging your minikin loving-cups, sufficient for the needs of mortal men. You cannot know, not Heaven-found, that in women there are hidden depths, cataracts and declivities, where only a god may take soundings.

And well for you that this is so, for if you forfeit the ecstasy, so also do you miscarry of the travail.

I knew, when they brought me the birth-stool, that what I awaited was god-begotten; that the cramped earthlings, ruddy Castor and Clytemnestra, would be thrust headlong out of the nest — as sparrows by a cuckoo's child — to let the exorbitant egg emerge. But who would have thought so frail a thing, received by the gentling, waiting hands, would crack with a roll of prophetic thunder? Or that I, eased of the nine-month weight, would turn from Helen and Polydeuces and weep for what was come upon me — the burden of a double nature?

For I knew, as the shining children broke the shell, that, having been clipped and plumbed to the void, I had taken on that of him that would not let me rest. Congress with Heaven demoralizes the earthly mind that otherwise would play with its toys, vestal, unknowing, blameless.

But with awareness, blame arises. And I, Leda, by reason of that one swan-moment, must take the blame upon me. For Troy, yes, but not Troy only; nor Agamemnon whistling for a wind, offering Iphigenia for it and receiving, from her death, his own; nor Hector dragged across the plain; nor Achilles heaped in his fire-blood ash; nor the drowned men feeding the hungry sea, turned on the spit of the wave.

Oh, I weep for these, but not these only. Nor for my daughter, Mycenae's queen, blood-stippled by the babe that milked her; nor Orestes, therefore, fleeing the Furies from hill to hollow to hill.

For them — and more. For myself I weep that, unwittingly — in the place where body comprehends body, where flesh stores up its own wisdom — what had been done in the green wood should leave its mark on the dry.

Oh, are living and dying not enough? Must we also endure the pain of knowing — the knowing that brings in its train Unknowing and makes us ask, without hoping for answer, 'Who am I? What is my purpose?' Why through me, Leda, should the fuse have run that, exploding, toppled Ilium's towers and made of Sparta a name of shame? Must cause ever carry on its back effects so much greater than itself, as a grain of sand carries the sea?

Would you beguile me, comforters? As well put cheek to a mummy's cheek! True, I have sons picked out as stars and have given birth to a matchless woman whom all men name the World's Desire and lust for in their dreams. But will a star spread a bed for me or bring me a mantle against the cold or heap a cairn at my grave-place? And the world's desire should be for Heaven or else no Heaven is. A matchless thing, sole of its kind, is not for mortal men. Let the gods have her, as they have us all. It is on us that they grow fat — if not on our souls, then on our life-stuff. And Helen brought them ten years of that, which they lapped up like cats round a saucer. Never tell me that she sits now in the women's court broidering bed-cloths for herself and Menelaus. The ghostly heroes beyond the Styx would cry out at such an ending. Rather let her be hung in the air to compete with the moon as Sky Goddess, or sent into the Underworld to plump up the pillows of Hades; or made into light that glows around the masts of ships when a storm is on its way. History must transmogrify her rather than let her be had by the worm.

But me, worm, you shall have, and welcome — maiden, mother

and grandmother, the soft flesh and the stubborn bone — to feed on and digest my story. Through you it will come up with the grass and the knowing bees be privy to it so that, humming, they may bruit it forth and let the world learn of the new time coming.

For, outworn heart in a time outworn, my ending foresees another ending. Here will I sit, worm, till you take me, and tell strange stories of the death of gods; how they will, all of them, depart, back into him that rayed them forth. And of how he, too, son of Earth and Time, will, plump with their forces, himself depart.

But where depart? Indeed, worm, there is no place that is not this place. Everywhere is here. It is all one. Nothing is lost. Age follows age as breath follows breath. God follows god as the day the night, new foot exact to the old footprint. So, may it not be that Zeus — the all-trickster, cold-hearted, self-sufficing — has only to stoop to the sandal's latchet of the One that is to come — he who, among the ten thousand things, is acquainted with love and sorrow?

And may there not arise a poet who, pondering an ancient tale, will ask himself the question:

'Did he, the white Swan sailing her inward waters, put on, before he let her drop, her humanity and her grief?'

First published in 'Parabola' on the theme of Holy War, New York, 1982.

Walking the Maze at Chartres

IN HIS book *Mont St Michel and Chartres,* Henry Adams quotes
from a letter written by one abbé to another telling how the stones
for Chartres Cathedral were drawn in carts, not by mules or oxen,
but by men and women of the nobility; and how there was an
understanding among them that this should be done in silence.
Silence without, silence within. If anyone uttered even a prayer
he was sent away. Reading this, I thought to myself how gladly
I would have been of that company and made up my mind that
in some future time I would go and see what had been made of
those stones.

This did not happen until a day, just after the war, when the little
train from Paris took myself and a scatter of friends through fields
of breast-high corn to the town. I remember it as quiet and self-
absorbed, almost a village, few tourists around. And there it stood,
the Cathedral, upon its mound, a great stone Melusine. I was not
to know until many years later why such a word should come to
me as I went in through the royal portal.

I had not come as a sightseer, merely to be within this sanctum
that had haunted my thoughts for so long. The others, as though
on roller skates, swept from one wonder to another, making
suitable exclamations, giving each as much attention as they might
to a picture post card. I heard them darting around the chairs, a
posse of transient bits of matchwood that mocked the eternal stone.
I sat upon one of these, gingerly, so as not to evoke a vulgar creak
of gratitude that at least, if there was to be a service, there would
be a congregation of one.

There was no service. Nothing but fading voices as my friends
dashed off on their tour of inspection, taking in, as they rolled
along, Moses, Melchizedek, Christ in Glory.

I sat on, beneath the crowding forest of stone, unselfed even of the self that had brought me, wholly given to the moment. Stillness enfolded me, without my help made me its own. I was, and at the same time was not — for how long, probably seconds, but a second can have a lifetime in it — when the hair on my head began to move, lifting towards the boughs of the forest. Up, up it crept, like ascending rain, my scalp rising, too, like the peak of a tent.

'Presently,' I thought, not in words, for I had no head — a vibration, a throb of the pulse, merely — 'presently I shall know something; whatever it is will reveal itself . . .'

And then the skaters came rolling back.

'Don't just sit there, time's running out!' But I had just been outside time. 'You mustn't miss the crypt.'

So I rose and went away with them — head solid now upon my shoulders — grieving for the loss of something I had not quite possessed.

'You've seen nothing,' they reproached me, as the train bore us away.

It was true. Not Mother and Child down in the Crypt, not Abraham and Samuel with the Tablets of the Law, not the Sirens regaling themselves from the Grail Cup, neither St George nor St Theodore. The great rose window of *La Belle Dame de la Verrière* had bathed me in its light, but the Labyrinth, which echoes it as the earth echoes the sky, had been hidden from my sight by the chairs. And if I had seen nothing — no thing — what had I been? No thing, either.

But time, as it must, came round again, bringing with it a sequel. Not long ago, a geometer friend of mine invited me and some of his pupils to go to Chartres and walk the Maze while he took measurements — a cardinal privilege, for in recent centuries, among the clerics of the Cathedral, the Labyrinth has been held to be a pagan symbol, one to be discreetly secluded from the laity lest their temple be profaned. The Maze might be used as a merry-go-round, worse still, little boys, being what they are, might decide to play hopscotch on it! They do not know, or make great ploy of pretending not to know, that the Maze *is*, among other things, a hopscotch! Childish similitudes of it have been found not only in Crete and Greece but in more than one layer of fallen Troy. Many a time I have hopped it myself, drawing the abalone-shaped circle on any level patch of earth as children still do on city pavements. 'Playing Snail' it was called, or 'Troy.' And in England one can see its wavy furrows in many a field, accurately shaped and turfed —

'Troy Towns,' the country people call them — to be walked through on festive occasions.

They have even wiped from their minds, these same clerics, the part of their ancient liturgy that required the Bishop, at Eastertide, to lead the Round Dance through the Labyrinth; to say nothing of the fact that it was incumbent upon every pilgrim to tread it — perhaps as a form of initiation — before he approached the altar.

I do not know how many of us were pilgrims as we swept in a chartered Parisian bus through the sweet well-husbanded countryside. But many a camera was ready to click at the first sight of the Mound — that mysterious eminence so old that nobody knows whether it was man-heaped as a pyramid is, or tossed up by an impulse of nature. That elephantine hummock of earth is known to have been a place of pilgrimage not merely before the Christian era, but before the Gauls appropriated it from the still earlier Celtic world.

And suddenly, in the distance, we saw it, its Cathedral like a ship sailing or, seen from another angle, a great bird brooding above its young.

Arrived, we became part of a sightseeing crowd, corralled by a human computer who knew little more than what had inadequately been fed into him. But I had spent years on the theme of Chartres and could, as I listened, tell myself the whole story of its building, all its exterior carven glories, the yin-and-yang of its lunar and solar towers. But when, in the Crypt, the ancient dwelling-place of Our-Lady-under-the-Earth, he offered us a miniscule Mother and Son where once had sat in the dark grotto the great black Virgin and Child, carved in the hollow trunk of a pear-tree by those 'pagan' fellows, the Druid priests, in the days when Bethlehem was merely desert — well, I had had enough. I jabbed my *pourboire* into the door-keeper's claw, fervently hoping that it would scratch her, strode away from the tawdry scene and waited to be rod-and-staffed into the Cathedral.

I paused in the entrance. Would my memory have failed me? No. I knew by the tingling at the back of my neck that I was, in a sense, coming home, back to something unknown but true.

There was the forest, dappled with the ineffable light that comes from the coloured windows themselves, not from the sunlight that filters through. But the high altar I could not see. A rectangular table, covered in scarlet cloth, and presumably used in place of an altar, divided the Cathedral in two. It was bare now except for a vase of roses, a trivial note in that place of awe: a priest, apparently having finished mass, was hurrying away, and from the ranked chairs came a series of groans as the scant congregation took its leave to a pious chorale from the organ. I listened carefully. Surely that was piped music, something not from a human hand, intentional and communicative, but brought about by a switch. I examined one of the carven pillars. Yes! In the hollow between two flutings of stone lay a long black casing, clearly carrying the wire. As if the soundless stone itself was not music enough!

Who are the pagans, now, you clerics? We who are going to walk the Maze or yourselves, Bearers of the Word, who, in a place that enshrines the Word, so misprize those who have come to hear it?

By now there was not a tourist in sight. It was clear that our geometer's contract had required that, for a certain time, the Cathedral should be ours. We alone were to be tainted by what was revealed when our little band moved the chairs away — a model of the universe, some say, where those that walk it are treading not the Earth only but Moon, Mercury, Venus, Sun, Jupiter, Saturn and the Fixed Stars, visiting upon the way the houses of the zodiac.

Perhaps. But I had not come as scientist or philosopher, but to learn what the Maze itself could tell me as it lay there, full in view at last, and seeming slowly to wheel or waltz beneath the flickering glass-light.

The measuring instruments set up, the crowd formed itself into a line that, without pause, fed itself into the entrance.

I waited, sitting on one of the dreadful chairs, taking off my shoes and stockings. Let me feel my bare feet on the stone, I thought, nothing between myself and it.

There were too many walkers. Inevitably, as they went round and round and in and out, it had to become a shuffle. And presently a young man withdrew from the motley and came and sat beside me. 'I can't do it,' he said. 'Not with so many people.' I suggested that he wait for me and saw, as he glanced at my bare feet, that he furtively removed his shoes, but not, however, his socks. It is hard for the young to be bare to the bone.

And soon the Maze was clear again, seeming to turn as though on a pivot, as the geometer, diminutive under the great arches, went round it, taking its measure. And, again, I — also microscopic — walking towards the swinging circles, knew the Cathedral for a Melusine, a Woman-serpent — the voluptuous brooding mother-stone alive with reptilian vibrations, telluric or cosmic, I could not tell. But I felt a tremor run through my blood as the Way opened before me. From this point I must walk through my life as at night, before sleeping, I walk through my day.

My foot shivers upon the stone and as I make my first turn leftwards I think of the pilgrims of long ago. Did they, too remember the Younger Son, who took his portion and went away into an unknown country? Am I he? Yes, we are all he, turning, as I turn, upon the path, at first so easy, so flower-bedecked, stone vibrant under the foot, lifting it forwards at each new lap.

But the downhill road runs ever upwards. Each circuit becomes more difficult than the last, with never a resting place. I remember that this is a Labyrinth, not a maze; it does not fool us with false clues. So, the way inexorably leads me on, through myself, as well as its own design; through the sweet that so soon becomes the bitter; the taking of what is not one's own, the discarding of that which should be grasped. Is it thus for all who walk this path? Fearful of living, fearful of dying, I fall upon the thorns of life, hugging my suffering to my breast as though it were a dead child that I cannot give up to the grave. Companionable souls, and dear, reach for my hand in the gallimaufry, while I remain, alone in the midst — knowing and hardly knowing within me that which is nearer than man's neck vein, which forever calls and, the call not answered, is therefore itself alone.

Now I have come to the outermost rim, the fearful symmetry that carries me out beyond Mars, Jupiter, Saturn and the zone of the fixed stars. I am lost and astray in the universe. But, at once, the way turns back on itself. Lap upon lap it bears me inwards to the flower-shaped central stone of the Maze. *Ciel*, it is called, and 'Jerusalem,' 'The Holy City,' *La Mort*.

Slowly I tread the straight path towards it, carrying all that I am and have been, coming at last to myself. Would Heaven have me, or Jerusalem? No! Well, Death, what have I to bring to you? Only this — my burden! And, as well, certain scraps of meaning. For if my life has happened to me, there have been moments — may they be counted — when I have happened to it. Let me not, therefore, be a Sabine Woman, part of your plunder, borne off in protest. I would encounter darkness as a bride and eat the pomegranate!

Ah!

My blood leaps at a soundless sound and I know it for what it is — the cry of a mutual shock of rapture and I am part of it. I should have known, as I trod the way, that if the centre is the end it is also the beginning. That cry conceived me and I assented, participating in the nuptial dance that compounded of two, a third.

So, dividing, I multiplied. I was fish of the sea, bird of the air, four-footed creature of the earth — and, all these knotted by a thread from the sun, I came forth, as all come, wailing. Alas, the sorrow of being born!

But I had said 'Yes!' In my marrow, I have always known it. And if Yes, then all must be endured, no plaint, no claim to any right, and nobody to blame. Ripeness is all. Oh, may I ripen!

Here, then, is the turning point when the pilgrim, like the Prodigal Son, must arise and go to his Father. So, from the Maze's epicentre, I am borne by the ascending forces that will lead me out of it.

Buoyant of foot, vibrating to the stone's vibration, I trace the same paths in another direction. Passing my impalpable self trudging inwards under its load, I feel a wry compassion. Let me repair the past, I pray. Let what is done in the dry wood renew what was done in the green. And at each turn, the burden lightens, inessentials fall away of themselves — 'I want!' 'I like!' 'I do not like!' Suffering, intentionally offered up, leaves in its wake a sort of joy; greater love hath no man than this that he lay down his love, no trace abiding. And, companions, look! I am following. Poet, seer, sailor, sage, I take your hands, no longer alone, for that which is nearer than hand or foot is also part of your dance. For the rest, like the monkish calligraphers, I illuminate the mistakes of the brush — laurel and rose, lily and rue — not erasing, adorning.

At the edge of my vision a shadow moves. The young man is following the path. May he be spied from afar! And the geometer with his measuring line makes himself air before me.

The last lap comes, then the straight line. The path that leads in leads also out. Was it your purpose, Artificer, that men should, by the same door, arrive filled full and depart empty — empty and fulfilled? Vacant of hand and heart and eye, I turn as the pilgrims must have turned to go from the Maze to the altar. But the huge red table bars the way. It will let no pagan pass.

No matter. Another Labyrinth spreads before me, beyond the rose window, beyond the portal. The World, men call it, as they harrow its circles, turning and turning, seeking its path. I shall find an altar there.

First published in 'Parabola' on the theme of Guilt. New York. 1983.

What Aileth Thee?

WE KNOW him, the Grail hero, under many names — Gawain, Perceval (Parsifal in Wolfram von Eschenbach's version), Bors, Galahad. Lancelot is not in the list for, though he is brought near to it, he is denied the full sight of the Grail because of his long liaison with Guinevere — though whether that event ever really occurred needs, I think, in spite of all the corroborative evidence, to be questioned.

Malory, quite probably, may not have heard of tantrism, but he could not have failed to be familiar with the ordinances of the Courts of Love. It is, therefore, quite possible that those two doughty combatants may have taken on a far more poignant and rigorous task — that of faithfully serving their mutual love while mutually foregoing the taste of its wine. Otherwise, how account for Arthur? The High King, *sans peur et sans reproche,* who with Merlin's help laid down the rules of knighthood — is it conceivable that he would have allowed his paladin among knights to cuckold him at his own Round Table and not reach for Excalibur? Did he look on consenting? It has always seemed to me that in this matter the myth is hiding a card up its sleeve.

Galahad, whom we may think of as Lancelot's unspotted part, is par excellence the Grail's true man, but he dies of his own wish so early in the story that he does not serve to carry it forward so that it can speak to *our* needs.

So let us settle for Perceval, the widow's son, sealed from the world by his mother's love and arriving tardily at court, a homespun and untutored warrior. He is received with mockery. Churl, clown, clodhopper, they call him. But his enthusiastic habit of bringing defeated vassals to the King and lugging in the bodies of hitherto unbeatable villains, stuffs their mockery back into their mouths. His bumpkin herohood forces them to accept him as a true member of the Round Table.

But, cloudily, in his innocent heart though not yet in his rustic head, he knows there is something more to knight-errantry than demolishing giants and rescuing damsels. He is called to something else — but what?

So he sets out, not choosing, merely letting himself be drawn to whatever adventure lies in wait. Wandering through woods and wildlands, following chimerical roads that cross and wind about each other with no apparent destination, he comes, on a sudden, to a magical tower, the great walled keep of Montsalvesche.

Not knowing it for the Grail Castle and all unlearned in knightly procedure, he enters it as he would any other and stands transfixed by what confronts him. This is nothing less than the ceremonial of the Grail feast. Before him reclines the Grail King, *Roi Pescheur, Roi Mehaigné*, unmanned by his secret wound and about him, in a blaze of moving light, knights and maidens led in procession by the Grail Queen carrying the Grail itself.

Undone at finding himself in such surroundings, he watches the pageantry in silence, partakes in silence of the sacred meal, in silence allows the shining figures to bow him to his bed place. And in silence he awakes at daybreak to find that the Castle has disappeared. He is alone in a vast spreading wasteland where all streams are dry and voiceless, trees naked of their leaves and no bird sings.

Bemused, knowing himself under enchantment, he makes his slow way back to the court to be accosted at the entrance by a boar-tusked female riding a mule. And there, amid his welcoming peers, he is arraigned for unknightliness. Why, the creature demands, having seen the Fisher King sore wounded and because of that wound the land itself wasted and wounded, had he not asked the healing question?

Unknightliness! The sting of it, to one who has valiantly, if belatedly through no fault of his own, set himself to master the courtesies of knighthood, of which to refrain from unasked-for questions is high among the list!

Within himself Perceval rages, even against the God he is seeking, and determines at all costs to find again the place of his misjudgement.

Now, the myth requires that the question be asked even if it means thereby that one of its own rules be broken. It gives him a second chance. After long years of searching he finds himself in the place where he had stood before. The miraculous ceremony is once more performed. And he, gathering all his forces, steps forth and asks the question.

'Sir, what aileth thee?'

We know the rest. The King is healed and therefore the land. Birds sing and the desert blooms. We know the rest, for the myth takes us back to the first syllable of recorded time, to its roots in the pagan vegetation rites of the death and resurrection of such heroes as Tammuz, Adonis, Attis.

The theme of the question is a late addition. It arose because it was required. Myth answers every need. It is not static, once and for all, a phenomenon caught in the web of the past but rather an ever-living process. It speaks to us with an ancient voice that is forever new and to understand it properly we will have to live it as it marches with us.

For the question is our own question. In our rational, fragmented, technological world, it is we, seeking deliverance, that need it to be asked; we ourselves must become the Grail hero who will set the waters free, not only in ourselves but in others. Secretly, we are all sore wounded and need that the wound be noted and the necessary words of power spoken.

What aileth thee, neighbour? Friend? Brother?

First published in 'Parabola' on the theme of Words Of Power, New York, 1983.

Re-storying
the Adult

THE analytical psychologist, James Hillman, has written of the importance of 're-storying the adult.' There are, indeed, books that purport to be written for children that, in fact, do exactly this for the grown-up. Not to mention the fairy tales, which are at all times available to him and which were never, in the first instance, written for children. It is they, the wise ones, who have purloined them.

'We love only what is our own,' said A E, the Irish sage, 'and what is our own we cannot lose.' But as we grow older what is our own is not so easily perceived. It becomes silted over with what is not the true story, like a penny lost in a puddle. For the adult to re-story himself a certain process has to be set in motion, a process in which he himself must relive intentionally what once was organically lived by the blood. He must take an active and enquiring part; no one can do it for him. To set him loose in a library full of myths and legends would do no good whatever. He would merely go on reading, reading, silting over still further that bright instructive penny. No. He needs to let go all his knowing, be as ready for Hell as for Heaven and bare his heart until, if need be, it is capable of breaking. Maybe, even, he will need a guide. He will certainly need to listen. The ear is ever more subtle than the eye.

'Shall I hold your hand?' asked a child of five whose father was about to read us 'Fitcher's Bird' from Grimms'. She had no fear, knowing the story, but clearly doubted my ability to cope with all the bloodiness that precedes the happy ending. I accepted with gratitude, realizing that since I myself at the same age had cheerfully encountered all those chopped-up bodies in the basin, much silting over had happened within me, many tables had been turned.

If I had the job of re-storying someone, I would go first to the great world epics, those reservoirs from which all the smaller stories have been fished — the *Mabinogion*, the *Eddas*, the Irish *Tain*, the *Nibelungenlied*, the *Iliad*, the *Odyssey*, the *Popol Vuh*, the Old and New Testaments, the *Mahabharata*, and the *Ramayana.*

Of the last, Coomaraswamy has observed that 'one might go so far as to say that no one unfamiliar with the story of Rama and Sita can be a true citizen of the world.'

If you, stranger, wishing to be such a one, were to take my hand while I recited this mighty saga, we would be together for days and weeks. But at least we can speak here of Hanuman who, in a sense, is the *deus ex machina* of the story.

'It may be questioned' — again I quote Coomaraswamy — 'whether there is in the whole of literature such another apotheosis of loyalty and self-surrender as Hanuman . . . the perfect servant who finds full realization of manhood in faithfulness and obedience, the subordinate whose glory is in his own inferiority.'

He must have been already ancient and come from afar — a character, perhaps, in search of a story — when Valmiki, writing early in our Christian era, lifted him from the unwritten annals of the folk. True, the *Ramayana* is full of other monkeys; Surgriva and Vali are powerful and princely apes whose subplot thrusts the action forward. But Hanuman stands apart from these, sole of his kind, seeking nothing for himself and, in serving Rama — who, it is ultimately disclosed, is an incarnation of Vishnu — becomes the meeting-point of an earlier system of nature-worship with the burgeoning order of gods and devas which was to influence the whole future of religion. So, let us speak here of t'.e *Ramayana* solely in terms of that meeting-point, finding the oak tree, as it were, in the acorn.

Briefly, Rama, ousted from his position as heir apparent to the throne of Ayodhya, sets off with his newly wedded wife, Sita, and his brother, Lakshman, to dwell in the forest as hermits. But the forest, if full of hermits, is also inhabited by rakshasas (demons) whose King, Ravana, by devious means, discovers the trio and becomes enamoured of Sita.

Choosing a time when the brothers are away hunting, he appears before her as a wandering yogi and as such is treated courteously. However, he quickly shows himself in his true colours — ten-faced and twenty-armed — and carries her off in his chariot, but not before Sita, perceiving five great monkeys sitting together on the top of a mountain, casts down to them her veil and a handful of jewels. Rama, distraught, comes upon the monkeys and swears friendship with their king, Surgriva, who summons his hosts from far and near, chief among whom is Hanuman. It is to him that Rama gives his signet ring, immediately divining that if Sita is to be found at all it will be by this humble monkey.

So, Surgriva's people range the world and learn at last from an aged vulture that Sita has been carried away by Ravana, a hundred leagues across the sea to Lanka. But who can cross those hundred leagues? Who but Hanuman, the son of the Wind, who, as a child, had seen the sun in the sky and, thinking it to be a fruit, had leapt three thousand leagues to pluck it.

He leaps. Mind, heart, and body steadied on the task, he disdains, in his impatience, to rest for a moment on a mountain thrust up by the kindly ocean, and alights upon the shores of Lanka, neither weary nor breathless. Like a cat he creeps through the sleeping city and comes at last to where Ravana lies among his resplendent queens. But his instinct tells him that Sita could not, indeed would not, be among them.

'Better I die than not find her,' he thinks. So he proceeds to meditate, making his mind one-pointed, ranges through the surrounding woods in his imagination and in his imagination comes upon her. Guarded by rakshasas, like a deer among hounds, she lies grieving beneath an asoka tree. Hanuman climbs silently into the branches and softly, so as not to startle her, recites the deeds and virtues of Rama, till at last, certain that he has her ear, he stands before her with joined palms and offers the signet ring. Modestly, ever the servant, he suggests that he carry her on his back across the sea. But, no. For all her joy at the signet ring, she will not willingly touch anyone but Rama, and the glory of her rescue must be her husband's. She gives him a jewel from her hair and begs him to return and tell Rama where to find her.

So, go he must but, monkey-like, he will not leave till he has left his mark — breaking the branches of the wood, despoiling the elegant pavilions. Inevitably, he is caught and brought before Ravana, whose one thought is to kill and eat him. But demons, too, have their chivalry; one may not eat an envoy. There is nothing, however, against setting fire to an envoy's tail. So Hanuman becomes a flaming brand till the Wind, beholding his son's plight, blows cold between the tail and the body while the son reduces half the city to ashes and slaughters a host of rakshasas. Then, quenching his tail at the edge of the ocean, he makes another great leap across it and lays Sita's jewel at Rama's feet.

Thus, with Sita found, the struggle for her rescue begins. Ocean, by its nature fathomless, suffers Rama and the monkey hordes to build a bridge of stones and trees and vows to hold it up. So, to and fro the battle surges, Hanuman, ever-excessive in the midst, breaking off hilltops to hurl at rakshasas; even, with Lakshman wounded and in need of healing herbs, leaping to the Himalayas and, too impatient with love to pluck them, carrying southward a whole mountain and replacing it when the wound is healed.

At long last — for the battle takes up almost half the story — Ravana is slain by Rama with a Brahma weapon, and it is Hanuman whom he sends to Sita to apprise her of all that has happened. The reunion of the pair and Rama's two heart-broken renunciations of his bride — in the name of custom and tradition — is another story. That of Hanuman ends with the departure of the helpful monkeys laden with goodly gifts. But he himself has no need of a gift, his passion is to serve. All he asks is that he may live on earth as long as the story of Rama is told. The boon is granted. It is, in fact, the gift of eternal life. For if, by mischance, the *Ramayana* should ever cease to be known, Hanuman could not but live on. Whatever it is or whoever it is that unwinds the myths of the world would make sure that he didn't disappear but moved from one cycle of stories to another. Inevitably, I think, he would find his way into the Jataka tales as an incipient Boddhisattva, not to be lost till all men are lost, nor to step into Heaven till he is sure that all men, absolved, are at his heels.

So, stranger, I give you an acorn. If you will re-story yourself its tree will become as high as the sky. Or, better still, remembering Blake — one of the great re-storyers —

I give you the end of a golden string
Only wind it into a ball,
It will lead you in at Heaven's gate
Built in Jerusalem's wall.

First published in 'Parabola' on the theme of Sun & Moon, New York. 1983.

The Hanged Man

THE TWELFTH TAROT CARD

'OH, young man, why do you hang there upside-down, smiling and seeming to dance? Your blood will all run into your head. You will have no chance of growing old if you persist in such folly.'

'I have already been old,' said the young man. 'And it does not appear to me that I am upside-down. The blood has indeed run into my head but it has also run out again, leaving it all but empty.'

'Empty? But you are not the Fool. The number of the Fool is zero, and zero contains all numbers.'

'Not the Fool, but a simpleton, set free of his too-much knowledge. Oh, there was nothing I did not know, no question I could not answer. I was ancient and heavy with my learning; knowledge ever breeding knowledge; propositions, measures, degrees; sciences, lore of every kind; the old and the new mixing, adhering; affinities and parallels begetting themselves eternally. Many men came to me for teaching. The universe was my bedside book. I elaborated on the secrets of life and death. What was above and below I knew. I was a prodigy among scholars.' He swung to and fro on his rope.

'And then there came to me one who asked, "Who is it, sir, that knows all this? What sustains your learning?" And there, for the first time, was a question I could not answer. No lexicon had prepared me for it. I looked within and found no-one. "Who am I?" I inquired of myself and nothing made reply. Oh, then, indeed, I was upside-down, a mere head walking the earth. "What shall I do?" I demanded of my erudition, aghast at the discovery that far from being more than a man, I was less than half. But my erudition could not tell me. It does not deal in such things. Then deep within me something wept — I who had never wept before, nor needed the gift of weeping — and I knew what had to be done. A tear is an intellectual thing, opening doors no knowledge can broach. It gave me the grace to remember Plato: *Man is a heavenly plant and what this means is that he is like an inverted tree of which the roots tend heavenwards and the branches down to earth.* And I said to myself, "I will be rooted."

'My tear also brought to me Lao Tzu, whom before I had thought of as merely a book. *The man of learning increases every day, the man of Tao decreases every day.* And I said to myself, "I will decrease."

'And that is why you find me here, foot-fast to the celestial root, swinging between Nonexistence and Existence. And while it is more difficult to decrease than to increase, I find that daily something falls from me, daily myself grows nearer to me. If there is anything I now need to know, a passing bee will apprise me of it.'

'But what will happen to you at last, hanging there, prey to every wind?'

'I do not know. The dancer and the dance are one. And, anyway,' the young man said, 'the matter is not in my hands'.

First published in 'Parabola' on the theme of Hierarchy, New York, 1984.

Miss Quigley

WE HAD nothing to do. And where there is nothing, something inevitably arises. Satan chuckled contentedly as one thought, single and triune as the Trinity, entered our three heads.

And not our heads only. It ran like an elixir through our veins, quickening them with illicit joy — erotic had we but known the word — a serpent coursing along the blood.

'Let us,' we said, as with one voice, 'go and steal Miss Quigley's apples!'

They were Stripeys, so-called because they were streaked with alternate bands of colour, the only fruit of their kind in the neighbourhood; ours were merely common cookers.

It was not that we disliked Miss Quigley. She had, for us, a unique distinction, the only person of our acquaintance possessed of a broken heart. This piece of lore had entered our private mythology to the accompanying tinkle of elegant china on various local silver tea-trays, from which we were given sponge fingers and told to 'Go and play, children!' Grown-up talk was not for our ears. Therefore, since, like all children, we were natively scandal-mongers, we lusted eagerly after it. So, we crept back, whenever we could, to hear how they lived in that other world — how, for instance, Major 'Bingo' Battle had a habit of 'lifting his elbow' which, mysteriously, was why he was so often seen holding on to tree or fence as he staggered along the road; how Mrs Scott-Campbell's baby, not being wanted by Mrs Scott-Campbell — the nods and becks made it clear to us — was not allowed to be born; we thought of that infant with commiseration, sitting forever in its cramped dark place, no exit allowed to it through Mrs Scott-Campbell's navel; how Mr Farquhar 'wasted his substance', which to us was the same as 'wasting away', and yet, to our eyes, grew not thinner but fatter; and how Miss Quigley's broken heart had to do with a fair-haired soldier whose portrait hung on her drawing room wall. Crack! Like a Dresden cup it fell; we could almost hear it shattering against the wall of her bosom.

Oh, no, we liked Miss Quigley and because we liked her it would be an added sauce to the adventure to hurt her by stealing her apples; to take the forbidden path through the bush 'Not unless there is somebody with you!' that led to her apple orchard. We were there, distant though it was, as though it was no distance, the serpent doing its work within us, lifting us, light as birds, into the trees.

We picked with care, choosing the best, thrusting the beautiful striped darlings down between our vests and our chests, scooping them under the elastic of our sailor blouses and bloomers, growing heavier and more lumpish every moment, bulging and shapeless as Christmas stockings.

Then, suddenly, a voice hailed us and there was Miss Quigley, her skirts frothing over the grass, coming towards the slip rails. 'Children, how lovely! Have you come all this way to pay me a visit?' She had a lingering way with words, as though reluctant to let them leave her, or as if she were speaking them in a dream.

We looked at her stonily, caught in the act, pressing our bodies against the branches, one with the bark and bole of the trees, as we waited to be denounced. But Miss Quigley was smiling. 'Won't you come in out of the sun? We could play the musical box.'

The musical box! Oh, it was our treasure, pored over rapturously whenever our mother took us to tea on Miss Quigley's 'afternoons'. Miss Quigley's father, it was said, had long ago brought it from Home — Home being England, where all good things came from — and, unlike common musical boxes, it played not one but three · tunes: a *Lullaby* to a child improbably called Brahms, *Barbara Allen*, and *The Blue Danube*. The thought of the musical box was too much for us. We would have that and the apples, too.

Cautiously, we climbed down and followed Miss Quigley to the house like a trio of old arthritic men bearing their knotted bodies along. Arriving, we refused, though reluctantly, her offer of lemonade lest, lifting our hands to take the glass, the apples fell out of our sleeves. 'Well then,' said Miss Quigley, girlishly, 'we shall have music wherever we go.' She waved her hand at a big brown box inlaid with silver and mother-of-pearl. Then she opened the lid and turned the screw.

We held our breaths as the long gilt cylinder began to turn, a golden hedgehog sending out its thin high hedgehog music. The infant Brahms was put to sleep, Barbara Allen — and serve her right — was buried beneath the briar. As we waited for the third tune, one of us said, for we did not know, 'Miss Quigley, what is a Danube?' 'Oh!' Miss Quigley clasped her hands to her breast. 'Oh, c-h-i-l-d-r-e-n, it is a r-i-v-e-r! Blue as an eye, blue as Heaven, blue, blue,' she murmured, dreamily. And as the hedgehog tinkled again, she began to waltz in time to the tune, holding out her arms before her as though she were clasping something, someone — was it the fair, red-coated soldier? Round and round she went with the music, her eyes gazing raptly upwards.

And, caught by her fervour and the swinging, swaying, dipping tune, we, too, began to waltz, arms out, clasping to our bony chests presences hardly apprehended. The future was gathered in our arms, invisible, intangible, prefiguring what would one day be — soldier, sailor, tinker, tailor, poet, candlestick-maker — and the apples fell out of their hiding places and went bouncing across the floor. Alas, we had forgotten the Stripeys!

The music stopped. So did we. Miss Quigley came out of her dream and slowly took in the scene. We waited for the inevitable, the serpent steeling us to face it. Miss Quigley swiftly left the room. Was she going to look for a horsewhip? No. She was back in a trice with three paper bags. Like marble statues we stood and watched her as on hands and knees, fossicking under chairs and tables, she gathered up all the apples.

'There!' she said, scrambling to her feet. 'One for you! And you! And you!' She thrust a bag at each of us. 'I'm so glad you like my Stripeys. I'm partial to them myself.' She swept her hand swiftly across our heads. 'So fair, so fair!' she said fondly. 'Goodbye. Give my love to your mother.'

And then we were out in the sunny day, tricked of our serpentine intention. With one accord we dumped the Stripeys and left the bags by the slip rails. They had no meaning for us now. We had come for booty and been given a gift. Without our wish, without our connivance, we had been found not guilty. Yet, for all that, not guiltless, either. Caught in a no-place between the two, we felt cheated, stolen from, and empty, the virtue all gone out of us. We went home by the bush path — the air spicy with the mingled scents of blue-bottle ants and gum trees — nothing in either hand or heart.

'Where have you been?' we were asked.

'Nowhere.'

'What have you been doing?'

'Nothing.'

'Not playing alone in the bush?'

'No.'

If we could not be thieves we could still be liars and face, as such, the consequences. However austere, they would be welcome and bring us their healing power . . .

We never went to Miss Quigley's again. This was a matter for comment.

'Why not? You like dear Miss Quigley and her musical box!'

They might have been questioning the Sphinx. For how to explain that these assumptions were no longer true, give reasons for what would be thought unreason? To explain is always in vain . . .

But all that was long ago. Now that I can speak my heart, I say to you, all you blond robbers of the world, robbers, indeed, of every colour, let you beware Miss Quigley! Everyone steals — a purse, an apple, a piece of knowledge, another's good name, another's love; and time, itself a thief, can be stolen, secreted from the diurnal round for that in us which is not diurnal and which exacts its particular price. But Miss Quigley at any level — she may even be yourself in disguise — will absolve you by tearing up the bill. Thus she betrays you at the outset, defrauds you of rightful retribution, the chance to repair both yourself and the deed; and worst of all worsts, she will trick you out of the reconciliation, flowing and flooding mind and heart, that comes with metanoia.

Theft and consequence are one whole transaction. But Miss Quigley, with her good intentions, will prevent the accomplishment of the process. For she is, herself, a master thief, slipping a hand into Cause's pocket to steal away Effect. Thus she paves for you — oh, so bright and shiny! — that well-known downward path.

But do not indulge her self-indulgence. No robber worth his salt will lightly be party to forgiveness before it is wanted or asked for. 'Take what you want,' says God. 'Take it and pay for it.' That payment, in the long run, will shrive you. You do not need Miss Quigley.

First published in 'Parabola' on the theme of Theft, New York, 1984.

The Way Back

LET me remind you of the ancient story, taken from the Upanishads, of Indra and his palace; how, heady with triumph after his defeat of the enemies of Heaven, he engaged the divine architect Vishnakarman to build him a mansion of such ever-increasing size and splendour that Vishnakarman despaired of finishing it, and appealed for help to the gods. Immediately thereafter, you remember, a radiant boy — Vishnu disguised — appears before the triumphant king, praising this marvel of architecture and assuring him that no other Indra has ever accomplished such a feat. Surprised, but indulgent — how could there have been another Indra? — the king smilingly asks to be told how many Indras the boy has known. 'They are numberless,' the child replies, 'as the universes that rise and fall.' And he waves his hand at the column of ants that at this moment, in martial array, is marching towards the throne. 'Can you, O king, make count of these? Yet each of them,' the boy declares, 'was once himself an Indra. Each one, by virtue of pious deeds, ascended to the world of the gods and now, after many incarnations, has become again an ant.' Startled, the king confronts the army till at last the truth dawns upon him and we are left with a repentant Indra, rehabilitated, wise, and humble. One could wish that all men, both high and low, could have such lordly preceptors.

But, rejoicing as one does with the king, as indeed we do with all that ends well, can we forget those others, the ants? For me they are the heart of the story. I need to be told what happens to them. In my mind's eye, I see the parading horde and ask myself — Is there one among them who in his secret lonely heart has the wit to enquire 'Who am I?' Him at the outer edge of the line, a sturdy sergeant-at-arms, maybe, bulbous-eyed, tiger-waisted, a pillar of the ant-heap? I imagine him, having heard the words of the ancient boy, breaking abruptly away from the column and, egged on by his own enigma, making hurriedly for the portal and the nearest blade of grass.

There I would find him, crouched and sombre, pondering within himself his whence and why and whither. And as one pilgrim to another, I would make bold to speak to him, lightening my heart to the stranger as one cannot do to one's nearests.

'Ant,' I would say, 'my plight is yours, my questions, too. But where shall we find the answers? From the moment of birth we are, all of us, on a voyage of exploration, not, as we fondly think, to new pastures — though these we'll doubtless come upon — but to what, a voice within tells us, is, in fact, our homeland. We think of it as the way forward but in truth, Ant, it is the way back. We return to whence we have come. And if there be answers, they will outstrip us. We will find them arrived before us.'

Would something of Indra stir within him as we sat in the shade of the blade of grass, I beguiling him with a story or two to illustrate my theme; perhaps reciting the *Hymn of the Pearl*, watching the round eyes growing rounder as he heard the tale unfold?

'There was once,' I would say, 'a Prince of the East whose parents sent him forth on a quest. They provisioned him aptly for the journey but took from him the robe of glory that was fashioned exactly to his shape — as all our robes are at the beginning — telling him that when he had gone down into Egypt and captured the One Pearl from the Sea Serpent he would not only have his robe again but would be, with his brother, heir to their kingdom. So he set out and when at last he came to Egypt he settled, hidden, close to the Serpent, watching for it to fall asleep so that he might take the Pearl.

'But, alas, it was he himself who slept, in the sense that he became one with the Egyptians. He decked himself in their garments, drank deep of their curious potions and ate the food of bondage. He forgot that he was a Prince of the East, made his oblations to the Egyptian king, and thought no more of the quest.

'At length his parents, made aware of his plight, sent him a royal message:

> Awake! Remember you are the son of a king who now comports himself as a slave. Remember the Pearl for whose sake you went down into Egypt. Remember your robe of glory that you may put it on again, and your name be read in the book of heroes, and you with your brother be heir to the kingdom.

'Then this letter, royally sealed, rose up and took the form of an eagle, and flew till it alighted by the side of the Prince and became, miraculously, speech. And the sound of the words awoke the youth. His freeborn soul leapt within him, and he longed to be with his kind. Now, at last, he remembered the Pearl and slowly began to enchant the Serpent, making a charm of the names of his parents. And the Serpent, rocked and lullabied by the spell, for the first time slumbered and slept. At once the Prince seized the Pearl, tossed aside his foreign garments and, guided by the voice of the letter, made his way towards the East. His robe of glory came to meet him, brought by a faithful messenger, and he ran to bedeck himself with it as though it were his lost true self. And so, carrying the treasure, he came to the gates of his father's castle and was given a hero's welcome.

'Ant,' I said, as the naked lidless eyes glistened, 'I have told the story shortly but the journey would have been long, I think.' How long, I wondered, would *his* journey be, what ardours, what austerities would it take for a man, much less an ant, to become again an Indra? The fearful thought turned upon myself, blackening my blood. But I continued my telling.

'The tales are many, Ant,' I said, knowing well that I was invoking them as much for my own sake as for his. 'There is one that reveals itself in pictures, as the eagle, remember, became the letter, of an Oxherd who has lost his Ox. And yet we learn, paradoxically, that the Ox has never been astray. It is the Herd himself who is in confusion, beguiled by dreams of gain and loss, right and wrong and all things that oppose each other. He must gather what he has of wisdom and set out in search of his beast. And, sure enough, in the picture called *Seeing the Traces*, he finds in the dust a hoof-print. This happens, we are told, because what he thinks of as the objective world is merely a reflection of his Self. He is still confused, unable to distinguish between truth and falsehood, but his senses, now more harmoniously related, bring him to the point of *Seeing the Ox* — which, when all is said and done, has really nowhere to hide. But *Catching the Ox* is a different matter, for the creature has returned to the wild and is restive and unruly. So, *Herding the Ox* is no easy task. The Herd must keep tight hold of the nose-ring while letting go that in himself which is wild and will not be tethered. At length, after a long struggle, harmony is established and the Herd rides home on the back of the Ox, joyfully playing his flute. *The Ox Forgotten, Leaving the Man Alone* shows the two now at peace with each other, the Man sitting on his verandah, the Ox grazing meekly by. And the eighth picture, *The Ox and the Man Both Gone Out of Sight,* is nothing but a large circle. 'All confusion,' we are told, 'is set aside and serenity prevails. Emptiness is fullness.'

'But are we to suppose, Ant, that that is the end of the story? No, I do not think so. In all tales that tell of a quest — you must have heard many in the ant-heap — something has to be brought home. This is the meaning of 'Happy Ever After,' where all things that have been separate are made into a whole and the fullness overflows to the general world. So, after *Returning to the Source,* which is shown simply as three flowering branches, the Herd appears to us again rich with all his emptiness and *Entering the City with Bliss-Bestowing Hands,* in fact, bringing himSelf. "Carrying a gourd," says the legend, "he goes into the market; leaning on a staff, he comes home. He is found in company with wine-bibbers and butchers, and he and they are all converted into Buddhas." Was there ever such a Happy Ever After?

'But, Ant, there is still another story. Do I dream that your great eyes glisten as a child's do when a tale is proposed? Well, this is how it goes.

'A certain rich man had two sons, and the younger said to him, "Give me my portion that I may go adventuring in the world." So the father divided his living and gave him his share, and he set out into a far country. There he wasted his substance in riotous living. And when a famine fell on the land, he was destitute and compelled to join himself to one of the citizens, who set him to feed the swine. So, since no man befriended him, he was hungry and would fain eat the husks that the swine devoured. Then it was that he came to himself. "Even the hired servants of my father have bread enough and to spare while I famish and waste away. I will arise," he said, "and go to my father." And that is what he did. He arose and took the long way back. But when he was a great way off, his father spied him and had compassion and ran and fell on his neck and kissed him. And the son said "Father, I have sinned against Heaven and in thy sight and am no more worthy to be called thy son." But the father ordered that the best robe be brought and a ring put upon his finger and shoes upon his feet. Also that the fatted calf should be killed and all should eat and drink and be merry.

'But the elder brother, hearing the sound of music and dancing and learning what movement was afoot, was angered and would not join the feast.

' "These many years I have served thee," he said, "and not transgressed thy commandments. Yet to me thou never gavest a kid that I might make merry with my friends. But he who has devoured thy living with harlots, for him thou hast killed the fatted calf!"

' "Son," said the father, "thou art ever with me and all that I have is thine, but this is my son that was dead and is alive again and was lost and is found."

'That is how the story goes and nobody cares for that elder son. Even children cry out against him. But to me, Ant, he is the heart of the matter. As I see the parable, he is the part of the younger son who has never left the father, the part that calls him to come to himself, to arise and journey home and be joint heir (again!) to the kingdom.

'And you, Ant, have you arisen? Is there something still of Indra in you that makes you move so purposefully from one blade of grass to the next, not trying to make a hurried escape but rather as one setting out. Shall we travel together, you and I, pilgrims both, valiant against all disaster?

'Who knows — yet something knows — if the stories I tell you are true? Men need such lively oracles in order to sustain their existence. Lay them to your heart, if you will. Even so, we take the road empty-handed, remember, without even a map to guide us; not dreaming that we carry treasure, nor hoping that someone will run to meet us. Cast off hope, if you have it, Ant. The burden of hope is too heavy. The way itself knows where it is going. The way itself will lift us forward. The way itself is all.'

First published in 'Parabola' on the theme of Pilgrimage, New York, 1984.

Sip No Sup
and Bite No Bit

'GOOD morning, Thade!' The man in the culvert straightened his back.

An English hedger and ditcher would have answered my greeting merely with a finger to brow or at most the wave of a hat. But Thade, being Irish, has to turn everything to drama. All encounters, for him, take place on the road to Damascus. He flung down his spade and clapped a hand to his heart.

'O Mary Hynes, O my share of the world,' (a line from an old Irish Poem) 'is it yerself?' he hailed me.

Well, was it? Could I swear on oath that it was myself calling to him from the lane? It needed a Socrates to answer, and even he, knowing it to be rhetorical, might cravenly have evaded the question as, indeed, I did myself.

Instead, I flattered him. 'That's a good ditch,' I said, eyeing the neatly tailored earth, the shorn green bank rising above it and the clipped hedge crowning all.

'Was I ever after making a bad one?' he demanded. 'When the rain comes it will be a river with fish in it sporting themselves.'

'But why so crooked?' I went on. For the line of the field, unlike the checkerboard land around it, swelled out in a rounded promontory before it returned to the straight.

Thade favoured me with a pitying look. 'And you with a mind as bright as a pin not to know the reason for it! It's a *rath* that's in it, I'm telling you, and where's the strong farmer that would put himself in fear of the Folk by crossing a *rath* with a ditch?'

I should have known. A *rath* is a fairy fort or mound and humans disturb it at their peril.

Leaping the ditch, I climbed the bank and peeped over the hedge. There it was, a daisy-pied circular knoll with a blackthorn tree spreading its shade above it. I shivered. I had seen other such mounds in Ireland and always a tremor in my blood — Emily Dickinson's 'zero at the bone' — had warned me to keep my distance, to walk around them, never across.

Clearly, the farmer who had first laid out the field — long dead he would be and full of lore — would have taken care to avoid this place by following its fairy contours and curving his hedge and his ditch!

'Come away down out of that!' cried Thade, helping me over the ditch with one hand and with the other tearing from the hedge a straggling frond of bindweed. 'I don't want you taken before me eyes. It's this will keep you safe,' he said, winding the frond round my wrist. 'A widdershins thing it is, the creature, climbing against the sun and the clock. And Themselves . . .' he nodded towards the mound, 'Themselves have no relish for it. It will never be abiding their spells. Sure, it has power of its own!'

I looked at the sorcerous dark leaves that seemed to cling to my hand. 'But Thade, you're not wearing it yourself!' If I was in danger, so was he.

'And am I not!' he scoffed at me, and took from his pocket a similar sprig along with an old rusty nail and something in a twist of paper.

'Bindweed, iron and salt!' he said. 'With those they'll never have me.'

'Do you know of anyone who has been — taken?' I was only half serious, asking the question — my rational mind making mocking of me — but Thade was wholly so.

'I do, then. A widow's son in the town beyant . . .' he jerked his thumb at the distant village. 'Handsome he was, a fine boy-o, the spit, barring a wing or two, of the Archangel Michael himself. He was taken below at the full of the moon for Them to work their will on.'

'And did the handsome young man come back?'

'Him, is it? An old bent fellow it was came back and him as hoar as the winter frost, wrapping his arms about himself and crying out to the world, "Nobody knows and I'll not be telling, what happened under the thorn-tree." '

' "Did yez eat anything?" they asked him.'

' "A sup of wine," he said, "in a cowslip and it only half full." '

'And that was it. That was enough. Eat their food and they have you.' Thade took a pinch of salt from his spill and solemnly made the sign of the cross. He was bringing every spell he knew to bear on the situation.

'It was that way,' I told him, 'with Childe Rowland. He was playing at ball with his two elder brothers and when it was lost their sister, Burd Ellen, ran widdershins round the church to find it.'

'Widdershins round a church! That would do it! They'd get her for that, for sure! And so —?'

Like all true Tellers, Thade is avid for a story told and therefore a perfect Listener. He turned his wheelbarrow onto its side, sat down and patted a place beside him. 'Now for the rest of it,' he demanded.

'Well,

They sought her East, they sought her West,
They sought her up and down,
And woe were the hearts of those brethren
For she was not to be found.

So the first brother went to the warlock, Merlin, who, of course, knew where she was.'

'She was with the Gentry! Where else?' said Thade.

'Yes! In the great dark tower of the King of Elfland. So, Merlin consulted with himself, told the eldest brother what to do and what not to do and sent him off to the Underworld.

But long they waited and longer still,
With doubt and muckle pain
And woe were the hearts of his brethren
For he came not back again.

So the second brother had to go to Merlin, who sent him away with the same instructions.

But woe were his mother's and brother's hearts
For he came not back again.

'Ha! They had to wait for the third, begob! The one and the two, where would they be, unless the three was in it? That's the law, I'm thinking.'

Oh, who can tell a Teller the tales? They know them before they are half spun.

'Well, now, ' I went on, 'came Childe Rowland's turn. He was his mother's youngest son — the youngest in those days was the heir — and she would not let him go. So he begged and pleaded till she agreed to girt him with his father's brand that had never struck in vain. And he, too, went to Merlin.

' "Once more and but once more," he said. "Tell how a man or a mother's son may rescue Burd Ellen and her brothers twain." '

'And Merlin gave him the same instructions. "The thing to do is this," he said. "Once you have entered the land of fairy, whoever you encounter till you meet Burd Ellen you must fell them with your father's brand. And what you've not to do is this — you must sip no sup and bite no bit or you'll never see Middle Earth again." '

'That'll be it!' Thade slapped his knee. 'As it might be in a nutshell. The widow's son over again. Go on now, with the telling.'

'Well, he did the things he had to do, inquiring the way of this one and that and cutting off their heads when they answered. And at last he came to a round green hill with seven terrace rings about it and a door set in the side. Three times Childe Rowland knocked and the third knock let him in. And there, in a great hall, was Burd Ellen, sitting on a velvet cushion and combing her hair with a golden comb.

'Up she sprang and kissed him, crying

O luckless fool, O woe, O woe,
That ever you were born,
For come the King of Elfland in
Your fortune is forlorn.'

'Forlorn. Forlorn.' Thade rocked himself rhythmically as though the words were a tune. 'And that indeed was what he'd be if he was after forgetting what he had not to do.'

'He did forget. He said he was hungry and Burd Ellen, under a spell as she was, could not give him a warning word. But over the bowl of bread and milk she looked at him so deep in the eye that he remembered and put it aside.'

'Ah!' cried Thade, triumphantly.

'And then there came a voice saying:

Fee, Fo, Fi, Fum.
I smell the blood of a Christian man,
Be he dead, be he living, with my brand
I'll dash his brains from his brain pan.

And in came the King of Elfland.'

' "Strike, Bogle, if thou darest," ' said Childe Rowland. And they fought till the king was on his knees yielding and begging for mercy.'

'Ah! That would be the length of it, the girl released and the brothers, too, riding safe home to Middle Earth. It's the way with all such tales.'

Thade was happy with the happy ending.

'Not all,' I said. 'We have to remember Persephone.'

'And who would that be?' Cat-like, he pounced on the unknown name as though it were a mouse.

'She was a daughter of the gods.'

'As it might be a child of the Dagda Mor?' His mind was carrying him back to the oldest gods of Ireland.

'In a way. But this happened in ancient Greece.'

'Far away and long ago. And she comely — when was there ever a fairy-tale woman that wasn't without a spot? — and taken away by the Gentry. Sure, they're everywhere in the stretch of the world, not only here in Erin.'

'No, not by the Gentry, but by Hades, Lord of the Underworld. She was picking flowers on the Nysian plain when he came by with his black horses, caught her up into his chariot and carried her down to the depths.'

'My grief, my grief!' Thade keened softly, as one bereft of a daughter.

'And her mother, Demeter, roamed the world, seeking for her lost child and vowing that no seed would sprout — for she was the goddess of growing things — until she had her child again.'

'And what of the pastures?' Thade demanded. The thought of a seed not putting on leaf was, to him, sacrilege.

'They were brown and sere; no corn thrusting up a blade, no green on any tree. And the people so cried against the gods that Zeus, the All-Father, himself was dismayed.'

'And who can wonder?' Thade interjected. 'If the land itself was not a-greening there'd be divil a man left to cry. And how would the gods be filling their days with no sons of Adam to work their wiles on?'

'Perhaps Zeus took that into account, for he sent his messenger, faithful Hermes, to bring the girl back to her mother. And once the two were together again, the grasses sprang up and the flowers bloomed and the fields were ripe to the harvest.'

'Well, that would be full of it; Childe Rowland over again unless . . .' Thade's face was suddenly anxious as of one fearing to hear bad news. 'Unless she had sipped a sup down there.'

'She had eaten a seed of pomegranate.'

'God save us!' He crossed himself.

'And for that, as Queen of the Underworld, she was compelled to live in it for a third of the year and the rest above in the light.'

Thade was silent, brooding long over the story like a blackbird on a nest of eggs. At last he sighed and turned his sombre gaze upon me.

'A Teller has to be told by the tales. It's them, not him, that has the wisdom, and him that has to find it. I'll not be forgetting that Greek colleen. Many a time, under a hedge or by a peat fire, I'll regale the company with her fate, which is also yours, and me own, begob, and theirs, too, if it comes to that.'

'How so?' It seemed an equivocal statement. 'We've never been down to the Underworld.'

'Faith, have we not?' he eyed me with pity. 'Tell me now,' he demanded sternly. 'Where's the kingdom of Heaven?'

Thade's digressions, for all that they often have sense and meaning, always catch me on the hop.

'You know that I know that, Thade,' I reproached him.

'If you do and if itself is in you, then isn't also the other place?'

'You mean the Underworld?' I was startled.

'I mean it, every living word. And we going down to it day and night, as we might be divers in the sea, cavorting among the comestibles, ay, and gorging ourselves upon them, too, till our bellies swell with the wind.'

'I hadn't thought of it like that.' But already I sensed his drift.

'Well, be thinking now, for yer soul's sake. If it's not in the canon it should be, by rights. I'm telling you, and the tale tells it, there's a darksome world within us, too. How else would we ever know the light? And the both of them calling back and forth like neighbours over a fence.'

I was silent. How else, indeed? I thought of my own crepuscular realm — Its 'comestibles'! Its pomegranates! And all its Dead Sea fruit! Would the other kingdom have a mansion for me?

'Arrah, it's as it should be!' said Thade, his face losing its doleful look as the story continued to blossom within him. 'Them two would be snug enough down by the roots, together all winter, weaving the Spring. And sure as we are sitting here she had to eat the one seed to give her the extent of the dark and bring her up green to the sun. That way she'd be knowing more, the creature, than ever her mother knew. So, let you not be grieving for her. Once ye have the pith of it there's nothing amiss in the tale at all.'

He flung a questioning glance at the sky.

'Mid-day!' he said. 'Time for me dinner. Ye'll take a sup and a bite with me?'

I hesitated, glancing instinctively at the fairy mound.

'Arrah, ye're safe with the bindweed,' he said, untying his knotted, faded bundle and spreading out its contents.

'Poteen, it is!' he smacked his lips. 'Me cousin has a still up the glen. And a loaf of soda bread, made by the woman.'

He unscrewed the cap of a dingy bottle and a colourless liquid ran into it, vibrant as mercury.

I felt like a fire-swallower in a circus as the sip darted down my throat. Who would have thought a mere potato would have such spirit in it!

'Keep at it!' Thade encouraged me, 'and ye'll have a gullet as supple and strong as it might be the tail of a cat. And now a little knob of the loaf. That's the sweetest part.'

'Paracelsus said,' I told him, 'that we eat stars with our bread.'

'Well, tell him from me, it's not much he knows.'

'I can't, he's dead hundreds of years. I read it in a book.'

'Book, is it?' he jeered at me. 'Sure, paper never refused ink!'

'Are you after telling me,' I mimicked his brogue, 'that because it's in a book, it's not true?'

'I am not, then. But the poor maneen, God rest his soul, didn't know the half of it. If there's stars in it, isn't there also the rain? And the clouds gallivanting over the sky with the wind at their heels, like a sheepdog? And the moon and the blessed sod itself and the sun over all, as it might be a tent? — That's the other half. Eat!'

And suddenly I was hungry. Congress with the immortal worlds vivifies the soul and the soul in its turn vivifies the body. I needed to taste on my mortal tongue the food of Middle Earth.

Thade raised his bottle. *'Sláinte!'* (Good health) he said, with a glint in his eye, and took a long, hard swig.

I acknowledged the toast and bit into my knob of bread. It was indeed sweet. There were stars in it. And all the cosmic rest besides. Nothing was amiss.

First published in 'Parabola' on the theme of Food, New York, 1984.

Lucifer

YES, without doubt, I outshone them all. But what, among archangels, is an extra shimmer? It would have been a thing of naught had I not boasted of it; so bragged, vaunted and dominated, so strutted before the Supernal Eye, that, taking away his angel name, they seized the rebel by the heel and flung him into space.

> From morn
> Till noon he fell, from noon to dewy eve
> A summer's day. And at the setting sun
> Dropped from the zenith like a falling star.*

Yet, for all that, I was not lost. Heaven has its husbandry. There is nothing that is not made use of. And you, Artificer, had need of me — even, perhaps, designed my fall — so that you should have a nether pole, a necessary antagonist, to sustain your creation's tension. The opposites yearning towards each other, forever striving to blend together — each being a part of each — must for ever be thrust apart. Planets must keep their appointed stations, the wandering stars their lawful courses by the tug between concord and discord; and men, to sustain themselves as men, must encounter the denying spirit to wake in them that which affirms.

So, setting me up against yourself, tossing me forth from light to darkness, from the blessed land to a place of travail, you deputed me Prince of this world, a potentate to be feared and hated, friendless except for a four-footed thing sent out into the wilderness with a burden of sins on its back.

To speak of me is to bring misfortune. My name is craftily obscured by those of earth under blandishments such as Old Nick, the Other One, or Clootie. In their minds I am a monstrous image,

* Milton, *Paradise Lost.*

fitted out with horns and a tail and a pair of cloven hooves. They cross their fingers and swiftly spit over their shoulders as charms against my evil eye. Dangerous places are named for me — the Devil's Dyke, the Devil's Leap, even the Devil's Punchbowl; and the four of clubs, a card that is held to be unlucky, is known as the Devil's Bedstead. When the wind blows wild they bar the doors, believing it not to be the wind but myself horsed upon the air, my hounds howling about me.

I am palpable or invisible according to their moods and needs. In their hearts and minds and secret parts, they encounter me inwardly. But some will insist they see me plain and kneel to swear allegiance to me, offering up their immortal souls if I will give them what they lust for. Yet, when I fulfil their utmost wish, they fall away, satiated, and go ululating for the World of Mothers or, as a last resort, yourself. And you are always there. Oh, hidden, as under the dove's wing, in the convolutions of all treacherous flesh, your imprint indelibly is there, do what I will to erase it.

A man will follow me all his days and at his last breath, when I think I have him, betrays me and calls upon Heaven. 'Deny!' I cry to the unbeliever and something within him, hearing the word, turns on itself and begins to question. 'Despair!' I whisper to the despairing and at that moment, in the abyss, they find the seed of hope. 'Curse God!' I advise the afflicted ones. 'Curse God and die!' And I wait to seize them. But a rebel spirit takes strength from their woes and bids them accept and live.

I urge the fool to persist in his folly and straightway he becomes wise and sups with me with a long-handled spoon. As adversary I invoke the hero that each man, even the coward soul, has woven into his sinews, expose him to every mortal danger and danger itself spreads a covering wing and fosters the rescuing power.

'Sleep on!' I encourage him who sleeps and he stirs uneasily in his dream, sensing the need to wake. In truth, Lord, as Remembrancer, I have served you well. Not one of those who enter your courts, especially your perfected ones, but has wrestled with me till the break of day and gone hence halting upon his thigh, seared and scarred with my brand. And the choir of angels, who know no sin, cast down their crowns before them.

What is man that, against all hope, he should find hope at his side? What is man that, between the stirrup and the ground, he should ask for, and be given mercy? What is man that, outfacing the two contending forces — your constant yes, my constant no,

he should receive — as balm to the wound, as dew to the leaf —
the power that reconciles them?

First published in 'Parabola' on the theme of Wholeness. New York, 1985.

Now, Farewell and Hail

IF ANYONE, in those early years, had asked me where I lived, I would not have been able to answer. For me, my homeland was Here and Now — not a place, not a time, a condition rather, or domain, enormous and yet intimate, close to the stars and the grasses. By night you went about cautiously lest the Pleiades catch in your hair; and by day lest you trod on a passing beetle that might well be a prince in disguise.

All was present and immediate, everything whole and complete, not a thing was missing. No road ever went on and on; it returned to its beginnings. The rainbow was not a mere semi-circle — it continued its course underneath the world, the two ends joined at the horizon. And there the pot of gold would be if you had the luck to find it.

The Sleeping Beauty awaited her moment within our crowding forest; the Argonauts saillied forth in their long-oared ships in search of the Golden Fleece, and the waves of the sea, if not seen by the eye, resounded when you put a shell to your ear. Tilly Saville, carrying the daily pail of milk, scattered the farmyard cockerels that forever crowed three times for Peter who somewhere, behind a shed, would be weeping; angels squatted on the roof top, ready to take your soul if you died; if there was an oak tree anywhere Bonnie Prince Charlie would be sitting in it; the Three Grey Sisters, from whom Perseus had to steal an eye and a tooth, were in reality my two great-aunts and one of their aged friends; Lord Nelson, behind my bedroom door, nightly scraped the wall with a pencil in spite of the grown-up assurances that the sound was merely the creaking of wood as the house stretched itself luxuriously after the heat of the day; there were serpents, any one of whom slithering by would be coming direct from the Garden of Eden; the sound of a shot would tell us that Nimrod was away hunting on the thither side of our mountain; tigers burned brightly in the nearby bush and God ubiquitously worked among us, forever unespied — playing the organ in church on Sundays, his feet bare on the pedals; unfolding the flower buds at the dead of night; peering through windows, listening at keyholes — how else could He know everything? — giving Halley's comet a push to speed it on its way to the stars; gossiping with the gossiping trees that no matter how hard you listened for it could never be caught in the act. Once He looked at me through the gap in the fence with the face of a golden sunflower, awesome, quizzical, resolute. I put up my hand and picked Him. This deed was reported to my parents who mildly —after all, it was only a flower! — expostulated with me. But when, in extenuation, I explained to them Who it was, they rose up on their high horses. No one, they said, could pick God and if they could, they would not. It was socially, if not ethically, unacceptable and not the kind of thing people did. I held my peace, knowing that this was not the case. Acceptable or not, *somebody* had done it. And, given the chance, would certainly do it again.

All things were possible in this world of Now. Near and far were alike to it. Huge, spherical and all-containing, it yet was so local and neighbourly that it seemed as though I could put out my arms and take it to my breast.

But the sun and the rain were at work upon me, drawing me up like the seedlings. And as I grew, amidst all the abundance, I began to feel a wanting. Lacking nothing, I came to know lack — a longing, even a nostalgia, for something I had never known. In all the completeness, I was incomplete, a cup only half-filled.

This ache, this lonely weight of heart came upon me always at sunset, when the long rays lay across the earth like stripes on the back of a zebra. 'There must be Something Else!' I would say. Achingly, I would say it. But all, I knew, was Here and Now, and if all, then within the all that Something Else awaited me, infolded, implicate. Was it an answer to an unheard question? If a question, how would I know the answer?

So, now grown to sapling height and pondering the riddle within me, I left my Now, my eternal homeland, or to put it more truly, I fell from it as ripe fruit falls from the tree, not of intent but inevitably, as if at the summons of an inner bell.

But who had fallen? Who had been summoned? I who had been a mere particle, a scantling of the whole I knew, had now become an entity, separate, a thing in itself, whose reflections threw themselves back at me from a glassy hall of mirrors.

Surprised at my new infinity, I turned among the images, delighting in each pose and posture, trying them on as though they were garments to see which was most becoming. Is this I? Or this? Or this? I could not choose. I was all of them, a multiple someone to whom life beckoned with auspicious finger, hinting at secrets to be revealed, promises fulfilled.

There were others, too, decked, like myself, in their own reflections, pressing towards a moving throng beyond the glassy walls. And, forgetting the weight I carried with me — for now it was no weight at all, a mere lostling among my findings — I with my flying bannerets hurried to join the dance.

Hand after hand swung me round — O tinkers, O tailors, O candlestickmakers! — and I was led into the general motley dancing to the tune of the world.

We had become our own images and were all, it seemed, on the way to Tomorrow which would give us everything we needed — importance, relevance, power, pleasure, every ultimate satisfaction. 'I want, I want!' was the general cry amid the fluttering oriflammes. Our friends were exultations, agonies, and the clamour always for 'More, more!' Yes, even for the agonies 'More!,' for the losing as well as the having — will the sailor come safely home from the sea, the hunter from the hill? — for thus we could reassure ourselves, 'I suffer, therefore I am. I suffer, therefore I escape the Void, the Non-living, the Nothingness.'

Thus I danced the day of my life, seeking, learning, experiencing, always-living-and-always-dying, until the long setting of the sun. And again, facing the falling light, I felt the old familiar weight and paused in the gallimaufry.

'Where am I?' I asked myself and from somewhere came a voice not mine, a searching echo, 'Where art thou?'

'On! On!' cried the dancers streaming by. But I stood still and let them pass, knowing that I had been hiding — hiding in the midst of the dance as in the rift of a dream, letting being take on the guise of becoming, homeless, looking for home.

'Where art thou?' That voice again!

And out, from under the leaves of Eden, I rose and was awake, awake and in my lost domain.

'I am here, Now, my eternal instant, that holds what was and will be.' I am here, Now, in the all that is here: Gilgamesh reaching for the scarlet flower and the serpent seizing it from him; Isis gathering back to herself the lost parts of Osiris; the Buddha watching the golden bowl making its fateful way upstream; Galileo muttering into his beard 'Eppur si muove!'; Prometheus bringing down the fire that men, laboriously climbing, must carry back to Heaven; a son of Adam setting foot on the moon, another walking the sky; Demeter searching for her stolen daughter; Stabat Mater, heart-stopped, breath-stopped, waiting to take upon her knees her dead and living son; Halley's comet still sweeping past; Aratus singing to his lyre, 'Full of Zeus are the cities, full of Zeus are the harbours, full of Zeus are all the ways of men'; the fox stealing into his hole, the crested wren swinging in her hanging mansion.

I am here, Now, a lost child found, with that Something Else, that painful riddle, again at work upon me. Perhaps it is not, indeed, a riddle but rather an intimation. There are things that may not be understood, except by standing under them, watching, waiting and empty, as a shell that the bird has flown. It could be that my lack is, on its obverse side, my treasure, that which calls and calls me back to the sole and living moment. I shall not be given to know its name nor even to ask to know it. Somewhere within me it is known, it has no need of words. And that which knows it also knows that I shall not stay long with you, my home-land. I shall fall away again and again, drawn by the magnet of Tomorrow and the treacherous hope that it exists, and carries gifts and surcease from care. Sages and seers, Now, dwell in your pavilions. To such as I it is given only to visit them from time to time and know that I have slept — slept and forgotten my meaning.

Death, be my friend! I came, waking, if weeping, into the world. Let me, waking, leave it.

And you, Sweet Lethe, run softly when I end my song that I may not drink deep of your tide. For there is a thing that I would remember.

Now is the day of everlasting. Now is the day of salvation.

First published in 'Parabola' on the theme of Exile. New York, 1985.

On Unknowing

IT IS not ignorance. Rather, one could say, a particular process of cognition that has little or no use of words. It is part of our heritage at birth, the infant's first primer. And the young child lives by it, gathering into its growing body and aboriginal heart a cosmography of wonder.

'The corn was orient and immortal wheat, which never should be reaped, nor was ever sown,' says Thomas Traherne of this period. 'I thought it had stood from everlasting to everlasting. The dust and stones of the street were as precious as gold; the gates were, at first, the end of the world.'

But soon the chattering mind takes charge and obscures Unknowing with information. For the ego, while presuming to ape what D. H. Lawrence called the 'truth of truth,' is avid, rather, for the truth of fact, relevant or irrelevant, and swells up, bloated, like the frog in the fable, as it records its dossier, the story of its ego-life. It has a name, if not a meaning, for everything and dares without compunction at any moment or on any subject to declare 'I know!'

But what if, in a momentary lapse in its knowing, it should stumble upon Unknowing? On Jalal-uddin Rumi, for instance:

> Sell your cleverness and buy bewilderment,
> Cleverness is mere opinion, bewilderment is intuition.

Or maybe it happens on a passage in *The Four Quartets*.

> What you do not know is the only thing you know,
> And what you own is what you do not own,
> And where you are is where you are not,
> Leading to a condition of complete simplicity
> Costing not less than everything.

Will it have the courage, or even the wish, to pay the price? Throw overboard all the information that Unknowing does not need? Let go and set itself to listen so that the condition of simplicity may arise?

That is not the way of the mind though it is ready to make use of all the Unknowing that, over the aeons, has become manifest.

For instance, it is from the Unknowing that all the myths, and, one may say, all religions issue forth and reveal themselves. Not invented but, as it were, summoned.

It is back into Unknowing that the mind-stuff of all the burnt libraries of the world repair. Never a page left to turn, but what the spirit of man has once conceived it can conceive again. All that is lost is somewhere.

Destroy the world, you men of the atoms, and Unknowing will retain the pattern. 'Trust that which belongs to the universe itself,' says the Tao. 'From that there will be no escape,'

Unknowing, if one can be open and vulnerable, will take us down to the very deeps of knowing, not informing the mind merely but coursing through the whole body, artery and vein — provided one can thrust aside what the world calls common sense, that popular lumpen wisdom that prevents the emerging of the numinous.

Unknowing needs that a man be in a certain state of grace, playful, artless, inwardly acquitted of opinion, not at all as children are but rather as fools or saints.

One thinks of Ryokan of Zen, playing hide-and-seek with the village children, secreting himself behind a woodpile, monkish sleeves drawn over his head. The game was soon over and the players called home but Ryokan still stayed hidden and when found next morning by a brother monk who asked him what he was doing, an eye peeped out from under the sleeve.

'Hush! Don't speak so loudly. The children will find me!' said Ryokan.

Or again, when thieves ransacked his house, Ryokan was at pains to thank them for leaving him the moon at the window.

We, too, in the West, have our quota of fools — Kasperle, walking forever through the world, his old grandmother on his back, the crocodile always at his heel, the abyss always before him. He lives with danger, safely, like the Fool of the Tarot, that zero of the pack, the nought, the nothing that, when added to any other number, inevitably exalts it.

And we must not forget St Francis who called the ass and the mouse his brothers and sang songs with the birds. Nor St

Catherine of Alexandria, the saint invoked by learned men, those mighty scholars who, being ignorant of the Unknowing, have need of such patronage.

And what about the fairy tales, diminutive kith and kin of the myths, in which, coming as they do from the same ancestral stock, Unknowers abound? Think of the third of those ubiquitous three brothers. He is always the simpleton, the one who, aware that he has little wit and needs help, is humble enough to accept advice from the frog, the dwarf, or the little old woman which the elder brothers have spurned. And help never fails to come to him from the cauldron of Unknowing, the treasure, the princess, the cup from the well of the Water of Life.

But it is not only in story or in calender that Unknowers are to be found. They appear among us in the streets and in the fields, their feet are upon the mountains — lunatics, lovers, and poets in their train; Blake seeing angels preening their wings in the trees, and singing songs on his deathbed; the Sufi camel-driver whose very toes cried 'Allah'; the centipede, who, when asked by the one-legged man 'How do you manage all those legs?' replied 'I do not manage them.'

Such as these are natural unknowers. But now the question arises — how can anyone intentionally attract to himself an epithet so impressive? What will lead us to that condition of complete simplicity?

We cannot wipe the mind clean of its knowing, as one would wash a face, for, indeed, paradoxically, we need that knowing. It is an essential part of living and not to be despised. Only when the mind attempts to usurp the whole realm of consciousness, of which, after all, it is but a fragment, are the possibilites of discovering Unknowing overlaid and lost.

The world belongs to silence and stillness. Unknowing, itself being empty, can be approached only in moments of emptiness which the ego-mind mistakes for boredom and hastens to assuage that condition with ever more learning. To it the phrase 'I do not know' is one of self-reproach.

But for one intent on seeking the Unknown, that 'I do not know' is the door to it, the 'Open Sesame' which to pronounce costs nothing less than everything. So, he drops from his busy awareness into the stillness whence life springs, into a void within him.

Only by such means can he come upon fullness, the fullness that the mind, with all its acumen, cannot even envisage. Thus, self offers itself to Self, as once Odin on the tree of Yggdrasil, and he knows without knowing whatever is needful to him — that there is manna in the wilderness, that the stone dances, and the rain it raineth every day.

Thus provided, such a one can lay himself down contentedly between the paws of the lion.

First published in 'Parabola' on the theme of The Body. New York, 1985.

The Garment

THE bell rang in the outer court, a peremptory, musical summons. And with much jangling of keys, St Peter unlocked the double doors, opened them a little way, and put out his head through the crack.

'Well?' he demanded. 'What do you want?'

A man in a long white robe stepped forward.

'I want to come in,' he said.

'What? Dressed up like an apprentice angel? Isn't that rather premature?'

'My garment represents myself,' said the man. 'You can read it as though it were a book. There is no stain on it anywhere.'

'So I see. That makes the book difficult to read. Nothing to declare, as it were. I'm afraid you have come to the wrong place. We only cater for sinners.'

'But surely I have a right to be here! I have led a blameless life.'

'We do not deal in rights,' said St Peter. 'Though there is grace abounding. Perhaps it would be more to the point if you told me about the wrongs.'

'There are none. Guilt has passed me by. I have never practised avarice, keeping only enough for my simple needs, giving alms to the beggar at the corner and tipping waiters generously. Moreover, I have envied no man nor been a source of envy. I eat sparsely, once a day only, a meagre dinner of herbs. And as for lechery, I deplore it. When I see a woman, even the passing swing of a skirt, I quickly turn my back on the scene or look in the other direction. Pride, too, I likewise abhor, bowing both to king and peasant, not setting myself above another nor boasting of my possessions. And I fill my days profitably, never an idle moment. Compared with myself, the ant is a sluggard; sloth finds no place within me. Last of all, I have never lost my temper'

'Alas, poor ant!' St Peter grinned. 'I feel for you, my good sir. You have told me a tale that is all perfection. But perfection is a heavy burden. I have not known one who could carry it.'

'But surely,' the man was clearly dismayed. 'You must take account of virtue!'

'Ah, virtue. That is a different matter. Virtue is always equivocal, a field of opposing forces. It is not merely lack of shortcomings and certainly not an unstained garment. It belongs to a man's totality, the bad along with the good. Did you think to approach the courts of Heaven without passing through — yes, and revelling there — the hostelries of earth? If you take my advice, you'll ring the bell at the Other Place. They would certainly teach you a thing or two, not least the meaning of virtue.' He pointed downwards with his thumb.

'Down there? Never!' the man shuddered. 'There must be some alternative.'

'There are always alternatives,' said St Peter. 'For instance, you could return whence you came and begin again at the beginning. The garment which you call yourself might then have something to tell me.'

The man drew his robe about him, with a fond possessive gesture.

'After all my self-denial!' he said, and sighed as he turned away. 'I never thought it was possible that this could happen to me.'

'You never thought — leave it at that.'

St Peter's face disappeared from the crack. The doors swung together again and a key turned in the lock.

And the sun rose and the sun set and the work of Heaven went steadily on, systole and diastole, the heartbeat of the universe.

And after a time, a lifetime, perhaps, the man who had gone dejected away came once more to the door.

'What — you again?' St Peter exclaimed. 'But what have you done with that vestal garment, yourself immaculate?'

For the man was clad in a threadbare robe, spattered with patches of brassy colour all shades of the spectrum.

'I am wearing it,' he replied, turning about like a spinning top in order to display himself.

'Are you, indeed?' St Peter chuckled. 'Well, this vestment has clearly done some living. Come closer so I can read it.'

He pored over the splashes of insolent colour as though they were a map. 'Ha! Yellow — bright as a wasp's wing! This is avarice, if ever I saw it! I would guess that the beggar at the corner no longer gets his lucky penny, nor the waiter his generous tip. And this strip of green must surely be envy. Covetousness seems to have burned in you for the chattels and qualities other men have. Warp and woof almost worn away.

'Now, what have we here in this patch of blue — greed, would you say, yes, greed indeed! No more dinners of herbs, eh, but gluttony at all levels, mind and stomach always a-clamour, calling, even when full, for more. And this — this broad explicit expanse of scarlet? Does the man who so deplored lechery still turn his back when he sees a woman, let alone the swing of a skirt? Who would have throught that virgin robe would have had such a tale to tell!

'And you are proud of its disclosures. See, the sin of pride declares itself here where the violet borders the red. Do you bow, now, both to king and peasant? I am inclined to doubt it. And what about the sluggard ant that you so far outdistanced? This splash of black where the thread shows through assures me that he who was never idle has lain in the very lap of sloth. And this torn flap of brilliant orange — what could it be but the sin of wrath? What tempers! What tantrums! What fits of rage! Well, well! Now let me see. Is there not something else?'

'What could that be? You have seen the lot. The sins speak for themselves.'

'I am looking,' said St Peter, gravely, 'for some small unstained segment — white, perhaps as the swan's wing — that would give them all their meaning.'

'What could that be?' the man inquired. 'I thought the list was complete.'

'That which completes is repentance and I do not find it here.'

'But these?' The man gestured widely at the colours. 'Aren't they enough? And what about *you*? Have you repented?'

St Peter gave him a long deep look.

'I have wept,' he replied, quietly. 'At the crowing of the cock.'

At that the man turned his head away and was silent for a moment.

'I thought to cast down a golden crown around the glassy sea. But that is not to be, it seems. I have never shed a single tear, nor learned aught of repentance.'

'It cannot be taught,' said St Peter, gently. 'It arises, of itself, in a man, when the time in him is ripe. Hitherto, as your robe tells me, you have let your life simply happen. You yourself have played no part in it. I have said there are always alternatives. Why not go and sit in the cave of your heart and confront whatever you find there — a caracole, maybe, of angels and devils. If so, you could join them in a dance, hand to one of them, hand to another, and so learn much that you now do not know. That garment will be your teacher.'

The man drew his robe about him, and strode away shaking his head, clearly misliking the proposition.

And the sun rose and the sun set and the work of Heaven went steadily on, systole and diastole, the pulse of the Universe.

And after a time, a lifetime, perhaps, St Peter, humming like a bee at his daily tasks — polishing the knobs of the doors, whitewashing the front step, shaking out the mat — looked up and saw a curious sight.

A man, naked but for some tatters of cloth, was sitting hunched up beside the entrance, head bowed, deep in thought.

St Peter tapped him on the shoulder. 'What's all this?' he demanded sternly. 'Keep away from that fresh white step. I don't want footprints on it. Why it's *you*!' he exclaimed, as the man turned, revealing a face that was now familiar.

The man assented wordlessly.

'But what are you doing sitting here with not a stitch of clothing on you but a handful of faded rags? What has happened to that famous garment?'

'It has gone,' said the man, 'except for these scraps. You told me to repair to the cave of my heart. This I did, but unwillingly. And as I sat there pondering, telling over the beads of my life, seeing what I had dared not see and dancing with the opposites, my robe disappeared thread by thread, worn out by the strain of that confrontation and above all by the grieving: grieving for my sins, yes, in the measure that was needful — all men, in some degree, wear my many-coloured gown — but mostly for that which had no colour, the white and stainless garment I was pleased to call my virtue. I had fashioned it, I saw clearly, to hide myself, my pretentiousness, from my own eyes, let alone Another's. And I wept for shame who had never wept. That I could presume to come to this place, assuming the rights of one called and chosen. Alas, the pity of it!'

'The pity of it, indeed,' said St Peter.

'Yet, for all that, do not pity me. With my garment in shreds I am emptied out of all that I was, and am content to be so. Who am I? I ask myself and do not know the answer — no more than the worm on the leaf knows or bread cast upon waters. And what, I also ask, is my purpose, without my protecting garment? That I do not know either but whatever it is I must try to serve it. If I have a meaning it is there.'

He hid his face in his hands again, lost in his own thoughts.

St Peter regarded him silently for a long and brooding moment.

'Blessed are the poor in spirit. You must come in,' he said.

The man raised his head, startled.

'But I am naked,' he protested. 'And of all men unworthy.'

'Your nakedness shall be your passport. And none are worthy here.'

St Peter flung the doors wide.

'Step over the whitewash carefully and make your way to the inner court. They will give you a garment there.'

First published in 'Parabola' on the theme of The Seven Deadly Sins, New York, 1985.

Out From Eden

I am sad.
He is sad.
You are sad.

So small a word to lie so heavy on the heart! So small, yet packed with a significance that nobody can define, not even the poets who use it with such familiarity. Antonio, in the first lines of *The Merchant of Venice*, shows us a man bowed down under the enigma:

In sooth, I know not why I am so sad:
It wearies me, you say it wearies you,
But how I caught it, found it or came by it,
What stuff 'tis made of, whereof it is born
I am to learn.
And such a want-wit sadness makes of me
That I have much to do to know myself...

Perhaps we would all know ourselves better if we could construe that word.

It is not depression, nor despondency, least of all is it self-pity, that coarsest of the emotions — greedy, sterile, all darkness, the ego prone upon its bed wrapped in a pall of selfhood. Grief and sorrow, on the other hand, though still not sadness, are life-giving and pulse with meaning; capable of receiving light, able even to engender it and thereby, through suffering, to transmute themselves into heart's ease and refreshment.

But if one were to mix and filter the whole gamut of emotions, the last, the quintessential drop would be sadness, which, being essence, had neither antonym nor synonym and cannot be analysed.

Blake, if you transpose the couplet, came near to it with:

Under every peak and pine
Runs a joy with silken twine.

and Keats, who wrote of 'Joy whose hand is ever at his lips, bidding Adieu' knew well what that Adieu was. Isaak Walton spoke of angling as a 'diverter of sadness' and Longfellow struggled manfully with it when he wronte in *The Day is Done:*

A feeling of sadness and longing
That is not akin to pain
And resembles sorrow only
As the mist resembles the rain.

Nevertheless, definable or not, the very infant knows it. The first cry is one of lamentation 'Alas, why am I here?' And the young child, for no apparent reason, will pause for a moment in its play, touched by something keenly sensed for which it has no name. But not the child only. We all experience it. Sadness lies at the the very core of being. Lay the heart bare of every other feeling and inevitably you will come upon sadness, ready, like the quickened seed, to put forth its green leaf.

Lovers in all their bliss know it and the tincture it leaves on their embracings and, unaware that it is part of love, turn to each other again and again hoping, but always failing, to efface the intrinsic stain. A man may wish for his heart's desire and be made sad at not recieiving it. But give it to him in all its richness and he will be sad at the having of it, at the very lack of lack. Another, gazing at the beauty of sunset, will be saddened at the burden of being; and a third, in the midst of rejoicing, will feel in himself an emptiness. We are so made that we can bear neither perfection nor imperfection.

It was not so, I think, in Eden when the lion and the lamb were together and we danced, purely for the sake of dancing, to the melodies piped to us by the wind as it moved through the Paradisal trees. But once the angel had waved his sword, with a new thing working in our breasts, we moved to a different tune. Wordsworth, looking down on Tintern, knew well what it was —

'The still, sad music of humanity.'
That is the measure we must dance to now.

O stranger, take my hand!

First published in 'Parabola' on the theme of Sadness, New York, 1986.

Le Chevalier Perdu

'IS there anybody there?' called the young man as he drew rein at the dilapidated shelter topped with a rusty iron cross. A weather-beaten shutter creaked open to reveal a greying head almost hidden by a coarse hempen cowl.

'Well,' said a voice from within the cowl, 'that is never an easy question. Let us put it another way. Is there anybody up there on that horse?'

'It is I, Perceval de Galis!' The youth was ringingly confident. 'I thought perchance I could borrow a cup to quench my thirst at the spring yonder.'

'You have a cup of your own, young sir.' The voice that came from the cowl was kindly. 'Merely put your palms together and bend to the water as it flows. It is the way I drink myself, having no other cup.'

'Then what is that?' asked Perceval, waving his whip at a roughly carved wooden vessel that stood on a table within the lodge.

'That, as you must be aware, is a chalice, not a mere crock to take to the spring. It is the custom, among knightly men, to partake of the Mass before they set off adventuring. And though I am hidden deep in the forest, an occasional paladin comes my way, and I must be ready to serve him.'

'But the wine,' said Perceval. 'Where does it come from?'

'I make it myself from fruits and berries fermented with a certain herb. And they bring me flour from a nearby steading to bake the unleavened bread. Oh, no more than a crust, but a crust is enough. One day you may need it yourself.'

'I well may. Indeed, it is written, I understand, that I am bound for knighthood. But I am the son of a poor widow and all unlearned in knightly things. That is why you find me here, searching through the vales. "Seek out Sylvanus of the Marshes," my good mother advised me. "Maybe he would take you as his squire and teach you what you need to know." '

'Sylvanus? Why he? Why not Lancelot?'

'Have you not heard? It is widely known. Lancelot is away in his wits. He has run mad amid the plantations, naked and raving in his nightshirt. Nobody knows if he will recover. Yet, before he joined the fellowship, it was Sylvanus — surely you know of him — who was thought to be the best knight in the world. No giant was a match for him; he killed the lion of Polgorran, the terror of the countryside, albeit it clawed his face in dying; he brought in chieftains to be the king's vassals and rescued damsels without number. As for dragons, he slew so many that I fear there will not be a dragon left when I receive my sword and spear.'

'Such creatures are the ferment of the earth. They are always with us, never fear, and will be till some shriven knight approaches the dragon without enmity, and the dragon lies down to be slain.'

'Let that not be soon, I pray the Lord. I envy such encounters.'

'You will not be disappointed, I think. They belong to the first degree of knighthood.'

'Degrees? I had not heard of those. Are there many that I must pass?'

'There are three. And the first is simply told. It is the degree of Induction. Every man born into the world is in a sense a knight. A quest is offered him at the outset together with all the great emprises that you so long to meet with. But not everyone, when he comes to manhood, is ready to take up the challenge. Most of them follow the enticements, which, make no doubt, are also offered, and loiter aimlessly at the crossroads or fall asleep by the wayside.'

'That would not be for me, I think. Acquaint me with the second.'

'Ah, that is the one you dream of now, all high resolve and chivalry — the doughty deeds, the righting of wrongs, the fellowship of knightly men, the jousts, the roisterings, the tourneys (with perchance a lady's sleeve in your helm!); fire-breathing monsters in every glade to be slain at a single stroke; giants sought out and crying 'A-mercy!'; beleagured castles freed from the fiend; recreant knights brought to court in chains; distressed damsels of every kind rescued and carried home. This is the degree of Action, and if you believe the chronicles the folk tell round their evening fires, most knights are content to go no further than the endless heroic round — the day filled full of deeds of prowess, the night with the telling of them and the feasting, and after that the sleep of the just threaded with dreams of the morrow's adventures, new dragons, new giants, and pastures new.

'But can a man remain young forever? Will he not go grey in these pursuits, ever feebler as to arm and thigh, his courtesy more and more strained as each damsel in distress grows heavier than the last? What will sustain his knighthood in him and lead it to its destined goal when these things come to pass?

'Oh, there is a means, though few men care or dare to use it. It is a matter, if you would know it, of pausing amid the gallimaufry and allowing oneself, committing oneself, to come to the end of the world. And when one comes to the end of the world, there is only one road to take.'

'And that is?' Perceval asked intently.

'Inwards. Into the heart of yourself. This is the third degree of knighthood. It is known as Contemplation. This does not mean retreat from the world — though more than one knight has pursued such a course — rather that in undertaking his worldly adventures he encounters them also inwardly. "Who am I?" he will enquire of himself, "this man who goes about righting wrongs?" Echo alone will make reply — there is no known word to match that query — but the mere echo may arouse the conviction that within his own essential self there is a wrong to be righted. So it is with the dragons, the ill-famed knights, the distressed damsels, the fiends. They have their reflections in his inner selves that need to be struggled with, exorcized, and, indeed, accepted. The quest from the very beginning has had as its aim the knight's self-transformation. Only one made new by grace or made anew by his own efforts will find what he has sworn to find, a glimpse of the Sangreal.'

Perceval's face was eager. 'That is my hope. Shall I achieve it?'

'You are young to be asking for oracles. There is, however, a mark on your brow that encourages me to reply. But, I warn you, there will be obstacles and not only in yourself. There is the matter of the Maimed King and the land about him laid waste and from you, Perceval de Galis, the right question to be asked.'

'The right question? I shall spend my life thinking about it.'

'No amount of thinking will encompass it. If you are to be a Grail hero, what you are, soon or late, will itself ask the question. Now, begone and pursue your adventure.'

'Then blessings on your head, Sir Hermit! I will no longer seek for Sylvanus. Any man of true fealty will instruct me in the matter of sword and spear. But if, under God, I achieve my knighthood, it will be to you I owe it.'

'No, to yourself. Be blessed and farewell!'

The shutter of the lodge closed as Perceval, full of the morning's encounter, gathered his reins and departed.

The man within took up the chalice and held it high for a moment. And as he did so, the hempen cowl fell away disclosing a face whose left side was striped and scored to the whitened bone as though some animal in its death throes had striven to claw it away.

First published in 'Parabola' on the theme of The Knight and the Hermit, New York, 1987.

Lively Oracles

BRIGHT ONE, moon of the mind, mother of the muses, be for me, as for Taliesin, Shining Brow, not the archivist of the common round but the soul's remembrancer. Leave yesterday in the hands of time and of time itself make one living moment. Remind me of what my blood has known since a sudden cry of mutual rapture opened to me the door of life and I began my journey.

Couched under the drumming heart-beat, hearing the sound of many waters, I was fish of the sea, fowl of the air, beast of the earth until I came forth, a child of Adam, a speck of planetary dust, weeping as all men weep.

Even so, Heaven was about me. Angels and cherubim played beside me, their feet not bending the tops of the grass. Cats composed tunes on fiddles, making music that only I could hear. Dishes ran away with spoons; rabbits, wearing neat blue coats, drank camomile tea at bedtime; king's horses and king's men tried and failed to mend a broken egg. And my shadow ran about me in the morning, changing its shape to match my own as I grew like a plant in the sun and the rain, with the lively oracles of men speaking to me in their ancient voices.

I waited for a hundred years sitting beside a hedge of thorn till the one hero without a name came to wake the Sleeping Beauty. I was eaten by my father in a stew and my sister, Marlinchen, gathered my bones to bury them under the Juniper Tree where a bird sang magic in the branches and I was whole again. I herded the King's geese with the Goose Girl — (O Fallada hanging there!); stirred the King's soup with Allerleirauh; sewed shirts for my brothers turned into swans; heard Rumplestiltzkin's cry as at last his name was spoken; drank of the water of the Well of Life; learned that one was one and all alone and ever more would be so. And at noontide my shadow stood under my heel. I was caught between it and the sun as the day of my life proceeded.

Lead on, Taliesin, and I will follow, remembering what you, too, like a bee, have gathered from the ages. I have been in the trains of Inanna and Ishtar, goddesses of the antique world, givers of life, givers of death, kin to the morning and the evening star, and seen them descend to the Land Below Earth, each rescuing a lover-son, Dummuzi and Tammuz. I have heard the wailing of Gilgamesh when, waking from a moment of sleep (Watch and pray, Gilgamesh!) he found the snake devouring his treasure, the flower of immortality. Men come and go. The serpent abides.

I was with Isis, sister-wife of murdered Osiris, searching the land for his scattered parts and burying them by the banks of the Nile — all but one, all but one — so that he, below, should be Judge of the Dead and, above, the Lord of the Living Waters.

With Drapaudi I bewailed her fate when Heaven closed its doors to her because, of all her five husbands, the tiger-waisted Pandav Brothers, her heart preferred Arjuna — Arjuna who drove to the battle of Kurukshetra with the god Krishna as his charioteer, reciting the Bhagavad Gita. 'Thou grievest for those who should not be grieved for, The wise grieve neither for the living nor the dead. Never wast thou not, nor I, nor these princes of men, Nor shalt though ever cease to be.'

I was among the populace when Sita, queen of the god-king Rama, required for a second time, alas, to defend her wifely virtue, called upon the earth for help and the furrow opened and took her in. I was warmed by the rays of Amaterasu, sun goddess of the Eastern Isles, when they lured her from sulking in her cave by means of a looking-glass. As she came forth, rapt at her own splendour, I watched as they tied a loose rope behind her. Only so far, Amaterasu! You may only go back to the mouth of the cave. Men cannot live in the dark for ever. They need you to shine on the world.

I was with those who stood gazing when Lao-tzu took his leave of the world, riding up the slopes of the sky on the back of a buffalo. I followed in Demeter's footsteps as she crossed and recrossed the Nysan plain, crying aloud to the gods for vengeance for the loss of her daughter, Kore. And the leaves fell and the herb withered and the corn put forth no life-giving seed. Mother, mother, do not grieve. Let the Spring come and your child will come with it, her arms full of crocus and narcissus, in her hand the sacred sprouting grain to be shown forth at Eleusis.

I was on the windy plains of Troy, with Helen watching from

the battlements, as Achilles and Hector met in battle. Was it better, O Beauty of the World, to see men fight and die for you than to sit at home weaving counterpanes for Menelaus' bed? You could not choose. No man chooses his fate. I saw tears leap to Odysseus' eye when, on the last lap of his voyage, the helmsman, spying land ahead, shouted the one word 'Ithaca!' Athene had brought her wanderer home. I was there when Odin hung on the Tree, nine days and nights on Yggdrasil — offering himself to himself. Who gave and who received? I trembled when Frigg passed the mistletoe by — of all plants the one not to be forgotten! — and when Hoder flung the magic sprig, I joined in the earth's lament to the sky 'Balder the Beautiful is dead, is dead!'

I have heard the Western Mountains singing songs of praise to the Great Spirit through the mouths of feathered braves. I stood by when the mighty Quetzalcoatl, plumy serpent lord, brought up the bones from the Land of the Dead and ground them with manioc and his own blood to fashion the primal man. I have been at the dark corroboree where the feet of men make a drum of the earth and heard them call to the Rainbow Snake to take them into the Dreaming. I paddled in Maui the Trickster's canoe when he cast his line for *ulua* fish and drew up a string of coral islands.

I heard Setanta make his promise when he killed the guard-hound of Culain the Smith — 'Sir, I myself will be your hound,' thus assuming his solar name, Cuculain, which of all the hero names of Erin is most sweet in the mouths of men. I have seen the white horses of Mananaan racing toward the Land of Youth, Tir Na n'Og in the Western sea, where

> *Boughs have their fruit and blossom,*
> *At all times of the year,*
> *And rivers are running over with red beer and brown beer,*
> *An old man plays the bagpipes in a golden and silver wood,*
> *Queens, their eyes blue as the ice, are dancing in a crowd.*
>
> W.B. Yeats

I was there with Merlin when Arthur drew the sword from the stone and regaled myself at the Round Table with all his company of knights, the Siege Perilous empty and waiting for the one that would come at last.

I have been in the company of Bran the Blessed, king of the land westward of Logres, and have dipped my ladle in his Cauldron of Plenty which foreshadowed, men say, the Holy Grail. And the Grail, the inexhaustible cup, that, too, I have encountered, deciphering in its winey depths a green hill topped by crossed branches cut from a tree in Eden with, hanging upon them, arms outstretched, their inevitable burden. And again, as I looked, I heard the earth lament to the sky 'Balder the Beautiful is dead, is dead.'

Take me no further, Taliesin, if indeed there is anywhere else to go; if indeed, in all our mutual remembering we have not been always at this point, where the vertical pierces the horizontal and North, South, East, and West are met. Go where we will — to Arcturus or Aldebaran — there is only one place, only one moment and here, where Heaven and Earth conjoin, all things are gathered in. The ancient springs arise here and memory, seeming to come from afar, is forever in this now. If there are to be new mythologies — and why should we need new mythologies? — they cannot but congregate to this point.

So à Dieu, Taliesin, Bard of Elphin! Where the centre holds and the end folds into the beginning there is no such word as farewell . . .

My shadow follows me as I walk westward. The sunset spreads it along the grass, taller and lordlier, now, than I. What will be remembered in it, this changing incorporeal shape compact of myself and the sun? When the tides of evening come flowing in we shall both be lost to sight. May the Lord have mercy on me and my shadow.

First published in 'Parabola' on the theme of Memory and Forgetting, New York, 1986.

The Unsleeping Eye: A Fairy Tale

I GIVE you something, you know not what, enrich it, you know not how, bring it back, you know not when. And, remember, I shall be watching you,' said the Sun to the newborn child.

And the infant serenely smiled to herself, content not to understand until the time should ripen.

I need not tell you that she was a princess. All women, in or out of fairy tales, are born princesses, being descended from the Goddesses who, by the very nature of things, had to precede the gods.

Inanna of Sumeria was the first to be known to us historically but there can be no doubt that she herself was merely a descendant, the latest comer, as it were, to the hidden genealogies of those who belong to the north side of the mountain and the south side of the river. Thus, with such a lineage, sovereignty was and still is the prerogative of woman, as long ago Dame Ragnell made clear to King Arthur's faithful knight, Gawain. This is a fact she either forgets, and thereby betrays it, or on the other hand uses it for some ego-purpose instead of bestowing it, once it is adequately acknowledged — and here again we must remember Ragnell — as a gift to those who belong to the south side of the mountain and the north side of the river. Nevertheless, it should not be forgotten that the Muse, while she inspires, herself also sings and dances, makes her own music and weaves her own stuff of poetry.

So, since the child was of notable lineage, there had to be a christening, a modest affair such as happens daily, and of course Wise Women were present — not twelve of them, a mere handful only, all of them silent, finger to lip, as they presented their gifts. There has been only one story where the largesse of these puissant ladies was publicly proclaimed. But that, it is clear, was a special

occasion. For the commonality such ceremonies are performed
in silence. It can take the recipient a lifetime to discover the nature,
not always benign, of these baptismal bequests.

So the child grew, ever in the eye of the Sun, content to be seen
and known by him as a mere piece of the world, without at all
asking to know whether she herself was anything other than tree
or stone or grass.

Occasionally she would ask herself, 'Why me? Why should I be
given a gift?' But never an answer came.

But inevitably there came a time when aspects of herself arose
that did not want to be looked at; things unbecoming, unknown
and unknowable, to the trees and the grass, that would rather run
and hide themselves than be seen by the Sun or, indeed, herself.

Then she would cry 'Go down! Go down! Let the width of the
world be between us.'

But the sun merely smiled and shone. 'It is you who are turning,
not I,' he said. 'The earth is as filmy as a bridal veil. For me there
are no Antipodes. I cannot help but see all, as I myself am seen.
That is the way of the law.'

She knew that this was true and felt the pain of letting herself
be seen and known, no rag to cover her nakedness. It was at such
times that the favours of the Wise Women came, in a sense, to her
rescue.

One such, it seemed to her, was the love of and the need to work;
to busy herself, like Allerleirauh, in making soups for the king;
to herd the geese along with the Goose Girl; spin wool and flax
with the Three Spinners or mull a stoup of wine for Homer.

As for the second gift, perhaps it was the satisfaction that lies
in what is small and passing, the unconsidered moment; the King
of Hearts on a city pavement, dropped from a pack of playing
cards, gazing benignly up at her, begrimed, serene, majestic; all
minor losings and findings; a rose, of all flowers most enigmatic,
unfurling, letting its petals fall, its secret still untold; shadows
moving upon a wall, the outside of the inside of their substantial
selves; lines of a poem leaping, unasked for, to the mind; the day
dissolved, absolved by the night.

But the third gift was the greatest. The Wise Women, it appeared,
had so arranged matters for her that she should find, as she went
her way, hand after hand held out to her of those who asked the
same questions that had burned in her since childhood. 'Who am
I? What is my purpose? Where is the abiding city?' And from each
she received — oh, never an answer — but a spark of instructive fire.

With these she went on, unwinding the way, through the dark forests, across the wide deserts, the Sun's eye always upon her.

And at length, since it happens in all the tales, she encountered the vermilion thread and became so enmeshed in its joys and sorrows that for a moment she despaired and cried rebelliously to the Sun, 'Whatever it is you have given me, I cannot carry it any longer. I must throw it away.'

'If you do, it will return to me. That, too, is the law. But you yourself will be lost,' said the Sun.

Of course she had not meant what she said. She had no intention of being lost and would go her way through the thrice-nine lands, no matter what it cost her. And it had, she saw, to cost her much, everything she had, perhaps, if she wanted to come to Happy Ever After. Those whose hands still led her on were quick to remind her that this was no simple matter. The fairy tales that end with this phrase have told only half the story. In their wisdom — they are manuals of sagacity — they leave the other half to the reader. It is he who must complete it.

Thus, wilily, they force him to search within himself until he comes to understand — and our princess was no exception — that it is not the advent of the Prince or the ship coming safely home to port, that brings about the denouement. She had to learn that happiness is not pleasure, though pleasure — and, above all, joy — are in its warp and woof. Rather it is a moral virtue, come to by grace and discipline and not without suffering, withal. It requires a poignant letting go of what has been most cherished and learning a new vocabulary — the grammar, as it were, of the heart. The 'I' that knocks upon the door must become, in answer to 'Who is there?' inevitably 'Thou'; Love, as noun, must become verb and lose itself in Loving; and Passion assume the syllable that makes of it Compassion. Only thus, when what was lost has been found, is it possible to enter the city with bliss-bestowing hands.

'It is all very difficult,' she said to the Sun, as the realization worked within her.

'Would you value it if it was easy?' he asked, shining upon her.

And, reflecting that the nightingale leans his breast upon a thorn to sing his song of joy; that the fly is forever wringing his hands; the mantis clasping his in prayer; that wormwood, for all its bitterness, contains a healing virtue — she knew that she would not. The fascination of what's difficult continually sustained her.

'I will go and sit in a rocking chair and commune with myself on these matters. I have made enough soup for the king and herded geese long enough.'

So she did that, fanning herself as she pondered with a leaf of coconut palm.

And children came and played about her as though she were part of their landscape.

'Why do you sit in a rocking chair?' a fair-haired boy demanded.

'Well, the rocking chair is the clock of the earth — tick-tock, tick-tock, it tells the time.'

And, not being scientists they did not enquire what time the earth was telling. When a thing is true, you can let it alone.

'And I use my fan of coconut palm to shade me from the Sun.'

'Ah, but he can still see you,' another child said smugly, 'The Sun can see through everything.'

This she knew only too well, but how did the child know it?

'The Sun,' the fair-haired boy was dreamy, 'the Sun has a mother's face.' And she knew he was thinking of some merchant's sign — the Sun Alliance, the Sun Insurance — hung high above a city street, a metal orb with its gilded rays, eyes downcast but all-seeing, mouth full-lipped and faintly smiling, tender, ironic, a little weary. The metaphor was apt.

'He'll be pleased,' another child joined in, 'when we bring him back his gift.'

At that the rocking chair stopped rocking.

'What gift?' she was startled. 'What gift did he give you?'

'But you must know that,' the fair boy said. '"I give you something, you know not what, bring it back you know not when." We do not know what it is. Perhaps it's a kind of riddle.'

The palm leaf fan fell from her hand at the shock of the revelation. She had thought that the sun had singled her out, given her something solely her own, for reasons she could not guess at. Her uniqueness fell from her like a garment, leaving her first with a sense of loss and then with a feeling of freedom. Whatever it was, all men received it. She was not alone.

She turned to the children to draw them nearer but they were off on another tack.

'Riddles!' they shrieked. 'Let's ask her riddles.' And they rained on her all the old conundrums.

'Who killed Cock Robin?'

'When is a door not a door?'

'Why does a chicken cross the road?'

And to each — as though she did not know! — she shook her head and let them triumph.

'Where was Moses when the candle went out?'

And of course she knew that answer, too, had even, as a child, felt sorry for Moses, left as he was in the dark. But now poor Moses did not matter. In her mind the riddle turned on itself. What, rather, of the candle? Or, to go further, what of the flame? One moment there it is and the next — puff! — it is gone. But is it possible, she wondered, that light can not exist, be nothing? Blown out, it must surely go to its source. And life — can it be lost either? The two are in a sense one. Life, too, must surely go back whence it came.

And suddenly her head knew what her body had always unwittingly known. The Sun's bounty had at last a name.

Gently, as though it were a newborn child, she sat and rocked her life in her arms, gratitude welling up within her. She might so easily have been lost to it, as the candle is lost to the flame.

The children were arguing together, confronted by their own riddle. How could they bring their life back to the Sun. He was so far and they so small.

'A ladder!' said the fair-haired boy. 'A great long ladder to lean against a cloud.'

She rocked and nodded her agreement. A ladder was indeed the answer. But she refrained from telling them that it need not be so very long. They must find that out for themselves. For she knew now that what she had to do — what they would all have to do at last — was to climb up through the length of herself, on each rung repairing what had been — the wrong roads taken, the forgettings, the long stretches of nothingness — and preparing what was to come. Only thus could she enrich the gift she had to bring back to the Sun. And the Sun would convey it where it belonged.

Tick-tock, tick-tock, went the rocking chair as she began her inward journey back through the thrice-nine lands to the beginning which would contain the end.

Look at her! She is still climbing. And, yes, — can you hear her — singing?

Therefore, with my utmost art,
I will sing thee,
And the cream of all my heart
I will bring thee.
George Herbert, 1593-1633

Rocking, rocking, she goes her way, with the Sun keeping vigil upon her. And on the children wandering home; on you; on me; and all the rest. A constant sleepless eye.

But, you will say, this is just a fable, a tale told around the hearth as the fire reddens and falls.

True enough. And enough of truth.

If you don't like it, don't listen.

First published in 'Parabola' on the theme of The Witness. New York, 1986.

O Children
of this World!

Beware the children of light
   That riff-raff crew,
They will pilfer your peace of mind
   And your money, too.
Not as thieves in the night —
   Deeper far their offence —
They make light of the things of this world
   By their innocence,
Toppling the sturdy house
   To its basic sand,
Turning silver and gold
   To dust in the hand.

On all your highroad journeys
   Wrapped against wind and snow
You will find them arrived before you
   Barefoot, by the low.
Your effect will be cause,
   Your right their wrong,
Your wisdom a little thing
   To be had for a song,
And your women, hard to please,
   Cold to you as the sea,
They will pluck in passing
   Like plums from a tree.

Beware the children of light,

They will turn you away
From all that goes by the clock —
'Now,' they will say
'Is then; here, there,
    And the frost is warm,
Sun icy and only danger
    Will keep you safe from harm.
Taste of the aloe's honey,
    Give your breast to the thorn,
Let the stone bird pluck at
    The living fern.'

First published in 'Parabola' on the theme of Addiction. New York, 1987.

On Forgiving Oneself

IT WAS in the middle of the dark wood — *rel mezzo del cammin di nostra vita* — that I first saw her.

Oh, I had had glimpses of her out of the tail of my eye ever since I had ceased to be of such as are of the kingdom of Heaven, that period when one is One and all alone with sun, moon, earth, and sky.

And I would put those glimpses by as matters of no moment, flecks of dust on a window pane to be rubbed off by a finger, and not even by my own finger. Surrounding love would do it for me. Life, after all, was on my side. It takes a lifetime to comprehend the untruth of this assumption. Life is not on anyone's side. It is for us to take up the fardels and put ourselves on the side of life and go wherever it leads.

So — I saw her. Plain? Well, not entirely, for she was veiled. A long blue mantle — the blue I have always associated with Demeter, empyrean, hyacinthine — enfolded her like an atmosphere.

And she was dancing, self-satisfied, self-absorbed. At the same time wanting, I was sure, to be looked at and admired. I would not look. I would not admire. My way through the wood was not her way. Nor was I going to turn aside to take part in such follies.

Yet it happened that whichever path I took she was always somewhere near it, a blue shape flickering through the trees, plucking any fruit that offered, or gathering the woodland flowers only to drop them incontinently when some new interest beckoned.

Or she would meet with other figures, each of them veiled in a different colour, and move with them round and round in a ring, till another circle caught her eye and she would break away and join it; or take the hand of a passing stranger and loose that to go with somebody else, wandering where the whim took her as thistledown goes on the back of the wind. Always dancing, always pleasing herself and at the same time — I could not but sense it — always searching for something — something more, something other, a lack that she could not fill. And I had the impression that if she was ever at the edge of my vision, I was ever at the edge of hers. She would like, I felt, to have gone my way if her own — could it be called a way — had not had her so ensorceled.

Once I saw her, solitary and motionless in the woodland, as if for a moment lost and lonely. And, again, she was crouching among dead leaves, blue shoulders heaving, hand under the veil flung out, a wordless cry for help as I passed. There are given tears, tears of grace and tears that should not be allowed to flow but drunk back, rather, to their source, letting their salt ichor serve to vivify the will. Hers, I felt, were not as these. She had clearly fallen on the thorns of life, but her grief — like her dancing, I was sure — was part of the drama of herself, the one demanding approbation, the other pleading for pity. I strode on, keeping to my path. Why should one linger by the wayside to condole with the self-condolent?

But, as one coming to a decision, she rose up from her leafy bed and stood before me barring my way. There was nothing of threat in the urgent gesture; nevertheless it was obdurate. A request, not a demand.

And I knew suddenly what she wanted, had indeed wanted all along — to have herself acknowledged. But why should I acknowledge her? Was this another of her games? Let her acknowledge herself! And I turned away, back on my track, only to find that the nimble-footed resolute shape had skilfully outflanked me. Again I turned and again she was there, inexorably confronting me. It was in a way a kind of dance, each intent on her own orbit while treading an identical measure. The road was narrow. The hyacinth-ine silhouette filled it from side to side. I could not pass her and I realized now that I did not wish to pass. If I was to find my way through the wood, I would have to come to terms with her, and accept her insistent challenge.

So we stood there facing each other, vibrant in the expectant stillness, the forest bird-song suddenly silent. Then she thrust a hand under her veil and drew it down from head to shoulder, her face emerging from the blue as the moon slips out from the edge of a cloud.

It was my face. The woodland, as though it were a glass, mirrored it back to me, line, shape, colour. And I knew that I had always known, and at the same time refused to know, what lay beneath the veil.

For a long moment she eyed me gravely and my face must have been a pattern of hers. Then she smiled, a smile that was shy and sorry but with nothing abject in it.

'Forgive me,' she said. 'I am what I am.'

As she spoke her veil slithered to the ground revealing a white under-gown that was tucked and puckered and stained with living. And, looking down, I saw that my own robe was equally tucked and puckered and stained.

It was then that something opened within me and the springs of perception poured forth their fountains.

The same face, the same garments, the other aspect of myself — and I had rejected it, believing, in my ignorance, that I could go on my pilgrimage unshadowed and alone.

But can one set out on the road to Heaven without taking note of the earth one treads on, that lifts the foot forward, giving it wings? How could Purusha make itself known without Prakriti to manifest it; the Self perform its hero task without the Ego to contend with; Spirit exhale its vital breath without Body to receive it? Both ends of the stick are necessary, and Soul helps Flesh no more than Flesh helps Soul. Would we have need of Nirvana if there were no Samsara? If she needed me, I also needed her, and I had barred my door against her, steadfastly refusing to take to myself what, after all, was my own. I could have lightened the load I carried by delighting in her self-delight, taking part in her varying rounds, sitting beside her — friend to friend, compassionate — so that her self-pity could turn about and become its healing opposite, the pity for all that is. By failing her I had failed myself.

'No, no!' I cried. 'It is you who must forgive me. I, too, am what I am. We are, both of us, walking through the fire. One single flame enfolds us both. So let us together proceed with our burning. There is no other way.' Arms wide, we bent toward each other. And a passing angel paused for a moment, standing imponderably on the air, to witness our embrace.

'Wherever there are two, there are three!' He smiled at us benignly. 'May that Third, the One that reconciles, unnameable, not to be seen or known, in mercy forgive you both.'

First published in 'Parabola' on the theme of Forgiveness, New York, 1987.

Zen Moments

DAITO KUJI

Before dawn, the little group of Westerners is setting out for the Zendo, fur-wrapped and yawning, their breath, substantial, going before them, leading them to the koan.

Will Roshi give them his sightless glance from the face behind his face, strike the bell for the next comer and send each away, answer unanswered? In this place there is no forseeing. All depends on the moment.

So they come to the waterfall. Tonight it is frozen, a shawl of marble, silent, not a stir.

Someone stands back and says 'Wonderful!', congratulating the full moon on its shining white reflection.

Neophytes, knowing nothing as yet of how to say nothing, they all agree — 'Wonderful!'

And out from the shadows comes a dancing figure, a small monk, cotton-robed, naked feet in sandals.

'Two-derful!' He clasps his hands, gazing with unction at the waterfall, caricaturing their rapture.

'Three-derful! Four-derful! Five-derful! Six!'

Black as a crow amid the frost, he caws with laughter as he hurries by.

Can that be it — the koan's answer on two feet, skipping among the trees?

Not wonderful. One-derful!

RYOANJI

Just sitting here on the low verandah, gazing at the stone garden — that is enough.

The islands rise out of the sea of white pebbles, each ringed by wavelets drawn by a rake.

From whichever direction you approach the enclosure, there is always one stone you cannot see. That is the garden's secret. The ever-changing Invisible — I will spend the day with that.

Tourists and schoolchildren come with their clamour and take it away with them, unnoticed. It does not touch the edge of the silence or move me from my stillness. I, too, have become a stone.

After 50 years, maybe, a monk mixes some green tea and gives it to me in a bowl.

Centuries later, another comes to rake the circles. He stops and regards me thoughtfully. Then he offers me the rake.

Oh, no! I press myself against the wall, wanting it to absorb, unmake me. Nothing in life has prepared me for this. Who am I to say, 'Let there be sea!'?

But he stands there, impassive, the rake held out. Oh, the arrogance of humility! Be simple and take what is offered.

I slip off my sandals and step down, the marble pebbles cool to my warmth. The Invisible changes as I go, drawing the rake round each rock. It is not I who am making it — the ocean is being made.

Later, at the end of the day, the monk comes to rectify my work, turning its tremulous water-lines into more accurate circles.

Yet it is not done by him, either. The islands themselves are plummet stones, flung down by an unknown hand, sending the waves out, ring on ring.

BEING SEEN, BEING KNOWN

'Never let me see you'
Said Roshi,
'Not sitting under
The fig tree.'

MIROKU BOSATSU

I had come to the Koryuji temple in Kyoto, hoping to stand alone before him.

But he was in a long room crowded with other statues and inevitably the ubiquitous schoolchildren came thronging in among them.

'I shall wait till another day,' I thought.

But there is only one moment, only one day. If not now, never.

Then I saw that the children, beholding him, had ceased to move, perhaps, even, to breathe. Each of us was alone before him, listening to the silence of that one uplifted hand.

SUNT LACHRYMAE RERUM

We sit on our heels on the tatami, the Japanese woman and myself, telling the stories of our lives. One can do this only with a stranger. Too near, and the perspective is lost. Only the far can be near.

A sound — not knock, intimation only — had come from the inner door. And there she was in her blue yukata exactly like my own — the only wear in a Japanese inn — bowing to me, like a branch bending.

'It is permitted to practise my little English?'

I rise and become another branch. 'It is permitted.'

And so we kneel before each other, the foot-square mirror at which I make my toilet reflecting each in turn.

There is no need for us to commend the cherry-blossoms — they are doing no more than their duty. Nor to chatter about the shrine at Ise. Neither of us is a tourist. We are just two women, gone beyond time, our talk a shuttle pulling weft across warp, no beginning, no end to the pattern.

The cauldron of plenty in each of us seethes with its ferment, sweet and bitter — the world to be carried and no plaint made; love to suffer long and be kind, not vaunting, not puffed up; the seed that we carry to be threshed, freed from its crusty husk; the aching question of who we are and for what made, answered only by its echo; the need to stand before the Unknown and never ask to know; to take our leave of the world, head high, no matter how hard the parting; and, coquetry no whit abated, offer the unassuaging mould an acquiescent lip.

Arms crossed, we rock from side to side. Hushing what? Ourselves, perhaps. And again and again she murmurs a word, as a counterpoint to her movement.

'What is that you are saying? Tell me.'

She rocks and seems to draw it closer, folding the word to her breast.

'A — Wa — Re.' She stresses the syllables as though teaching a child.

'A — Wa — Re. It means, in our tongue, The Pity of Things.'

I look at her long and in silence. Then I rise and bow.

'Do you know that what you have said is our word "aware" '?

She looks at me long and in silence. Then she, too, rises and bows. And at the door bows again.

There is nothing to say. We say nothing.

First published in 'Parabola' on the theme of A Sense of Humour, New York, 1987.

The Interviewer

HE HAD written from a distant country asking if he might come and see me to talk about a series of books known to us both for an article in his newspaper. He would not take much of my time, he assured me, just an hour or so between plane journeys.

Yes, I replied, knowing that the compliant word, written down, would not reveal the reluctance it might contain, if spoken. I am shy of interviewers. They try to ferret out from one's heart things that even the stethoscope can not be privy to. But, to come all that way! I could not refuse.

So he arrived, hurrying out of the sky, as it were, clearly eager for the fray, a blue silk handkerchief peeping out of his breast pocket and his arms full of blue flowers.

My favourite colour — a good omen, I thought. Perhaps he was one of those journalists, rarely, admittedly, to be found, who have themselves something to contribute, perception, a streak of understanding.

And he had! Taking me warmly by both hands, 'These books,' he declared, 'are not invented. That is why they are so interesting.' Here was another good omen.

'How could they be?' I asked, laughing. 'You invent motorcycles and atom bombs.'

'So tell me,' he said eagerly, settling himself into a chair and taking out his notebook. 'Where did you get the idea?'

The good omens took to their heels. How many times had I heard that question from people of all ages. Must I face it again?

'Where does anyone get an idea?'

'But it must — it can't help it — come from somewhere.'

'Why not from nowhere?' I suggested.

He waved this aside as frivolous.

'Well, did you ever know, at some point in your life, anybody like her?' He named the book's chief character.

'What? Someone who slides up bannisters? No, never. Did you?'

'Of course not! How could you ask that? I am being serious.'

'So am I,' I assured him. 'Never more so.'

'But you have to face the facts, you know.' He was gentle but determined.

'I don't see why. And there *are* no facts. Or none that I am aware of.'

'Oh, yes, there are!' he insisted. And with something of a flourish, a gesture of triumph, he took from his notebook a newspaper cutting. 'I have here an interview with your sister in Australia. In it she says that you told her about this character when she was a very small child.'

'Well, if she was so very small, I myself could hardly have been much larger. But it's not true, I'm afraid.'

'It must be. It's here in black and white.'

'And black and white makes things true? Printer's ink on a scrap of paper?'

'Then what *did* you tell her? If you could recall that it might give us a clue to what came later.'

'I have no idea. Stories are like birds flying, here and gone in a moment.'

'But this one must have stayed with her. How else could she remember?'

'A matter of hindsight, I suppose. A linking — or mislinking — of one thing with another.'

'Well, *what* thing? Think back, think back, think back!' he urged me. 'The time, the place, the season, the weather.'

The weather!

Suddenly he was no longer there. Oh, he was substantial in his chair, but in essence he did not exist for me. I was hearing a cataract of rain stabbing a corrugated iron roof with sharp resonant sword-thrusts. And beneath it the silence that had fallen as the three children ceased their playing.

For *she* was standing by the door, her blue robe hanging from her shoulders, hair in a walnut braid down her back, her face white and distraught.

'I have had enough. I can stand no more. I am going down to the creek,' she said. And she went out, closing the door behind her.

If I had run after her, she would have certainly turned back. Mother in her very essence, she would never have allowed the barrage from Heaven to be unleashed on her child.

But at the age of ten — or almost — I was as green and tightly folded as a bud on a winter branch, not knowing what would later ripen; what woman-stuff, now in embryo, would comprehend the inner ferment that tonight had clearly reached its climax and urged her out into the storm — the husband dead at forty-three, she herself eleven years younger, left to be sole resource, the one loved object, of three ebullient children; the commodious house full of helping hands exchanged for what, by comparison, was about as capacious as a wren's nest; no stables, there were no more horses; sugar and flour, once bought by the bushel, tea in mahogany boxes embossed with Chinese ideograms, were now bought in packets from the grocer; bread from a baker's basket instead of out of the oven; a whole spacious bushland way of existence suddenly expunged and a new life laboriously to be made.

Such a making did not trouble the children. For them it was all adventure as long as she was there, the playmate, the comforter, the constant pillar round whom their lives revolved.

And, indeed, would have been adventure for her, with all her lively zest for life, had she not had to do it alone.

The sound that the door made in closing was as if a bell had tolled. It made the silence in the room seem louder than the rain.

Large-eyed, the little ones looked at me — she and I called them the little ones, both of us aware that an eldest child, no matter how young, can never experience the heart's ease that little ones enjoy.

And I knew that what they needed from me was what we all needed from her — security, reassurance.

I put a log on the failing fire, brought an eiderdown from a bedroom and we lay together on the hearth rug, the warm downy quilt around us like a bird's wing shielding a hatch of nestlings.

There was no need for me to think of a story for suddenly he was there before us, the little horse — a colt, rather, finely made with narrow withers — I can see him now — mane and tail neatly trimmed, hurrying off on some pilgrimage.

'He's white!' said one of them.

'Grey!' said the other.

'No,' I told them. 'Spickled and speckled like a guinea fowl.'

And there we were, all gathered behind him, watching him moving over the ocean, sparks of light flashing from his hooves as he trod the smooth dark waters, head thrown up, scenting the way.

'Perhaps he is going to his home!'

'No, he's coming from it,' I said, 'to a place that has no name. He can see it far away in the distance, a great big cloud of light.'

'Will he get there safe and sound?'

'Of course! He is a magic horse.'

(The creek is not deep. There are crayfish in it. Surely no one could drown in it, unless, like Ophelia in the picture, they lay down and let it cover them.)

'If he is magic, can he do everything? Fizzle up the world in a frying pan?'

'Yes!'

(But the creek flows into a wide pool. Nobody knows how deep it is. We are not allowed there without a grown-up. A thrown stone has many rings around it.)

'Can he fly into the air without wings?'

'Yes!'

'And dive to the bottom of the sea?'

'Yes!'

(What happens to children who have lost both parents? Do they go into Children's Homes and wear embroidered dressing-gowns, embroidery that is really darning?)

'Perhaps he will never get to the light!'

'Oh, he will. Remember, he is magic.'

(Will rich relations come and get us and turn us into poor relations?)

'Is there corn in that land for him to eat?'

'Yes, and a bundle of hay.'

(Perhaps they will send us to different places, one here, another there. No one will be a little one.)

'And a pail of water, all lit with light?'

'Yes!'

(Maybe she has gone from the creek to the pool. How long does it take a person to drown? Oh, I will be good, I promise!)

'Could he carry us to the shiny land, all three on his back?'

'Yes!'

I had to say Yes to comfort them and also to comfort myself. But the horse was so small, not yet ready for burdens. I knew that he had to go alone. And, somehow, they must have known it, too, for the three of us moved more closely together, drawing the eiderdown tightly, tightly around us, watching him toss up his speckled head as his hooves, dainty and precise, struck ever brighter sparks from the dark, with never a splash from the water.

I tried to think only of the horse and what would happen when he arrived. I was afraid of my other thoughts.

The logs slipped sideways with a falling sound as they reddened in the grate. And at that moment she came in, rain streaming from her clothes and hair, looking young, forlorn, and lonely but somehow with her mind made up.

The little ones leapt and ran to her, crying, laughing, embracing her, drawing her into the warm room, squeezing the water out of her gown, kissing her in every possible place.

And she gave herself to their ministrations, accepting the welcome gratefully, leaning on their joy.

As they ran to find towels and dry clothes, she looked at me expectantly, waiting for me to go to her.

But I turned away without a word and went to light the primus stove — a thing I was not supposed to do, it was only for grown-ups. When the kettle came to the boil, I filled a rubber hot-water bottle and took it to her room.

They were in the big bed, all of them, the little ones huddled on either side, holding her tightly, safely, between them as they told her excitedly the story of the horse. She looked at me across their heads and lovingly held out her arms.

But I stood silent in the doorway and with all the strength I could find in myself, flung the hot-water bottle at her and went to my own room.

'Oh, you cold-hearted child,' she cried. 'The others are so pleased to see me. What has happened to you?'

I could not answer. It was true, however, that I was cold, not only in my heart but throughout the whole of my body. I lay in my bed still as a stone, feeling and knowing nothing . . .

All that was Now. It was still Now when I roused myself and found I had been thinking aloud, and also that I was weeping.

I looked across at the Interviewer who, when I had last been aware of him, had been madly scribbling in his notebook.

But his chair was empty. And in my lap lay the blue silk handkerchief and a note on a strip of paper. He must have quietly slipped away and left me to my tears, the tears that had stayed unshed within me, forgotten, concealed, biding their time till something they needed called them forth. And as the blue handkerchief absorbed them — that had been a delicate gesture — I knew they were not for myself only.

The tight green bud had long unfolded and now I could go with her through the storm, silently sharing what then had moved in her mind — the bed, once proportionate to conjugal life with its whispered, sleepy confabulations; Yin breath and Yang breath flowing together; naked foot over naked foot; the day dissolved, absolved by the night — was now as wide as a desert. What had once been borne by two had now to be carried by one. Fulness had become emptiness.

I wept for her and at the same time could now allow myself to rejoice that she had come back through the door to be still the pillar, the sharer of all joys and sorrows, loving and loved for the rest of her life.

I put the handkerchief away and took up the strip of paper.

'I have my answer,' it said. 'The horse! The horse that can do everything! It is wonderful that from so much sorrow such happiness could come.'

His answer indeed! I flew to the door, hoping that I could catch him. But the little street, like his chair, was empty — only, at the end of it, a young man leaping into a taxi. I would like to have shouted wildly, 'Stop!' But what would the neighbours think? A citizen held to be relatively sane shouting 'Stop!' to nothing!

Besides, I knew he would hurry home to tap out on his typewriter his gleanings from the morning. Tomorrow they would be in 'black and white' on a host of breakfast tables, a fallacious account of a book's begetting transmogrified into fact. Nothing could stop that happening.

But if I could have brought him back I would have told him that there are no answers, there are only questions.

Fallible creatures that we are and being ourselves in question, we inevitably demand answers to ease the lack within us. All things must be capable of explanation, every effect must have a cause, each problem a solution. It is thus that we arrive at conclusion, for conclusion brings about the ending that we mistake for an answer. 'That's finished,' we say, mendaciously. 'We can go on to something else.'

But nothing in life — nor, perhaps, in death — is ever really finished. A book, for instance, is no book at all, unless, when we come to the last page, it goes on and on within us.

You, I would say to the Interviewer, took the magic horse for an answer, the clue, the code to be cracked. It did not occur to you to enquire from whence that idea came to the child. Or whether at some point in her life she had encountered such a creature. Nor, indeed, what lay beneath the horse, the cause of which he was the effect. And the cause beneath that cause. Doubtless, had you pursued this course, you would have had to fall back on that too much bandied about Unconscious, which people with little knowledge of psychology, and even those with much, make use of as a sort of psychic rag bag in which to throw any old concept.

I have pondered long upon that phrase — is the Unconscious unconscious of itself? — and never felt quite at home with it. There seemed to be something lacking.

Then I read in a book by Sri Mahada Ashish of Mirtola that in his view it should properly be translated as The *Unconscioussed*. But would such a large ungainly word take root in common parlance? I tried it on several scholarly minds, but while its accuracy was accepted it was not received with enthusiasm. They would stick to their old-fashioned fallacies.

Later, however, one of our leading analytical psychologists, being quoted in the magazine *Resurgence*, set all my unease at ease. 'It means,' he said — and I verified this with one of his *confrères* — 'it means, simply, the Unknown.'

The Unknown — our beautiful Anglo-Saxon word, intimate, reverberant, profound, not so much to be understood but stood under while it rains upon us — that is something I could well live with and, indeed, have revered, cherished, and tried to serve for many a year and day.

Call it the Unknown and one can conceive of the creative process as being a next door neighbour to it. Though, with the general decline of language this phrase, too, is too often used without discrimination and applied to the scribblings of every passing rhymester.

C S Lewis, in a letter to a friend, says, 'There is only one Creator and we merely mix the elements He gives us' — a statement less simple than it seems. For that 'mere mixing', while making it impossible for us to say 'I myself am the maker,' also shows us our essential place in the process. Elements among elements, we are there to shape, order, define, and in doing this we, reciprocally, are defined and shaped and ordered. The potter, moulding the receptive clay, is himself being moulded.

But let us admit it. With that word 'creative', when applied to any human endeavour, we stand under a mystery. And from time to time that mystery, as if it were a sun, sends down upon one head or another, a sudden shaft of light — by grace one feels, rather than deserving — for it always comes as something given, free, unsought, unexpected. It is useless, possibly even profane, to ask for explanations. Somehow, somewhere, the Unknown is known, perhaps — who can say? — to the wild bee!

First published in 'Parabola' on the theme of The Creative Response, New York, 1988.

Well, Shoot Me!

SHE stood before me, surly, beautiful, predatory, a falcon feathered with human plumage.

'I'm going to shoot everybody over the age of twenty-five,' she said. Even her voice was a falcon's, harsh, keening, lonely.

'Except you,' she added, whether from a momentary lapse into politeness or from real conviction born of our friendship, I could not tell.

But why me? Who was she, I asked myself, to say to one 'Come!' and 'Go!' to another; to arrogate to herself the winnowing fan and submit to the holocaust a host of martyrs the latchets of whose shoes I couldn't even hope to unlace and leave me out of it? Was I to be the sole white ewe and good stepmother who all my life have loved, cherished and loudly acclaimed the Black Sheep and the Wicked Fairy, who carry the story forward?

Well, let them have the world, I thought, she and her companions. Let them take the planet and ride it bareback. With all their energies at the mid-heaven, they are thirsting for responsibility and full of constructive imagination. And whatever of value is lost in the carnage they will rediscover and make their own. Eden recurs continually. Each generation experiences its guileless morning, equivocal noon-day and the drumming out in the evening.

So — let ice break and rivers rise! But what would I do in all the ferment, the falling dams and the melting snows, if I were the sole elect survivor? With whom share the antique dream, to whom say 'Do you remember?'

My gorge rose stubbornly. A bugle sounded from my childhood and the tramp of martial feet. 'Up from the meadows rich with corn, clear on the cool September morn.' And I heard the voice of Barbara Fritchie.

'Shoot if you must,' I told her. 'I refuse to be an exception!'

A gun I thought, is quick and final — no time for the treacherous second thought. Better this than to be hanged or bombed or to fade out with a whimper. It would just be BANG, and I nowhere and everywhere, riding a feather, gone into air. Indeed, in thought, I was already away, lost to all the swagger of living, yet not quite nothing, an essence, a seed — how much is there, ultimately, of anyone? — eyelessly acquainting myself with the lie of the galaxy, hearing with my no-ear the drumming vowels of the universe. Consonants, I suddenly realized — though with what? — belong to earth, but *A, E, I, O, U* are cosmic sounds. Sung or spoken as a chord they compose and forever repeat the word that we, knowing and partly knowing, transcribe as Alleluia.

But none of this journeying was true, alas! I knew it as I came back reluctantly, yet, it must be admitted, with a certain sheepish pleasure, to my body and found that the girl had not pulled the trigger.

'You're weakening,' I accused her. 'Hesitate, and the moment is lost. I shall probably still be hanging around when the time comes for someone to shoot *you.*'

'Me?' She was startled.

'Well, you're already nineteen. The rest is merely the blink of an eyelid. All over twenty-five, you said?'

But that was different, obviously. Could I not see that the two situations were in no way parallel? It was simply a matter of cutting out the dead wood. After that no one would *need* to be shot. It was ridiculous to suppose, even unimaginable, that some day *their* forests would require thinning.

'So — you'll all expire of old age — peacefully, in your beds?'

Such a conception had evidently no relish for her and, anyway, it was academic. Who really believes that they will die, except in those hero moments when the quality of life is so unalloyed, so brimming with possibilities that one can say Yes even to death?

Well, if indeed those moments were true for anybody other than a teenager, how was it that I — not single-handed, she allowed me that — but with the assistance of my generation had made such a hash of things? Her large incriminating gesture showed me the whole turning planet as it threw itself forward into space audibly groaning beneath its load of trouble.

My impulse was to turn away, to shrug off whatever sins of commission or omission had brought about that awful ululation, to cry aloud 'Not I!'

But I could not. I remembered the legend of Indra, the Hindu god, who threw a net over the world and at the point where each thread met another, he tied a little bell. After that, no thing, no creature, could make a movement without setting the whole net ringing. Knowingly and unknowingly I have rung the bells — Was I there when they crucified my Lord? Am I my brother's keeper? — and must say *Mea Culpa*. Yes, say it and digest it but not because of it bow my head and hurry to a nunnery. The world has to be faced and lived in and there, on one infinitesimal speck of it, stood I, confronting the falcon girl before me and hearing from a distance my own young voice asking the same indignant question. Why have you made such a hash of it?

'If our ears were tuned to the ether,' I told her, 'we could probably hear Methuselah's children making the same indictment.'

'You mean — people have always done it? Rebelled against their parents?'

If the habit was as old as that, it might be the groovy thing for her to take another tack.

'Of course. It's a law. But why lay all our troubles on parents? They provide a door for us into life; that, and nurturing, is their function. Afterwards, it is up to us. We can't blame them if the door opens on scenes we hadn't bargained for. It was not my parents, but the generation before them, great-aunts and their kind, who sat like black crows on my horizon, old, rich, and righteous. My lifelong dislike of authoritarianism and my predilection for seeing life through my own eyes — these I owe to them. To disagree, in that occupied territory, was to be something less than dust. Even to agree — in those unguarded moments when one's principles nodded — was to be granted a strictly limited claim to existence. They had already seen, known, and been the best. Life, therefore, for the young, must inevitably be a swiftly declining asset. Pterodactyls, I dare say, and brontosaurs, must have reasoned along the same lines, unaware that Time was already at the draughting-board, planning to supersede them with the roebuck and the hare.'

'And you didn't ever want to shoot them?' Really, I could hear her thinking, how un-with-it can you get?

'Well, no,' I cravenly admitted. 'Only to circumvent them.'

I was sure that, in the nature of things, their reign would come to an end. But in that I was mistaken. Men die but types persist. I had only to look into the perambulators to realize that life, having invented the pattern, was bent on repeating it. There they sat, reiterated suckling dynasts, regarding the world with lofty stares, their infant burbles already proclaiming that whatever card anyone else might play they would certainly trump it. Perhaps these identical babies, greying now and with double chins, today's intransigent conformers, were the ones she was gunning for!

Well, if they were, they would be dealt with. She was not, she reminded me, alone! And, indeed, I could grant her that. The young need never again be lonely. Never before, among them, was there such community.

'Well —' She sounded a little defensive. 'Life owes us that at least. We didn't ask to be born.'

'Are you sure of that?' I asked her, mildly.

She stared. 'Of course we didn't. Did you?'

'Oh, *I* did. I even think I insisted. If my being here is merely some cosmic aberration, I am not accountable for my actions, I have nothing to answer for. That would be saying Yes to chaos. No, no, to give the thing dignity and reason, I have to assume that I chose it.'

'I' she said, blandly, 'have plenty of reasons. The search for happiness, for one. Though it's never,' she added, reluctantly, 'in the place where you look for it.'

'Exactly my experience. One pursues a maiden and clasps a reed. Perhaps it's not a thing in itself but a by-product of something else — like the scent of coffee when it simmers. Or maybe it's a state of mind — not exactly to be pursued but in some propitious moment suddenly happened upon.'

'Well, what about Love, Love, Love?' she went on. 'That's also a reason.'

'Oh, indeed, the first and the last. But very difficult to practise. The greatest of all disciplines.'

Difficult? No, she wouldn't have that. It was *there*, evergreen, spontaneous, like grass in fields or sun on roof-tops.

'For me it's a long apprenticeship. A lifetime,' I said, 'seems hardly enough.' But I could no more have convinced her of the truth of this than I could persuade a bee, in a maze of flowers, that nectar was hard to come by. She shook her head.

'Everything's simpler than you think, you and your contemporaries.'

'Of course. One can overcomplicate as well as oversimplify.'

'All I want is to go to bed happy and wake up happy in the morning. That . . .' she hesitated. 'That and for life to have a meaning.'

'If you leave out the 'a' I would agree that that's the heart of the matter. To insist on one sole meaning is to close the door to every other possibility. But who are my contemporaries? What gargoyle regiment had you in mind? As far as I am concerned they are the very old, the babies in their cradles and everyone in between. We all breathe the same atmosphere and live by the same clock. Time and air do not distinguish between us. It is man who compares and sunders, not things as they are in themselves. Once I'm dead I am no longer anybody's contemporary. But until then I refuse to have time and space cut into snippets, this for me and that for you. If reconciliation is, as Whitman said, the word above all, then separation is in the nethermost pit, the word below all words. It destroys and kills, because it prevents the possibility of relationship and that reciprocal exchange of substance — like the royal stuff of the queen bee — which the generations need to receive by rubbing against each other. If we are talking of meaning, surely this idea of non-separation is one of its aspects. Life, for me, would be a desert if there weren't often children at heel, students sitting on the bookshelves for lack of sufficient floor space, you yourself dropping in to argue and my loved ones of all ages, all warriors of mental fight . . .'

'Oh, you and your old Blake,' she broke in, not unkindly, but impatient that Jerusalem is so long a-building.

'Well, how about the Beatles, and their "Strawberry Fields Forever"? I would welcome that. And "Living is easy with your eyes closed." No pop group has ever gone deeper — or so deeply into truth.'

'Yes, all right. At least it's modern.'

'Oh, much better. Call a thing modern and it's immediately old-fashioned. Something more modish is dogging its heel.'

'But don't you want what is *new*?' she cried. 'Don't you long to be free of the past? You're against conformity — all right! Then you must be for anti-conformity. Everyone has to stand somewhere.'

'I don't see why. Your anti-conformity, after a time, is bound to become conformity. I've always tried to slither between them, like the Argonauts through the Clashing Rocks. It's a difficult, dangerous, flowing process, always changing and always new and one fails continually. Is this freedom? I don't know! But to be in readiness for it, to make the dash through the opposites, I need to go widdershins round my mind, stand on my head, as it were. One gets, thus, another point of view, discovers at moments the endless moment and a Himalaya in every paving stone. And as for the past — is it really the villain? Can we be sure where the causes lie of which we are effects? The source of the river is the spring, we say. But how do we know the sea has not beckoned it, sending the underground message that starts it on its journey? Your cause may not be in the past. Perhaps it is the future that has called you up, all of you, from artesian deeps, to create a new order of things. Such beginnings obviously need endings; and mine it seems has come! But let me say, as you stand there with gun-arm raised — and trembling if the truth be known! — that I will not lower my flag before you though I'll gladly carry yours, too. There is a certain *A, B, C* of things that I have learned — the hard way and for that reason precious — that I will not relinquish or deny. I would like to have gone further in the alphabet — does anyone get to *Z*, I wonder? — but as things are, well, *C* is much. I'm ready when you are.'

'Don't be silly. I said I wouldn't shoot you.'

'Partiality makes one squeamish. If the rest go, then I go, too. That's what *I* said.'

'I'm not shooting *anyone!*' she shouted. 'To separate is to kill, you said. So killing is separation. But I'm not giving in. I'm going to see things through *my* eyes. And I'll fight anyone — you included — to get my own kind of *A, B, C!*'

Young, vulnerable, resolute, the falcon lifted its wings. I wanted to rush out and chalk up on a wall — 'Artemis lives, Pallas Athene lives, Brunhilde is not dead!' But I would not load the loaded moment.

'There's shortbread in the blue jar. Take a piece as you go.'

'I'll be back,' she flung out, elaborately casual. Was it a promise or a threat? Either way, she would be welcome.

'Any time,' I said.

First published in 'Parabola' on the theme of Repetition & Renewal, New York 1988.

Monte Perdido

ALL mountains are sacred mountains.

This is not merely because, being the closest earth can get to Heaven, temples so often are built upon them. May it not be, rather, that the planet, when newly arisen, and sensing with the awareness that pertains to matter its essential incompleteness, thrust up from its uttermost deep these urgent hylic supplications to what, for it, were the uttermost heights? The living being, sustaining evolving living beings, itself needed to evolve.

Created by forces from above, it needed, as the organic life that was to colonize it would need, sustaining help from that from which it had come. Thus, temples, monasteries, shrines arose, with sages, lamas, priests and monks, ecclesiasts of every religion chanting, as the millennia passed, the planet's original incantation.

But not all men throughout the ages have been aware of their insufficiency, nor the fact that it lies like a seed within them. For these, nowadays, the mountains are merely scenic localities resorted to by tourist rather than pilgrim; playgrounds for their feats of endurance; snowfields to be gambolled in; eminences where they may gigantically carve their ephemeral human images upon the abiding rock. Even so, is it possible for any man alive, when confronted with a mountain of any kind not to know himself, if but for a moment, in the presence of a presence?

The Druids were well aware of this and before their role was appropriated by high priests of various sects, they gave their own Druidic names to the highlands where their teachings flourished.

One of these was the Lost Mountain, so called because for the greater part of the year the sky came down and hid it from view — above descending to below — in answer, perhaps, to the planet's primordial prayer. But for some time now the Lost Mountain has been clearly marked on the maps and man has contrived to find his way almost effortlessly through the mist-cloud.

It may be that in the intervening years the celestial mood has changed, the sky no longer involving itself with this particular piece of earth. There is now a shrine half-way up, even a rustic stall or two where food may be bought on the way to the snow-cap.

But this I know only by hearsay. I have seen the mountain only in dream, or perhaps in a vision such as sometimes comes when mind is drawn down from head and plexus into the bowl of the abdomen, that central ground of the human body that in Zen is known as Hara.

Whatever the means, I believe I have seen with the inward eye the Lost Mountain as the Druids knew it, sky-clad, tenebrous, benighted, its hidden shape merely hinted at. And from where I stood, alone on the plain, something leaned on the unseen slope, no ladder but a kind of staircase, steep, narrow, vertically divided.

On the left side, steadily climbing, were people of many different ages, clothed in all colours of the rainbow, but a rainbow faded and bedimmed as if from being too long in the sun.

They took the stairs, slowly, for they were steep, some drawing others in their wake, leading them by the hand. And it seemed to me that each of them was in some way impaired, hobbling, breathing with difficulty, finding the going arduous but nevertheless intent on the climb. Were they, like the planet long ago, reaching up to their source?

Then, as I watched, the right-hand stair, which up till now had been quite empty, was suddenly thronged with figures — not angels, but energies, rather, in human shape — hurrying, almost flying, down and skimming off in every direction as soon as they reached the earth.

One of them, the first to alight, hastened with quicksilver steps towards me. Instinctively, I held out my arms and was caught in a bodiless steely embrace that had more of combat than caress for my very bones seemed to bend to it and the whole of me to vibrate.

From whence had it come, this vital force, this elixir of energy — mountain-top or firmament — to vivify thus my corporeal stuff and, indeed, my inward being? Who was I, that I should receive it? What was it disclosing to me? A message? An injunction?

And, as if my wordless thought had been heard, an arm of light, loosing itself from the embrace, gestured towards the left-hand stair. I knew immediately what it meant. I was to take the pilgrim path and join the climbing throng. And the elixir, permeating my every part, assured me that I was not only willing, but eager for the venture. Perhaps, though unconsciously, I had been so all my life.

The shining shape freed me from its clasp and I went towards the Lost Mountain, aware as I did so that something within me — not my body — was, as it were, halting upon the thigh. This was no new phenomenon. I had long known it, this inward limping, but had let the pleasures and problems of life exempt me from the knowing. Now I could hide from it no longer. The moment had come to face it.

To be healed one first has to be wounded. If the cup is empty it must be taken to be filled at the Well of the Water of Life. Where there is lack one must look for fulness.

I could sense the vibrant brightness behind me as I approached the staircase; and I knew that to find it again I must give myself up to the dark and be ready to face the unknown. As I put my foot on the first stair, a hand reached down and took mine. Help was at hand. I was not alone.

So I began to climb.

First published in 'Parabola' on the theme of The Mountain, New York, 1988.

The Endless Story

ONCE upon a time there was a king who had a beautiful daughter. That is not to be wondered at for all kings, in all the tales, have daughters that are beautiful. And, as usual, princes came from everywhere to seek her hand in marriage. But the king decreed that no man should have her unless he could tell an endless story. Anyone who tried and failed would have his head cut off. But the winner would get with her half the kingdom.

'What if I do not fancy him?' the princess wanted to know.

'The question does not arise,' said the king. 'Princesses are not supposed to choose. They take whatever befalls.'

So, naturally, the gallants came, each with a tale that went on and on, but eventually came to an end. And, of course, the heads fell right and left. At last people began to think that the king had lost his wits.

'The thing is impossible,' they said. So the princes ceased to come.

One day, however, a very poor man decided to try his luck. 'After all,' he said, 'What have I to lose? My stomach is so often empty that in any case I shall shortly die. Between starvation and beheading there is really little difference.'

So he came to the court, the king's proposition was read aloud, and he began his tale.

'There was once a farmer who built a barn, so big that it stretched for half a mile and its roof almost reached the sky. Now, in this roof he made a hole, small enough to admit one locust, should a locust happen to pass. Then he filled the barn to the roof with corn, not an empty space anywhere. And a locust did, indeed, come by. It crept in through the little hole, came out with a single grain and told his brother how he had found it. Then the brother came to get a grain and went away and told his cousin. And the

cousin came and took a grain and told his uncle about it. And
the uncle took another grain and told his sister where to find
one.'

'Get on, get on!' said the king, yawning. 'I want to know what
happened.'

'I must tell the story in my own way' said the man. 'There is a
time for everything.'

'So the sister came and took out a grain and flew off to tell her
aunt. And the aunt got a grain and told her mother and the aunt's
mother told the news to her cousin and they all came and took
out each a grain.'

'For heaven's sake, get to the point. You are wearing me out with
cousins and aunts!' The king was exasperated.

'You did not ask for a point,' said the man. 'You asked for an
endless tale.'

'Well,' he continued, 'the cousin then spoke to a friend. "There
is corn" he said, "in a friend's barn. You get in through a little hole
just large enough to admit one locust." And the friend found the
hole and also a grain and flew off to tell his eldest son. And the
eldest son took a grain for himself and told the second son. And
the second son . . .'

'Enough!' cried the king. 'I can stand no more. This is indeed
an endless tale. Take my daughter and half the kingdom and let
me hear no more of locusts, lest they bring me to my grave.'

So the princess, according to custom, went away with her suitor.

'You are a clever man,' she said. 'But tell me, now that we are
alone, how the story continues.'

'Where was I? Ah, yes. The second son came and got a grain and
he told the third son and so it went on. And as fast as the corn
was used up the farmer sowed more seed in his field, and the wind
blew, the rain rained, the Sun shone and the snow fell and with
every harvest he filled the barn. And the locusts continued to breed
locusts and each came in through the little hole . . .'

'This is not what I wanted to hear. Now that you have me and
half the kingdom, you do not need to go on and on. The part that
I am waiting for is Happy Ever After.'

'A figment of the imagination. I do not believe in it,' said the man,
who himself was without imagination.

'There you are wrong,' the princess said. 'To live happily ever
after is in itself a virtuous act. I will not stay with any man incapable
of that.'

So, breaking all the rules, she left him and went upon her road, not towards her father's house but in the opposite direction. And presently a traveller met her, comely of mien and clearly on a pilgrimage. He looked at her long and hard and took her by the hand.

'Leave this place and come with me and I'll tell you the rest as we go.'

'Will it be about locusts and corn?' She had had enough of both.

'Well, locusts do indeed exist and corn has its uses when made into bread. But my mind is on the Milky Way, and the fire beneath the depths of the sea, and Aristotle's Dialogues and the matter of Orpheus. Should he or should he not have looked back? Also, if it comes to that, the question of who are you?'

'I am the daughter of a king.'

'Trappings, mere trappings. I am interested only in essentials — for instance, that bauble on your head. You should never cover your hair.'

'Do you not know,' she asked him, smiling, 'that women are supposed to cover their hair for fear, it is said, of the angels?'

'Well, angels are merely the lusts of men and I like my angels to have their fling.'

So she drew off her royal jewelled net and went with him without demur, perceiving that it would not be easy but demanding nothing better. She did not ask who he was. The blood flowing in her veins assured her that from now onwards she was beyond the reach of choice.

As to his trappings, they were those, she saw, of a learned man. He would teach her to know what she understood and she, without letting him guess it, would help him to understand what he knew. In that way they would discover each other and in doing so find their own meanings.

So they went on together.

'You must hate me as much as you love me,' he told her. 'Only that will suffice.'

And she realized that what would suffice for him was to be the order of their days. Whatever might suffice for her would have to adapt itself to that. Furthermore, it came to her, as something felt rather than known, that all is really no better than nothing, that the heart of a woman, entire and undivided, is a heavy burden for a man to carry and that too close is to be too far apart. Only the far can be near.

So, without comment, she accepted both ends of the stick for the sake of the stick itself. The whole, alone, would suffice for her.

After that the word love was never spoken between them. As far as they were concerned, there was nothing in it that would correspond to Cupid's darts, nor of the glue that sticks together the chapters of a romantic tale. Rather, it was the ultimate goal, the durable fire towards which they went, travelling through the land and their lives, sleeping contentedly by night and by day contentedly wrangling.

Nevertheless, her nature was such that she longed for the small intimate gestures that sweeten relationship — grace-notes, as it were, to the melody — and instinctively she would reach out her hand to pick him berries from a hedge or ripe fruit from a tree — and then, remembering the two ends of the stick, hastily withdraw it. But once, as they passed a silversmith's workshop and forgetting what she had undertaken, she took up a little silver ship, its sails plump with the wind.

He eyed the craftsmanship with pleasure but made no move to receive it.

'If you give me gifts' he told her, gravely 'you make it impossible for me to give them to you.'

Hurriedly, she set it back on the shelf.

'You could sail to the ends of the Earth,' she told him.

'I have seen the ends of the Earth,' he replied. 'I am now concerned only with walking through it.'

And she saw that all she could give him was herself if, indeed, he could, or would, accept it. At the same time she had to *be* herself for her sake and also for his, so that the woman-stuff in her might waken what was in him of woman. If to please him she attempted to alter herself, something in him would also be altered and they would lose each other. She had to be as she was.

'Look, Rest-harrow!' she cried one day, excitedly falling to her knees in the grass of some farmer's field. 'Oh, it is so rare a thing. It only grows where the plough has been.'

And he, half puzzled, half indulgent, looked down at her, marvelling.

'What curious creatures women are! The finding of a small pink flower can make them content for a whole day.'

'Can the Milky Way do as much for you?'

'It can set me off on further questions and questions are better than contentment.'

But she saw that there was envy in him and exasperation that this should be so. At the same time his mind was hard at work analysing all that was moving in him.

'We will celebrate it in the village tonight and dance at the Festival.'

'Not I,' he said. The idea was grotesque. 'One flower is very much like another. There are better things to celebrate. Besides, I have never learnt to dance.'

'It is not a matter of learning,' she told him. 'It comes as easily as walking. One of my father's bards has written "The first and last duty of man is to dance." ' *

'A bard should be busy with higher matters — what spells the Druids knew and the songs the morning stars sing together, not rustic cavortings to the rhythm of a bagpipe.'

Nevertheless, the night found them in the village square under the eye of the Watchman, she tripping and turning, lost in the music, he standing at the edge of the dance, possessively regarding her as she danced from hand to hand, his foot, all unknown to him, tapping out the tune.

When it was over he received her eagerly into his arms as though he had been given back something that had been lost.

'You danced!' she cried triumphantly. 'Within yourself — I saw it! One moment more and you would have been with me, at the very heart of the motley.'

'Nonsense!' He would not admit it. But the music was clearly alive in him as he drew her away, held closely against him, to the lane that led to the river.

They leaned against the earth embankment, arm in arm, watching the water, as the lines of foam leapt over each other, hurrying to the sea.

'Even the waves are dancing!' she said.

'It's cold they'd be, sir and lady.' A man's voice spoke behind them. 'And swift too, the tide's on the ebb!'

They turned to find the village Watchman eyeing them anxiously.

'Cold, cold and dark you'd find the black waters. Any kind of life is better than that. Let the two of you sleep the night away. Hope comes in the morning, you'll see.' And edging himself more closely to them, he flung out his arms as if to seize them.

'Thank you, Watchman, but have no fear. There will only be fish in your river tonight. You can go back and cry your "All's Well" '

'Then I hope it will be a true cry!' The man turned unwillingly away, glancing back from time to time as he returned to the square.

'What was all that about?' she asked, surprised at the intrusion.

'Can't you guess?' He laughed at her. 'The fellow had seen us

* James Stephens.

leaving the dance and followed us, sensing a pact between us and hoping to prevent it.' He made a gesture towards the river. 'Down there! You and I together, making an end of it all.'

She was shocked. 'How could he imagine such a thing?' The very thought made her shiver.

'How indeed?' He laughed again.

'Even so . . .' His face grew thoughtful and she saw that something in him was taking a certain pleasure in imagining the drama, seeing their bones of coral made, hearing the sea-nymphs ringing their bells. 'Even so, we would have become a village legend told around the turf fires as long as the grass grows green. Something for poets to rhyme about.'

'I've no wish to become a legend. I prefer the present moment.'

'Here and gone in the blink of an eye!'

'And here again at the next blink.'

So, splitting moments as though they were hairs, he discoursing on time and eternity, she, while absorbing his erudition, maintaining that the one and the other were components of the essential Now, they left the river that might have made them a bardic theme and went towards the night. And the night resolved all differences and sent them, newly arguing, into the newness of the day.

Thus, living with the contraries, they came to know each other. She felt herself growing within him, putting on new leaves, like a plant, and knew — though she would not let him know that she knew — that he, albeit unwittingly, dwelt within her as in a tent, ripening as a fruit does, unknowing, unaware.

Once when they came to a country town he stopped beside a market stall and came away bearing two small objects — a carven wooden cow and a hen — which he put into her hand.

A secret joy flooded her. He had given her a gift!

'Why these?' she asked, folding them closely to her breast.

'What else?' he said, with his mocking laugh. 'You have not, as I have, seen yourself when we make our way past the steadings. The fox creeps cunningly through the bracken, the otter splashes in the stream, the roebuck goes leaping through the glen but it is these, the two most stupid of all creatures, that catch your eye and enthrall you.'

'Ah, but it's these who are the wise ones! I could watch them for ever.'

'You could, but that's the woman in you! Only a farmer would look at them twice and that because they are useful to him.'

'But remember how thoughtful she is, the cow, brooding, pondering, bearing all things.'

'That is merely chewing the cud — ruminating, it is called. She hasn't a thought in her head.'

'The bards know better. They say of her:

"And blown by all winds that pass
    and wet with all the showers
She walks amid the meadow grass,
    and eats the meadow flowers."†

'I would like to live my life like that.'

He considered this. 'Well perhaps you do. But if you are eating flowers in the rain it would be wiser to wear a cloak and that the cow does not have.'

'I meant it as a metaphor.'

'Ah, metaphors!' And what metaphor have you for the hen, the gossip of the farmyard? Cluck, cluck, cluck she goes all day and if there isn't anybody to hear it she cluck, cluck, clucks to herself, foolish bird.'

'Not when Chanticleer is beside her. She is then as mute as a stone. And, too, when she is mothering. There is a saying among the folk that the little hen hatches her eggs because her heart listens.'

'There's your metaphor, the listening heart.'

'Well, all female creatures have it.'

'But not that feather-brained bunch of feathers. I could never believe it. She probably sleeps the time away while her speckled heat-conducting plumage brings the chicks to birth.'

'Sleeping or waking, I think the heart listens. An ancient bard has declared it.'*

He eyed her thoughtfully.

'I shall have to ponder on that' he said. 'And on you and your folk and your ancient bards and all your farmyard friends.'

'Will Aristotle make room for such things?' She tossed him the question lightly.

'That will appear,' he tossed back to her, as they went on, putting the road behind them along with the summer days, their differences playing upon each other and making one composite sameness as of sunlight and its shadow. And soon the time of gold was upon them, with fruit heavy on the trees and morning grass white with frost.

† R L Stevenson.
* The Tao. The Song of Solomon.

A day, sparkling as though with stars, found them beside an apple orchard gazing at the rosy globes giving off light, like lanterns.

'Pick one!' said a soft, sibilant voice, and they turned to find a sleek narrow-headed man regarding them quizzically.

'Are they yours?' she asked, rapt at the beauty of the scene.

'Not mine, but I am in charge of them.' And with a gesture towards the fruit, the man slipped silkily away.

She hesitated, half afraid. What if the farmer came and protested? Even so, unable to resist, she put up her hand and picked a lantern. It lay like a crimson orb in her palm — a world, she thought — and bit into it.

'Are you not going to share it with me?' The voice at her side was sardonic.

'That would be breaking your rule,' she mocked him. 'I am to give you no gift, remember?'

'This is not a gift,' he replied. 'It is something you cannot fail to offer and I, like any other man, cannot fail to accept such a fruit from a woman. Surely your bards have told you that! It makes us privy to the opposites — good and evil, light and dark, yes and no, I will, I will not. Failing the knowledge that these bring we are nothing more than the beasts of the field. You a simple cow, perhaps.' Now he was mocking her.

'And you the cock that crows in the morn, telling the world that the Sun has risen. As if,' she bantered, 'it did not know! The very sod trembles to it.' She thrust the apple into his hand and watched him eat the rest of the world.

'That fellow was more like a snake than a man.' He flung the core away. 'Did you notice he had no lids to his eyes?'

'No, it was his voice that moved me — the enchantment in it! I could not refuse.'

'If enchantment, then also danger. They, too, are opposites and instruments of fate.'

'I accepted one for the sake of the other. Let fate do as it will.'

'It must do so. It cannot help it. It was fate, after all, that brought us together.'

'And perhaps the locusts!' she said slyly.

'Locusts again!' He was mystified. 'More of your bardic law, I suppose.'

'They belong to an endless story,' she said, secretly delighting in the fact that there was one thing she knew that he did not.

'Well, we all belong to an endless story, bards, philosophers and locusts, though I would hardly call the locust a philosopher.'

'How can we tell? Maybe he, too, concerns himself with the fire beneath the depths of the sea!'

He laughed the absurdity away and then again he was serious.

'I wonder,' he said, and there was wistfulness in his voice. 'I wonder if there will come a time or, indeed, a question, however small, when we have nothing to argue about — a christening cup for a grandchild, say?'

'No,' she said promptly, with conviction. 'Even in such a case you, for reasons doubtless logical, would demand that the handle should be square and I would want it round.'

His eyes glittered. He sighed with relief. They would never sit cosily by the fire nodding in concert over this thing or that. There would still be cut and thrust between them. He would never be bored.

So they went on, the apple doing its work within them, the endless story unwinding. But the far-off, thought-engendered child was never to be part of it, nor yet the silver cup. One day, as they clambered over a stile, he gave a sudden cry of pain and put his hand to his heart. 'I must see an apothecary,' he gasped, leaning heavily on her shoulder. But herbs and simples could not bar the door that was now swinging wide before him.

He took the situation philosophically, lying, self-communing, in his bed while she sat quietly beside him, trying, in spite of all she felt, not to distress him with her distress and to summon up what of philosophy she could find in herself.

Once he spoke, reaching for her hand.

'I have come to the conclusion that he was wrong. He should not have looked back.'

'Orpheus?' The memory of their first meeting flew like a bird to her mind.

'Yes. He should have known that she would follow.'

'As far as the wind blows and the sky is blue.'

'But, instead, he condemned her to the Underworld. One does not forgive him for that.'

'But, even there, he would not have lost her. She would be mindful of him.'

'The mind is not enough,' he said. 'The mind does not suffice.'

And she saw that at long last he had let fall the strong pole that had supported him all his life; that now he was vulnerable to other parts of himself.

'There is something to be said for the heart. It, too, perhaps, has its reasons.' He smiled, as though mocking himself, and turned his head away.

She knew that he would not turn again. Unlike Orpheus, he would trust her to follow or, at any rate, not to leave him. His hand was still within hers when they came to the end of the chapter — though not of the Endless Story.

So, she retraced her steps alone, walking through the thrice-nine lands with birds swooping and crying around her, doing her keening for her.

She would go back to her father's house, cherishing all that had happened to her. It was not so much remembering as a kind of not-forgetting. She would not allow to fall into Lethe the concord she had known, nor the fateful meeting with her other self.

Her father could give her away as he would — prince or pauper, it did not matter. She would live with either contentedly, making no demands. For she knew, from her familiarity with the tales, that to live happily ever after is something that in a single lifetime cannot be realized twice.

Such a happening is not in the nature of things . . .

Written for 'Parabola' on the theme of Tradition and Transmission, 1988.

The Black Sheep

'NO NO,' said my mother, '*Jacob* was the good son.'

But I preferred Esau. Is there a child who can hear 'Bless me, even me also, O my father,' and not groan for Esau? And what, after all, had the poor man done? It is a bad thing to be hungry. It is a difficult thing to be the eldest — the pomp, the responsibility, the burden of setting a good example. What firstcomer, with a combative, ambitious brother at his heel, does not sometimes long to forget it all and settle for lentil soup?

Besides, there was that business of the goatskins. 'Wasn't that cheating?' I asked my mother. And she, ever honest, squirmed and twisted, struggling with her sense of justice, her wish not to set herself up against authority and her natural irritation with an argumentative child. She could not explain, if indeed she realized it, that Jacob was the great fox of history, the crafty turner of all moral tables, the man of paradox who by stealing a thing that was not his, came to consort with angels — those going up and those going down — and by struggling with one of them, made that thing his own.

She cast around in her pool of maxims and thankfully fished one up. 'Esau,' she said, as though settling the matter for ever, 'Esau was the black sheep of the family.' Well, that was something I could accept — and without disloyalty. If Esau was a black sheep, so were all my best-loved friends — Ishmael and the Prodigal Son, Dan in *Jo's Boys*, Peter Rabbit, my Uncle Cecil and Major Battle.

Uncle Cecil's blackness was a grown-up secret, a thing of nods and becks and hints. All we really knew of it was that he had married — a last straw apparently — a lady whom my mother described as 'some sort of Hindoo.' But we well understood Major Battle's weakness. 'Not before the children,' said the gossips, tossing their heads and sipping the air in the manner of thirsty geese. And the children, neither shocked nor surprised, said to each other: 'Whisky!'

What *was* a black sheep, I asked myself. Obviously, in the general view, one full of iniquity. If so, might I not be one myself, in spite of the tireless efforts of parents, teachers and friends? But was the general view the right one? Can a leopard change his spots — and if he can, should he? Was a black sheep just a white sheep dirtied or black in his own right — accepting his colour, proud of it and his three bags full of wool? Did there exist another world where black sheep thought of their erring lambs as the white sheep of the family?

No answer came. Perhaps the question was its own answer and would drop its fruit when it ripened. I was still many years away from discovering the Chinese symbol of the Great Ultimate, black fish with white eye, white fish with black, the opposites reconciled to themselves and to each other within the encompassing circle. It was in my future, however, and because it was there it sent back messengers from time to time as a river at its sea-mouth sends back news to the source.

One thing seemed certain — even the nursery rhymes declared it — that for white to be truly white, lily and snow, it needed its dark opposite. Frost and jet between them — attraction, repulsion and interaction — brought forth the ten thousand colours. Good, it seemed, in life as in story, was pallid and colourless. It needed to be touched by bad to blush and know itself. Where would poor Cock Robin have been — an ordinary bird in an ordinary bush — if he had not met the sparrow? All unknown to history; and his funeral dirge — oh, the birds of the air a-sighing and a-sobbin' — unwritten and unsung. Who cares about the goodness of Flopsy, Mopsy and Cottontail until it is contrasted with the behaviour of their brother Peter? It does not exist till then.

Indeed, Peter Rabbit in his own miniscule way is one of the true black sheep of literature. Like Alcott's Dan, he retains his integrity against all odds, refusing firmly to conform, withstanding every genteel effort to sickly him o'er with white. Poets are made of the same stuff. There is no easy way home for them, either. They must cut their own path through thorn and thicket, like Uncle Cecil and Major Battle.

No matter on how small a scale — Homer in a paragraph, the world in a grain of sand — the relation between the antagonists was always exactly the same; Jemima Puddleduck finding her *raison d'être* only when she encountered the foxy-whiskered gentleman, Tom Kitten merely a kitten till Samuel Whiskers and Anna Maria wrapped him up in the dough.

And when I came to the fairy tales there was no change in the established pattern, the landscape merely widened. 'I can't think,' said my mother, 'what makes you so fond of Rumpelstiltzkin! The miller's daughter is so much nicer.'

Much nicer, but much less interesting. There were, however, certain maidens who were something more than comely ciphers, those like the Goose Girl and Little Two-Eyes, brave and defenceless as wounded hares; and the peerless, fearless Sleeping Beauty, grasping her fateful spindle. But I care for them and their lovely princes far more now than I did then. If I am true to my memory, the heroes and heroines have all one face, bland and featureless. It is the lineaments of the villains — dwarf, giant and stepmother, wicked fairy, dragon, witch — that leap to me now across the years. Each one is different, each is its own — pitted, grained and cicatriced, battered by passion and power.

Can I have been one of the Devil's party, as Blake said of Milton, finding Adam and Eve so tenuous, Satan so solid, in 'Paradise Lost'? Was I, like Blake's Black Boy, 'bereaved of light'?

It was possible. And if so it had to be borne. What hero — and I, too, was the hero of a story, my own — could do without a villain? It was the dark ones, after all, on whom everything depended. They awoke the virtues, imposed the conflict and, by strictly throwing the story forward, brought it to its strict end — the achievement of Happy Ever After. Their frightfulness, for me, had a kind of splendour, absolute and without spot, as it were. It was something one could completely count on, even, in a way, respect. You, monsters who are about to die, I salute you!

This uncompromising black and white of the fairy tales was what I needed as a child. It gave me a kind of reassurance. Children, beneath their conforming skins, have aboriginal hearts, savage, untutored, magic-ridden. When the old drums beat below the surface, their feet cannot help stamping. It can be frightening, even appalling, to a child to meet in himself the ancestral ghosts. 'Who am I,' he will ask, 'in this situation — caught between the world of the sun and the dark corroboree? Am I alone, unique, eccentric, the only one of my kind?'

'No, you are not,' say the fairy tales. And they bring out their comforting brood of dragons, each with a paladin prince to match. They put the thing in its proper perspective; for every inner insubstantial shadow they provide a palpable counterpart that will bear examination. Cut out the spectres from the tales — there are those I hear, who would gladly do this while sticking to Herod and the atom bomb — and you cut out their healing meaning. When one knows that the outer world has dragons — a couple, perhaps, at every corner — it is easier to contemplate the ones within oneself.

Neither Grimm's stories nor any myth frightened me as a child — not gorgon, Minotaur nor chimera, nor the terrible, beautiful 'Juniper Tree.' But the sea-captain behind my door, limping on his left leg and tapping the wall with a pencil — he was another matter. 'You see,' said my mother every night, grandly flinging the door wide, 'he's not there — and you know it.' I did, indeed, but she was speaking of a real captain. Mine was, alas, inside my head, and that door she couldn't open.

'But Grimm is so coarse and blood-bespattered — can you bear the cruelty?' people ask me. I can and could. These stories have grown and are not invented; they are old trees rooted in the folk, massive and monolithic. There is nothing in them that is subjective, or personal or neurotic. Simple, tribal crypto-grams, their cruelty is not for cruelty's sake but to show that life is cruel. 'This is how things are,' they say — and how mellifluously they say it! 'The battle of black and white is joined and must be fought to the end. Sit under our shade or go your way, it is all the same to us.'

They make no requirements. One can choose. And how much rather would I see wicked stepmothers boiled in oil — all over in half a second — than bear the protracted agony of the Little Mermaid or the girl who wore the Red Shoes. There, if you like, is cruelty, sustained, deliberate, contrived. Hans Andersen lets no blood. But his tortures, disguised as piety, are subtle, often demoralizing. It is all subjectivity here, a great performer playing the organ, with emphasis on the Vox Humana. Ah, how pleasant to be manipulated, to feel one's heartstrings pulled this way and that — twang, twang, again and again, longing, self-pity, nostalgia, remorse — and to let fall the fullsome tear that would never be shed for Grimm.

I enjoyed it. I even wallowed in it, yet I never could quite understand why I felt no better for it. Perhaps I missed the pagan world with its fortitude and strong contrasts. I and my soul were one there, but Andersen seemed to separate us. He suggested instead — how coaxingly — that I should not try to fight with dragons but just be a dear good child. He reminded me, sweetly, of the rewards and what, alas, awaited me if I should happen to fail. But his characters were so enervating, I needed more bracing companionship — a giant, perhaps, and a witch or two. There were no black sheep in Andersen — he would have found the idea distasteful. (You can't count the Ugly Duckling, for he was really a swan.) They were all white sheep, some clean, some dirty, but a homogeneous flock.

Nor could Hans Andersen have invented, I thought — he wouldn't even have wanted to — a villain strong and dark and lovely and worthy to be loved. For me there was such a one in Grimm, the 13th Wise Woman in 'Little Briar Rose,' or, as she is more popularly known, the Wicked Fairy in 'The Sleeping Beauty.'

To begin with, she was a victim of chance. The King had only 12 gold plates. Someone had to be left out. It might have been any of the others but it happened to be she. And because of that, to the end of time, men would scorn and point at her and spit upon her shadow. None of them would stop to think that if she had not brought her gift of death, Beauty would neither have slept nor awakened. There had, I knew, to be instruments — things were made wrong that they might come right — and the lot had fallen to her. For this unluck I pitied her, and because I pitied her I loved her, and because I loved her she had to be blameless.

'You love the Wicked Fairy?' said my parents, raising their eyebrows at each other. Had they a crow in a swan's nest? It seemed only too likely. I had to bear the opprobrium, since I couldn't deny what my heart said. And because I bore it, the Wicked Fairy — or so it seemed to me then — loosed for me many many secrets. I saw that she and her 12 sisters, constantly exchanging roles, played every part there was. Myth, fairy-tale, life — it was all the same. The 13 wise women were nymph, mother, crone, goddess; Kore, Demeter and Astarte, the Witches, the Fates and the Furies. They birthed the babe, blessed the bride-bed and swaddled the corpse for its clay cradle.

Their business was the whole of life. And in another story on another day, the 13th would perhaps be the Good Fairy and another sister would turn the key that set the wheel in motion. She did not need my love and pity, but I had to feed them both in myself in order to see her plain.

Plain? She was crystal! A tall, glass, shiny mountain from which I could see with a new eye the world of fairy-tale. Hero and villain, white sheep and black, there they stood in their fixed positions, opposite and separate and yet not unrelated. Rather, they were two ends of the stick, thrust away from and drawn to each other because of the stick itself.

And what of the stick, the space between, that divides and also connects? Here again was my old question and I carry it with me still. Somewhere, I thought, in my childishness, there is a place between North and South, where all opposing brothers meet, where black and white meet, where black and white sheep lie down together, where St George has no enmity to the dragon and the dragon agrees to be slain.

'What happened to Esau?' I asked my mother.

She smiled as one bringing good news.

'After Jacob wrestled with the angel, Esau came to him with his arms wide and fell on his neck and kissed him.'

So — the wheel had turned. The story had run its full course, through discord to harmony, through conflict to Happy Ever After.

'O my shadow,' I said to myself, 'I will not let thee go except thou bless me.'

First published in 'The New York Times', 1965.

A Radical Innocence

'LET'S try fantasy!' said the editor, scratching his head for a subject.

'But that is a word I do not like. It has come, through misuse, to mean something contrived, far from the truth, untrustworthy.'

'Well, what about this? How can we, in our technological age, foster imagination in children?'

'That's large — and, for me, too pompous. I would just say feed and warm them and let the imagination be — though wonder, I think, is a better word. Or, perhaps — *pace* William Wordsworth — intimations of reality.' Does it *need* fostering, anyway? And is technology your only villain? What about education? We learn very quickly from books and teachers not to respect our childhood wisdom. Wasn't it Aldous Huxley who said —

Ram it in, ram it in,
 Children's heads are hollow,
Ram it in, ram it in
 Still there's more to follow.

Can it be for this that we stretch our wings, to fly from what is a real treasure to the dubious world of facts? Hasn't it ever surprised you that the cinema will happily rush us from seed to blossom, from beginning to end in the space of a second, but never attempts the more interesting adventure — the following of the lily, say, back to its basic bud? Yet it's all there, the bud is the clue, you have to go back to that. No: back is, perhaps, the wrong word. You need to be there as well as here — simultaneous experience — to recapture what was. And to know that it is.

As to preserving this experience; I can only speak for myself, of course, but I have always been grateful that nobody, as you put it, fostered my imagination. It was not deplored, neither was it

... given room. It was taken as a matter of course — another fact, like whooping cough, another fact, like daylight. Every child has it as a natural inheritance, and all the grown-ups can do is to leave him alone with the legacy. It is the child's own incommunicable experience — perhaps the only thing that is truly his own — and should not be spied on or disturbed.

This, I think, was what AE, the Irish poet, had in mind in 'Germinal' when he imagined a child playing in the dusk — that magical moment between day and night — and the grown-ups calling him in from his dream.

> *Call not thy wanderer home as yet*
> *Though it be late.*
> *Now is his first assailing of*
> *The invisible gate.*
> *Be still through that light knocking,*
> *The hour is thronged with fate.*
>
> *Let thy young wanderer dream on:*
> *Call him not home.*
> *A door opens, a breath, a voice*
> *From the ancient room,*
> *Speaks to him now.*
> *Be it dark or bright*
> *He is knit with his doom.*

He knew that it is in the crack between opposites — dark and light, yes and no, here and there — that the real thing happens.

My childhood was full of such moments — wasn't yours? — and all that I am now somehow relates to them. Of course (and this is inevitable) I was called home from them to supper and bed and the life of the lighted house. But a clever child, a quick, cunning, foxy child, learns to smuggle them in with him and keep them alive in some inner secret cupboard.

'Children, it's late!' my mother would cry, in a voice full of clocks and water-heaters. (Not 'What are you doing — let me share it!') And my father would come striding, giving his impersonation of Zeus in a rage that we never could quite believe in. And then the dusk would catch him and he would fall silent, searching the sky for the first star till he, too, had to be called.

In this question of imagination, of the kind of fate that throngs the hour, so much depends on the quality of the grown-ups. I am grateful now, though I wasn't then (gratitude is a late growth) that I grew up in an atmosphere in which tradition was still part of life, laws few, fixed and simple, and children taken for granted; not 'understood' in our modern sense, not looked upon as a special race but as growing shoots of one whole process — being born, living and dying. My parents never played down to children, nor, on the other hand, did they treat them as equals; we were all just lumps in the family porridge. My parents had, I see now, what W B Yeats called 'a sort of radical innocence,' as though by some thin spider thread they were linked with their own youth. When they joined a game it was not at all for our sakes but for their own enjoyment.

Altruism — that impure emotion — had no part in their natures. If he lost the throw in a game of chance, my father would stalk off in a huff, saying some one had cheated. And beating my mother at Old Maid was like slapping a goddess in the eye; a most discourteous act. In our family life it was their moods that were to be respected, not ours. It was clear that they had their own existence — busy, contained, important. And this, as I now see, left us free for ours. There is no greater burden for a child than parents who want to live *his* life; contrariwise, when they are content to be simply landscape and leave the child to make his own map, there is no greater blessing. His mind can turn in upon itself (and I don't at all mean introspection) wondering, pondering, absorbing the world, re-enacting in himself all the myths there are. And for this he needs nothing — no thing, no person, unless, perhaps, another child.

Not long ago I came upon two little girls sitting motionless on the floor, gazing in silence at a cardboard box. Gradually it dawned on me that they were watching television. What they were seeing I could not tell — more things in heaven and earth, I would guess, than are dreamt of in the philosophy of *Top Cat* and *Wagon Train*.

And I remembered how, for a long period in childhood, I was absorbed in the experience of being a bird. Absorbed, not lost, knowing, had I been faced with it, that I was also a child. Brooding, busy, purposeful, I wove the nests and prepared for eggs as though the life of all nature depended on the effort. 'She can't come, she's laying,' the others would say, arriving for a meal without me. And my mother, deep in her role of distracted housewife, would come and unwind my plaited limbs and drag me from the nest: 'If I've told you once, I've told you a hundred times, no laying at lunchtime!'

Not, 'You are mad. I fear for your future. We must find a psychiatrist.' Simply, not at lunchtime! Could she, too, once have been a bird, I sometimes wonder now? Not that one ever could have asked her, she would have thought it fanciful. But her homes were always a bit like nests, warm and well-fitted to her shape, rounded as though by the thrust of feathers — and mine are just the same. Even a hotel room becomes a nest for me, something perching in the fork of a branch, or hanging from a leaf by a thread like the mansion of the golden-crested wren.

She had, too, flashes of inspiration, when the streak of poetry in her Scottish blood broke up the daily pattern. Picnic breakfasts miles from home; or a table-cloth spread out on the carpet and supper on the floor. The sudden lively moments! She would have called them merely moods, but they seem to me now a kind of wisdom, as though she knew instinctively that nothing brings so much energy as the breaks in a regular routine. Full of the saws and customs that are handed down from the generations, innocent, honest, predictable — it was from her we learned, far more than from our less dependable father, to be ready for the unexpected, even to the point of knowing that truth can be juggled with.

'Is this Mrs MacKenzie?' asked my father, pointing with the carving knife at a chicken on the dish. (The fowls fattened for the table were all called after friends and relations.) 'If it is, I'm not hungry. I was fond of her.'

'No,' said my mother, 'it's Nancy Clibborn.' And fixed us with a hypnotic glance as though we were serpents and she a snake-charmer.

'Good!' he exclaimed, slicing a wing. 'I never could abide that woman — far too thin and scraggy.'

And we, who that very morning had assisted Mrs MacKenzie to the chopping block, were left to sit in silent judgment. The facts, indeed, had been distorted. But we knew somehow that this was a matter less of morals than of expediency. Men — it was simple — have to be fed, otherwise everyone suffers. So we sat there like the three wise monkeys, seeing, hearing and speaking no evil. It is fortunate for grown-ups that children understand them so well.

But there is always one law for the rich and another for the poor. And we, in similar circumstances, did not get off so lightly.

'You told me a lie!' my father accused me when I denied leaving Lord Nelson and Lady Hamilton, two rag dolls — christened by him — out in the rain all night. It was his air of righteousness that had made me lie, and now his righteousness frightened and shamed me. 'I am disappointed,' he said sincerely, as though he were Adam upbraiding Cain.

Then he flung what he hoped was the last straw — 'And letting them catch their death of cold!' But miraculously it saved me. Great and little, there they were, and standing in the crack between them I was whole again and free of guilt. All that mattered to me now was to rush Lord Nelson to the fire and dry his kapok body.

If I speak of my parents it is because parents are a child's first gods and responsible, whether they know it or not, for many seeds of fate. Later they dwindle to human stature and later still, when the process of nature reverses itself, the child becomes the parent's parent. I never had the opportunity to become, in this sense, my father's mother, for he died while still very young. But for me his death was a germinal moment, strongly fixing my memories. And gradually, as hearsay was added, I came to believe that I saw him plain, in feeling if not in fact. I remember his melancholy, which was the other side of his Irish gaiety, and know that it was catching and inheritable. When he had taken a glass, he would grieve over the sack of Drogheda in 1649 till everyone around him felt personally guilty. We, not Oliver Cromwell, were responsible for the blood and slaughter. He was Irish, too, in argument, determined to have the last word, even — or perhaps specially — with children.

'Get that damned dog off my chair, or I'll send him to live in the stables!'

'Father, such language!' we protested, protecting a precious mongrel pet.

Criticism he did not like. And from his own flesh and blood — really, it was too much.

'Mealy-mouthed piety! If a man can't say "damned" in the bosom of his own family, where *can* he say damned, I'd like to know!'

'It wasn't "damned", it was "dog", we said. 'We never use that word to Tippu. He thinks he's a little boy.'

'Then he'll have to learn better,' Father retorted. And proceeded, in a voice that would have melted marble, to teach the necessary lesson. And that, for us, was the end of Tippu. He left us, for less than a handful of silver, and slavishly followed at Father's heel. He became, in fact, a dog.

Arguments, yes. But no explanations. I cannot remember that he, or anybody else, ever explained anything. It was clear from their general attitude that our parents had no very high opinion of our intelligence, but at the same time, apparently, they expected us to know everything. We were left, each on our desert (but by no means unfruitful) island, to work out things for ourselves.

'Father,' we said to the back of the newspaper. 'Doesn't God have a wife?'

'No.'

'Then who does the cooking?'

'Nobody.'

Extraordinary! One son, no wife and cooks for himself.

'Father, what is God's other name?'

'Other name? He hasn't got one.'

'Not the duke of? Or even mister?'

'No, I tell you, just plain God.'

'Then why do you call him Harry?'

Down came the newspaper with a crash. His eye gathered its battle fervour.

'I've never done such a thing in my life! Tell me the time, place and circumstance when you've heard me call God Harry!' He was probably seeing himself as we saw him every Sunday, in his tussore suit with the crimson cummerbund, gravely singing the last hymn as he handed the offertory plate to the vicar. A pillar of Christendom, the ideal church-warden. Would such a man have spoken so? Never in this world!

'But you do, Father, every day. By the Lord Harry this, by the Lord Harry that — you're always saying it.'

'Jumping Jehosephat!' he cried, rolling his eye at Heaven for help. 'Haven't you heard of figures of speech?' And he threw the newspaper at our heads and went calling, as usual, for my mother.

Well? Figures of speech were Greek to us, and we were left with the suspicion, already familiar, that we still had a lot to learn. But this, in itself, was a kind of education. Had he explained, we would have been furnished with an indigestible piece of knowledge but very little the wiser. As it was, another question was laid down in us to grow and breed and seek its meaning.

It cannot have been long afterward — though time is different at different ages and this can play the memory false — that for me, at least, the answer came.

It was dark, midnight or early morning, and the room was cobwebby with sleep. The cloudy grown-ups were pulling us from the cocooning blankets — even the baby from the cradle — and urging us to the window. There in the sky, over the mountain, as long, it seemed, as the mountain itself, was a huge bright tail of stars. It pulsed and glowed and wavered and I had the feeling, though I heard nothing, that it made a humming sound. We were told, in whispers, to look and remember for we would not see this sight again for another 70 years, the time the great tail would take to circle the universe. Then they said it was Harry's Comet.

'Halley, not Harry,' my mother insisted, later correcting what she called my mistake. But I merely assumed she was bad at spelling, unable to tell an R from an L. For by this time, the Lord Harry and his comet had become part of my own private mythology, a voice from the ancient room. Seventy years! I would have to be old as my great-aunts, who themselves seemed as old as the Grey Women of Perseus, one eye and one tooth between them. Even so, if he was coming back, I would wait for him.

Waiting for Harry! That is one of the things I have been doing all my life — imagining him out there on his appointed course, trailing his tail among the galaxies, while children crowd at the windows to see him and babies are plucked from the cradles. he came to mean, in spite of his apparent beach-combing of the universe, something stable and purposeful, a wanderer only in the sense that his wandering was according to law. The stars, for me, were his witnesses. Somewhere among them Harry was moving, faithfully pursuing his mysterious treadmill to the end of the world and back.

Where is he now? In Andromeda? Or wrapping his tail round Orion's head, a transient fillet of gold? It doesn't matter. He can't help turning and returning — some time, I suppose, in the eighties. They've begun already to mention his name — always (will newspapers never learn?) always spelling it Halley. And do you know what they plan to do, in your technological age? Shoot a rocket right through his tail to see what it is made of! And then they will say it is only stardust. This troubles me. What will the children think, I wonder? Who will reassure them?

'Don't look at me!' said the editor.

'Why not? You're the very man! If I'm not here when Harry comes back — think of the slips between cup and lip! — you must tell the children. Say . . . that nothing is *only* this or the other; that stardust alone can't explain a comet; that there are laws and eternal patterns and Harry is part of them.'

He gave me a look that seemed like a promise.

'O.K.' he said. 'I will.'

First published in 'The New York Times', 1965.

The Death of AE: Irish Hero and Mystic

HIS story is the story of a soul, and therefore cannot be bound by geographical limits or biographical events. I come into it merely as a recorder, a sort of apprentice *file* of his last years, and the days that led up to his dying.

I met him at a time when it was growing late in his life and while it was still early in mine.

I had been brought up by an Irish father and a mother of Scottish extraction in a home in the wilds of Australia where, amid the Antipodean sounds there sounded continually the rhythms of another hemisphere, the place they both called 'Home.' The Celtic Twilight had cast its long blue light over my childhood but by the time I had crossed the ocean it had practically turned into night. I was fortunate to catch it, as it were, by the tail.

One of the first things I did on arriving in England was to send AE (George Russell), then editing *The Irish Statesman*, a small poem, tentatively, with no covering letter of explanation, just a stamped addressed envelope for return. And the envelope indeed came back — but with three guineas in it! Not only that, but there was, too, a letter from AE saying he felt the poem could not have been written by anybody who was not Irish and a suggestion that if I was ever in Ireland I should come to see him and bring some more poems.

If I was ever in Ireland — and I bent towards it all my thinking life! And anyway, I was about to visit my father's relations and that would make it possible to accept the invitation.

At Merrion Square in Dublin I was welcomed as though I were an expected Avatar. I was overwhelmed to find myself in a painted forest, every wall a woodland; to have the one unchipped cup picked out for me, the poems I had brought at once accepted and an invitation given to come again on my way back to England.

I went off to my relatives in the southern counties in a maze of happiness and wonder. How could it have happened that this world I had dreamed of for so long had, in the person of AE — whose famous initials I seemed always to have known — drawn me into it?

Only a month or two before, I had stood in the Australian bush, listening to the silence — a pursuit I had been about ever since early childhood. Be still long enough, I thought, and the trees would take no notice of me and continue whatever it was they were doing or saying before I happened upon them. For nothing was more certain, to my mind, than that they lived a busy and communicative life which ceased — as at a command given — whenever I appeared. I have never lost it, this sense of the secret life lived by forests that withdraws itself at the sound of a footstep. And the painted woodland of AE's office, all of it from his own hand, had its own particular kind of silence. If one sat with it long enough, would one hear what it was saying? Would I ever get the chance to listen?

But now I was off to the long green hills, of which I had been so often told, and a family that, I soon discovered, had no need for poetry, except in a book; by whom Cathleen ni Houlihan — perhaps because they lived with her, cheek by jowl — was dismissed as an aberration and where twilight was simply twilight, a patch of time between night and day. Moreover, my enthusiasm for these things was cause for family murmurings. Was Robert's streak of Quixotry — going off to Ceylon to plant tea and then to Australia to plant sugar — showing up in his daughter? It was earnestly hoped not.

'I don't approve of you taking up with men who see fairies,' said my uncle, shaking a sombre head. 'And going to London to be a writer — well, you'll meet such frightful people. There's a terrible great boastful fellow — his family lived in a white-washed cottage, over there, across the fields . . .' a wave of the hand described the landscape. 'If you meet him, be courteous, but do not pursue the acquaintance. He calls himself Bernard Shaw.'

'Bring her to me. Let her have the choice,' Shaw said, delightedly, when AE later, and with relish, recounted this incident to him.

But all of that was still in front of me and I set out from the home of my family in happy anticipation of my dreadful London life.

I walked through Dublin to Merrion Square and AE and the painted woods. Hadn't I been pressed to return? But I found I could not touch the bell. I was face to face with my diffidence, my inability to believe in my fortune, or to dare to trust my luck.

'It was just politeness,' I told myself. 'A great and busy man like that — he'll not want to be intruded upon.' And I turned away and went back to London.

Three weeks later, answering a knock at my door, who should I find standing there but AE, and under his arm a great parcel of books.

'You're a very faithless girl,' he accused me. 'You said you would come on your way back and then you never turned up. I had these waiting for you.'

'These' were his collected works, each of the many books inscribed.

So — it was true. I had to believe in my good fortune and not waste any of it in asking a useless 'Why?' If there was an answer, it would come in good time. From then on I was as much at home in Dublin as in London and in both cities AE fished up friends for me from his inexhaustible cauldron. For, as well as being his own best friend, he had a talent for friendship, even something more than friendship, for which we have no word. He said once: 'We can hardly tell where our own being ends and another begins or if there is any end to our being. We are haunted by unknown comrades in many moods, whose naked souls pass through ours and reveal themselves to us in an unforgettable instant.'

And, to his mind, these friendships had antecedents. I was to discover this one day when walking with him in Regent Street. I must have made some remark about the strangeness of our meeting — two people from the ends of the earth! He stopped in mid-stride, his round blue eyes growing rounder still with surprise at my ignorance.

'But surely you don't imagine,' he said, 'that this is the first time we've met!'

Well, I did imagine it and was thereupon introduced for the first time to the idea of reincarnation as he understood it. That I did not myself have any inkling of having known him before did not disturb him in the least. He could remember for both while I, listening to his reiterated chantings of the *Bhagavad Gita* and snatches from the old Celtic legends, was happy to accept what I was being told without trying, merely with my mind, to verify it.

But other things I could comprehend. 'We only love what is our own and what is our own we cannot lose.' That needs no verification. Nor did his Law of Spiritual Gravitation. 'Your own will come to you' was a constantly repeated axiom and in a letter to me, dated April '32, he wrote:

Ireland as a nation I have no further interest in. Indeed, I have no interest in nations at all. I feel I belong to a spiritual clan whose members are scattered all over the world and these are my kinsmen. And I would sacrifice any nation, my own quite readily, to promote the interests of that spiritual clan.

As a member of that clan, however humble, I was permitted to see much of the Ireland that he nevertheless loved. I stayed with him often in his beloved Donegal, at Janie's-on-the-Hill above Dunfanaghy — a white-washed cottage where at night one would hear the cows moving about in their stalls below the attic bedroom and in the daytime Janie churning butter or clanging the lid of the iron cauldron that swung on a chain above the peat fire and in which everything was cooked: bread, meat, cake, soup.

Much wisdom was dropped into my ears over mountainy mutton and dark brown bread. Once, talking about poetry, he said: 'All artists should take the vow of poverty, that is, the inside vow. It does not mean that if somebody leaves them a hundred thousand dollars, that they refuse it, but that they stand ready at any time to desert prosperity or fame if these conflict with the spirit.'

Or again, as he later was to write to the Scottish poet, Hugh MacDiarmid: 'We have nothing to write about truly except ourselves. I use the word "ourselves" to include the conscious personality and that vast ocean of life that envelopes us and in which we find our most intimate understanding of the minds of others.' John Eglinton said of him: 'His mind was a natural inhabitant of that region of thought in which myths are "true"'. So, there would be tales told from the *Táin*, while the heroes of Ireland strode invisibly through the room. And, once, teasing me from a pensive mood to laughter, he told me the Story of the Three Druids who decided to live together in hermetic silence. At the end of the first year, the first Druid remarked 'This was a good decision.' At the end of the second year, the second Druid replied 'It was.' And at the end of the third year, the third Druid said 'I must get away from all this chatter.'

From Janie's, he would take me with him on his excursions to friends in the neighbourhood or to those parts of woodland or strand that set up in him the strongest vibrations. Was he intentionally educating me, I wondered! No matter: it was being done, with or without intent.

Once, as we were setting out one morning, I saw, looking down at the little stone-fenced fields below us, an enormous footprint of flowers among the grass. The shape was unmistakable, as though somebody of great size, coming from Uranus, perhaps, had landed on the earth for a moment, taken a step or two upon it and set off again, leaving his mark.

'Look, AE,' I said. 'Someone has been here overnight.'

He glanced calmly at the footprints. 'He has.' he said. 'It often happens.'

So, there was nothing I could show to him and everything he could show to me.

On another occasion, when we had been asked to lunch with his closest of all friends, Mr and Mrs Hugh Law, who lived about a mile away, he glanced down at my London footwear.

'You can't go in those,' he said firmly. 'Our way lies through the deep bog. Haven't you anything stronger?'

I hadn't.

'Well, you'll just have to wear a pair of my boots.'

His boots! But he was twice my size and I wanted to look my best. A cry of horror broke from me but he was away, up the rickety stairs, to return with several pairs of socks, two huge seven-leagued boots and copies of the London *Observer* and the *Times*.

I found that I was to wear them all: Sock upon sock, then the boots, and the *Observer* round one leg, the *Times* the other, securely fastened by AE with what looked like a cow's halter but which turned out to be merely string.

I knew it was a loving act. Kindly meant. All for my welfare. So I bore it in seething silence and followed him, less like a lamb to the slaughter than some ungainly dinosaur cub, readier to kill than be killed.

We came to the bog. AE, serenely chanting Eastern scriptures, walked ahead of me, almost tripping, his feet sure of every step: even his boots knew the way. The other pair — I could hardly be said to be wearing them — evidently did not. I was stuck fast in the bog, as Brer Fox to Tar Baby, and giving vent to more vitriol than I had known there was in the world, let alone in myself. I *hated* the *Bhagavad Gita* and, as for the shining Celtic heroes, let them rot in Hell.

My silent violence must have communicated itself to him as I stood there, unable to move. For he turned, gave one look at me and, to crown all the indignities, burst into peals of laughter.

'I'm a fool!' he declared. 'You don't want a philosophy. You want

[handwritten letter concluding with the signature]

A E .

P L Travers in paper leggings and AE's boots, at the conclusion of his letter to her of 1 July 1927

a life. Slip your feet out and come barefoot. I shall enjoy escorting
a dryad to lunch.'

'But your boots, AE!' I was now contrite.

'Leave them. Let the bog have them.'

And the bog got them — unless he went back and retrieved them
later. All I could see was the newspapers, hurriedly sinking into
the peat as though ashamed, as I had been, of being so burlesqued.

On another occasion and another year, setting out on a painting
excursion with myself at his side — I do not know in which role
he saw me, as daughter, acolyte, apprentice, or as all three — he
thrust into my hands a paint-box, chalks and sketchbook.

'But I can't paint, AE!'

'Of course you can. Everyone can do it.' Later, Augustus John
said the same thing to me: 'If you have one gift you have them
all. One comes to the surface but the others are latent.' And it is
recorded that when they had both been in the same art school,
Yeats said of him that, in spite of being hailed as a budding genius,
or rather because of it, AE refused to accept it. He was set, he said,
on making his mind strong and vigorous and calm and could not
afford the moving emotional life of the artist. 'I prepare myself,'
he declared, 'for a cycle of activities in some other life. I will make
rigid my roots and branches. It is not now my turn to burst into
leaves and flowers.'

Nevertheless, burst he did, no sooner finishing one picture than
starting on another. But one felt that this was less a series of
emotional excursions than his way of finding out about the world
he lived in.

So, having arrived at his chosen position, a long yellow tongue
of sand, laced with a thread of moving water that changed its
colour as the sky changed, I sat beside him, making an occasional
sweep of a crayon but more intent on watching his way of working
than on what was in my sketchbook. Somehow, it seemed to me
that he was seeing more than landscape for he kept looking up
intently at some thing or person that, as far as I was concerned,
was not there.

'Do you see them?' he murmured, half turning to me and then
looking raptly up again.

'No,' I said, awed and regretful. I felt he would have liked me
to see whatever it was that he was seeing, and that in some way,
all unripe, I had failed him.

I put aside my sketchbook and climbed up into a nearby tree,
watching intently as there crowded, swiftly, into the canvas

creatures from some other world: bright, authoritative, beckoning. It was then, as he paused to mix a new colour, that I saw smoke rising from where he sat. Was this part of the process, I wondered? Was he to be wrapt from my mortal eyes? I remained as still as a moth on my branch, watching the course of events.

But the smoke continued to thicken and blacken and the smell of burnt serge rose up like incense.

'AE!' My cry shattered the silence. 'AE! Be careful! You're on fire.' Hand to my mouth, I waited for what would happen next, cursing myself for having, with my mortal voice, broken into an immortal moment.

Calmly, moving serenely from that world to this, he looked down, beheld the smoke and took his pulsing pipe from his pocket.

'My poor wife!' he said, remorsefully. 'She'll have to reline another pocket. Never mind,' he beamed, 'I got them down,' and spread out before me a canvas alight with starry figures.

'And also this, which I rather like.' He turned a page of his sketch-book and there was I upon my branch, not at all part of the scene but in a way witness to it. As if one had stood, unseen, at the portal of Paradise.

All that was his country world. His famous weekly evenings in

P L Travers by AE, sketched on the painting excursion

Dublin were yet another one. Everybody was prodigally made welcome in that room crowded with pictures where, he once told me, Maud Gonne used to sit by the fire, braiding her loose gold-brown hair and keening for the wrongs of Ireland.

Friend met friend there and, as well, enemy met enemy. It was a crossroads. One was reminded of the chapter in *The Candle of Vision* where he speaks of how things and entities draw to themselves their own affinities. No sooner does one become aware of certain stirrings within than he meets others with the same search; or one takes a book from a shelf and finds there what he has already himself thought, or envisaged; or one seeks no friends but discovers many. 'I need not seek,' the passage goes, 'for what was my own would come to me. I knew that all that I met was part of myself and that what I could not comprehend was related by affinity to some yet unrealized forces in my being . . . There is no personal virtue in me other than this, that I followed a path all may travel but on which few do journey . . . None need special gifts or genius. Gifts! There are no gifts. For all that is ours we have paid the price. Genius is not bestowed but won.'

Conversation blossomed in that room. People came and went, drinking from his generous chalice and wandering off to give place to others. And always, moving among them, diffidently bringing in tea and cakes, almost invisibly replenishing cups, a fragile, grey-haired feminine figure came and went, speaking little and to few before disappearing into the beyond of the house.

When I learned that she was AE's wife, I followed her one evening, asking to be allowed to help. Gently and shyly, she put me aside. 'No, no, you go back in. People come to see George, not me.'

But I persisted. And at last, to my delight, she allowed me to help fill the tea-pots and slice up the cake. We became, demurely, friends, sharing the myths and stories like two Old Wives, discovering mutual favourites in her flower garden. For what was he without her? Or, at any rate, from what established contentment did he draw — and bestow upon others — his strength?

After her death, the house in Rathgar lost for him its *genius loci*. Added to this, the demise of his weekly paper, *The Irish Statesman*, gave him the sense that Othello's occupation was gone. It was then that he came to England to live and this, together with his lecture trips to America, gave many people grounds for thinking, even loudly saying, that he had left Dublin for good. But it was not so. He never really withdrew from that root. He constantly assured me of this, as he surveyed the dark walls of his London lodgings. 'In a year or so I may return. I shall want to go to Donegal for three or four months of the year.'

But his many lives of poet, painter, mystic, prose writer, economist, editor, — for all that there was left to do — were gathering into one. The Prodigal Son had already, at some unnoted moment, turned, and was bent towards his Father. Indeed, the very fact that he sensed himself now bound for Heaven, seemed to make him ever more in love with earth, with the planet itself which he continued to write of as a living being with its own eternal memory that could be tapped in meditation.

It had been his custom, when in Dublin or Donegal, to boast to me that Ireland was full of springs of life — Fountains of Hecate, he called them — that the countryside of England lacked. But when he came to live in England and explored the stretches of moor and woodland where his friends lived, Constance Sitwell's in Northumberland, my own in Sussex and those of others, he had to admit, albeit grudgingly, that Hecate was in England too.

His life in London and in America — where farmers, after he had lectured on economics, kept him for hours reciting poetry — was as overflowing as ever, outwardly with friends, many of whom he had not seen for years, and inwardly with poetry. But he was not well. A doctor friend of many years standing, went over him with a pendulum which did not appear to inform him of anything unduly serious. Nevertheless, each time I saw him, which was often, he seemed a little greyer — greyness of skin rather than of hair, with something of his vividness fading. I begged him to see another doctor. Characteristically, he was unwilling: it would hurt the feelings of the man with the pendulum.

But when I went to meet him after his hurried flight from America — his last trip — all the colour had gone from him. He knew he was ill, told me of his symptoms and now he agreed to see a specialist. And again, nothing drastic was prognosed and he was put on a diet of milky food. We agreed that he would leave London and come down to the country where I could take care of him. A date was fixed and I went hunting for one of those turntable sheds so that he could sit in it all day and write, turning with the sun as it turned.

But on the day when he was expected, there was no AE. Only a post card saying he had been hurriedly sent off to a nursing home in Bournemouth.

I waited for news, day after day expecting to hear, wondering what I should do. And at last, on the telephone, was the voice of the pendulum doctor. 'Where the hell are you? Why aren't you at his side? He's asking for you hourly. He hasn't a fortnight to live.'

And I realized that again I had let myself be caught — as long ago on that first encounter in Dublin — in that base, timid streak of myself, diffident and self-distrustful, the fear of being in the way, not wanted. I had not rung the bell in Merrion Square, though I had longed to do it, and I had not rushed to Bournemouth. In the first instance, he had brought me his books; in the second he was asking for me. Again I had not trusted my fate!

I was in Bournemouth as quickly as four wheels could take me and the surgeon was waiting for me. He had examined AE as he had not been examined before, found he had cancer and had operated to give him ease for the time that was left to him. He told me that when he had broken the news to his patient, he had been given a long blue look and words of acceptance of such serenity that he had had to leave the room in tears. 'I have had a very interesting life, I have done nearly all the things I wanted to do. I have rejoiced in the love of friends. What man could want more?'

In the hall of the nursing home, a small man, reddish as to moustache and looking like some shy hedgerow animal, came to greet me: 'You may know of me as John Eglinton.' I did know of him and his clear tidal rhythmic prose had made me think of a tall, languid man, exquisite as a lily. But John Eglinton was now Willie McGee, one of AE's oldest friends and his best biographer. 'I'm glad you've come. He keeps asking.' His voice was gruff with shyness. 'And I can't make up to him for you.' He turned me towards AE's room.

Confronted with reality — with what inevitably is — one does not falter. It sends one its own courage. I opened the door. Serene as Socrates after the hemlock, his long shape was deep in the bed, his beard newly tinged with gold, a remade image of himself. I was sent at once to the chair beside him and laid my head on his pillow. He put up a slow hand to my cheek. 'Kind, sweet girl,' he said smiling. He had had no doubt that I would come.

He was prepared. He knew exactly what he wanted done and was setting about the business of his dying as he had set about his life, practical, unflustered. There was his lawyer to be sent for from Dublin to arrange for his burial; close friends to be apprised of what was to happen so that they should not read of it in the newspapers. A pile of letters lay on the table and fresh batches came with every mail. I was to read them to him and take down the answers dictated by a voice firm for all its frailty. From time to time he would take a rest and we kept a communicative silence, his hand resting on the copy of Tennyson John Eglinton had brought at his request. His first encounter with poetry had been the Tennyson given him by his father. He was thus completing a circle.

Then he would sleep a little or the nurses would come to do what had to be done. One of them said to me wonderingly as she came out of his room: 'There's Somebody in there, isn't there?' as though she were remembering — and yet could not quite remember — a legend she had heard.

'Yes,' I agreed, and said no more. I felt that he would have been happy enough with 'Somebody' and recalled how he had said to his old friend Charles Weekes who had protested that by editing a small provincial paper he was lost to the world: 'I will go back to the stars without any flourish of trumpets. I am not going anywhere I can be seen.'

And yet, while life at its highest point was being lived in that room, there was, in a sense, a flourish of trumpets. The summer days were radiant and there was about them an air of festival. People came and stayed at nearby hotels, happy to see him for a moment and then congregate on the nursing home's lawns. He was not unaware of this.

'Have you been swimming today?' he would ask and because I felt that that made him part of the shining days, I went swimming and talked to him about the tides. Then again I would stand beside him, taking down more letters: 'I am not curable by medical or surgical means' — he did not spare his friends as he did not spare himself. Sometimes he would hand me a special letter: 'I think you would like to keep that.'

Only once, to one who wrote asking to see him, did he tell me to say 'No.' I gently pleaded with him to retract. But he again refused: 'he has had his share of me. That is enough.' Now, looking back upon those days, I see that he was determined to deny himself any emotional deathbed scene; that he needed all his strength for dying — reconciliation would come later, once he was free and away. He had written in *The Avatars:* 'There must be a lordly way out of the body by one of those secret radiant gateways into light. If we do not find this way, I think we must return again and again to the body until we have mastered the secret of death and can take that lordly way out by our own will.'

This, clearly, was what he was trying to do. And except for that one refusal, he saw everybody. I telephoned one whom he had called 'the nicest nasty person he had known' thinking she might like to come. 'Well, but what could I do for him?' she replied. Nothing. There was nothing any of us could do, but much that he could do for us. The mere sight of him, growing more golden every day, was a lesson in living and dying.

There was one friend, however, from whom he urgently wanted to hear. Each day, as I opened the letters, he would ask me 'Nothing from Yeats?' And at last, seeing his disappointment and that this was the one thing he wanted, I dashed off a wire to the poet. 'AE dying and daily looking for a word from you.' It struck home. 'Give my old friend my love,' wired Yeats. And with that AE seemed content. He had come to the end of his wanting.

That day the nursing home seemed to be the still centre of a shining, turning world. His friends were scattered upon the lawns, laughing — nothing here for tears — waiting in the hope that one or another would be sent for to have a glimpse of him. But I noticed that in the high windowed porch a bird was flying backwards and forwards as though restrained, in spite of the windows, by something only birds know from making its way to freedom. It could have flown out but it did not. And remembering the axiom that if a bird flies into a house it will bring death in its train, I thought to myself 'He will die tonight.' And in my heart, if not in my mind, I urged him not, for our sakes, to stay a minute longer.

Oliver Gogarty had wired to me — 'Is there time for me to see my friend?' And I replied 'Come quickly.' He came. 'Be ever blessed for this,' he said, as I led him to the door. And before it closed, I had a glimpse of Dublin's Mocking Bird, its Wag, its Comus, kneeling in tears beside the bed as he kissed the drooping hand.

Gogarty was the last of the visitors. When he had gone AE asked for a drink and was able to move his pillow into an easier position. Why should one not die in comfort? And when a package arrived from Scotland he was able to take a morsel of its contents into his hand and sniff it, saying 'Ah, how good!' It was evident that with this moss and peat and heather — part of his beloved planet — he was soon to be one and a nurse took me by the hand and led me away.

I had hoped I would be allowed to stay to the end. But no: 'It would be too hard for you,' she said. And while I was ready for what was too hard, I felt it was also my part to be ready to do what I was told, and not by any request or protest disturb the harmony.

So, I joined the others — there were about eleven of us — in the big downstairs room that had been put at our disposal. I do not think that one of us was less than happy. He had let his myth sustain him to the last and to me it was a vindication of the Iron Age that such a man could live and die in it. And it was clear to all of us that the Pilgrim, whatever his destination, was content to go towards it. There is a time for tears but this was not it.

So we sat and waited, knowing that upstairs an Event was taking place. At last, about eleven o'clock, the doctor with the pendulum came in quietly and said: 'It is all but over — the death rattle has him.'

And at that I cried out. I heard myself say 'No, no, it will not be like that.' That was not the secret way. He had said to John Eglinton that he was not afraid of death; all he objected to was being what he called 'Thrust out' of the body instead of leaving it as he chose.

'That is not the way of it. Go back!' I cried. 'It is not over.'

Clearly assuming that I was unhinged and with the air of one who pacifies an hysteric, he shrugged and turned away.

After twenty-five minutes, he came in again, shaken and surprised. 'She was right,' he said. 'The rattle ceased. He has quietly breathed his life away.'

At once, Con Curran, AE's lawyer, stood up and said

Let us now praise famous men
and our fathers that begat us.

and we departed.

As I came out, the bird came soaring from the porch. It, too, had found its secret gateway into the light.

And it *was* light — such light as there was, perhaps, on the first day. Never before or since have I seen such a moon. It came up slowly out of the sea, full, golden and enormous, dazzling as the sun.

And I remembered the chapter of the *Bhagavad Gita*, the Eighth, that he had recited to me so often. I have his copy, given to me by his son, Diarmuid, and one particular passage is marked and remarked with different inks and crayons.

I will declare to thee, O best of the Bharatas, at what time yogis, dying, obtain freedom from rebirth. Fire, light, day, the fortnight of the waxing moon, six months of the sun's Northern course — going then and knowing the Supreme spirit, men go to the Supreme. But those who depart, in smoke, at night, during the fortnight of the waning moon, and while the sun is in the path of his Southern journey, proceed for a while to the regions of the moon and again return to mortal birth. These two, light and darkness, are the world's eternal ways; by one man goes not to return, by the other he cometh back upon earth.

Those markings of inks and crayons tell us what he hoped for and worked towards and also that we shall not see his like again. And the great moon, reflecting the sun on its Northern journey, would stand witness for him at whatever tribunal might await him.

The journey back to Dublin was a royal progression. Small gatherings stood at wayside stations to salute him; the High Commissioner for Ireland ceremonially met him at Euston and later he lay in state in the hall of Merrion Square — this man who asked nothing, who was frugal in all things — except in his prodigal giving of himself — lay in state, not in any worldly sense, but merely as a last courtesy to his friends.

With Yeats and de Valera among others in Mount Jerome, Michael O'Donovan, later to be Frank O'Connor, spoke the oration, taking the words from an Eastern scripture:

He saw the lightning in the East
And he longed for the East;
He saw the lightning in the West
And he longed for the West;
But I, seeking only the lightning and its glory,
Care nothing for the quarters of the earth.

So, in the earth and yet gone beyond it, we left him. In his obituary notice, Oliver Gogarty ended with this quotation from the Classics:

Now, Apollo was ever with Admetus — until today!

There could have been no better phrase — the Olympian herdsman, tending the flocks of the mortal man!

These notes are written by one who counts herself fortunate to have spent some time in the fields of Admetus during that notable sojourn.

First published in 'The Celtic Consciousness', ed Prof R O'Driscoll, Braziller, New York, 1981.

Grimm's Women

NOT long ago, a young woman whom I know slightly caught me up in the street and said breathlessly, 'Tell me something. How can I learn to be a woman?' I was surprised, for it seemed to me that the mere fact of having been born on the side of Yin was sufficient. A woman was what you inevitably, and willingly, became, as the seed becomes the flower. She had had, I knew, several lovers. Surely from these experiences, satisfying or otherwise, she could have learned something that would help her to define her aim. I cast about in my mind for some instructive book, and my good angel tapped me on the shoulder. 'Read Grimm's Fairy Tales,' I said, and left her, open-mouthed and incredulous, standing on the corner.

For Grimm's — or any other collection of traditional tales or myths — is a mine of feminine lore. Every woman — maiden, mother or crone, Kore, Demeter or Hecate — can find there her prototype, a model for her role in life. Take such apparently passive heroines as Cinderella and the Goose Girl, to whom good fortune seems to happen through no connivance of their own, simply as a matter of luck. But their passivity is only skin-deep. Cinderella, in Grimm's at least, is wise enough to know that nothing is to be got by wishing. It is only by performing the necessary rites at her mother's grave that she goes to the Prince's ball. And the Goose Girl would still be tending geese if it were not that she could understand the prescient lamentations of her dead horse Fallada.

Think of Little Two-Eyes, of 'One-Eye, Two-Eyes and Three-Eyes,' who tells us wordlessly that Three-Eyes, seeing more, and One-Eye, seeing less, are both monstrosities; that to have the ordinary complement, the power to see things as they really are, is what brings on the happy ending.

Then, of course, there are the beauties, Snow White for instance and Dornroschen. It would be a rash woman who modelled herself on either of these. For each of them, before becoming a candidate for Happy Ever After had to surmount inordinate obstacles. And to these may be added 'Beauty and the Beast.' This is not really a Grimm's story, but it deserves to be mentioned here because of its stern admonition that a thing has to be loved *before* it becomes lovable. One can think of easier roles to play than this.

Think of the apparent simpletons such as the Miller's Daughter, whose father boasted untruthfully that she could spin straw into gold and who had to discover unsuspected powers in herself before she could guess the name of Rumpelstiltzkin; or Clever Elsie, who in spite of her absent-mindedness could 'see the wind coming up the street and hear the flies coughing.' And then there are the heroic roles like that of the sister in 'The Seven Ravens,' who had to go to the end of the world, to the sun and the moon and the stars and back in order to save her brothers; and Allerleirauh, who to escape the concupiscent advances of her father put off her regal habiliments and became — until her true condition was discovered — a lowly kitchen maid.

These are all star-crossed heroines, but they do not by any means exhaust the possibilities of the tales. Anyone looking for a model of worldly eminence will find it in the Fisherman's Wife, to whom the flounder granted all wishes except the last. She became successively King and Pope, and it was only when she insisted on being God as well that she found herself back in her original hovel. Or, if we are after occult knowledge, we can go to the Twelve Dancing Princesses, who nightly explore the mysteries of the world below our world.

Then there are all the grandmothers, usually of giants, who by dint of ancient feminine ruses discover the answers to their grandsons' riddles, thereby saving the life of many a man-sized hero. And we must not forget the potent witches such as those in 'Rapunzel' and 'Hansel and Gretel': nor the numerous queens, jealous and carnivorous, who demand that their daughters-in-law or grandchildren be served up in a savoury stew; nor the ever-present stepmothers — think of the one in 'The Juniper Tree' — whose aim is always to enlarge their own children at the expense of the stepchild. There are, too, the true mothers, usually killed off early so that the story may take its inevitable course, who counsel, conserve and protect. Both the true and the false are variants of Kali, the Black One, the supreme mother-goddess of India, life-giver and life-taker, whose power the Hindus believe

— and the Grimm Brothers mutely acquiesce — abides in every woman. And lastly, there are the Wise Women, co-extant with the Three Fates and sib to the Greek Pythonesses and all the priestesses of the Great Goddess, who have power to bless or curse at will, who birth the babe, and stand by the bride-bed and ready the corpse for its clay cradle.

The prototypes are endless, and there is no woman alive who cannot be assimilated to one or other of them. When one is confronted with such manifold powers and possibilities, attempting to assassinate a President, becoming a Madison Avenue executive or holding up a bank teller with a machine gun seem poor cheap kinds of activity — fit only for men.

First published in 'The New York Times'.

Christmas Song for a Child

Child in the manger laid,
  Take now your myrrh and gold
And incense, as we kneel
  With the Three Kings of old.

Child, on this winter night,
  Do you know that we mean
To crucify you
  When the leaves are green?

First published in the 'New English Weekly'.

About The Sleeping Beauty

ARE there thirteen Wise Women at every christening? I think it very unlikely. I think, too, that whatever gifts they give are over and above those that life offers. If it is beauty it is of some supplementary kind that is not dependent on fine eyes and a perfect nose, though it may include these features. If it is wealth, it comes from some inner abundance that has no relation to pearls and rubies, though the lucky ones may get these, too.

I shall never know which good lady it was who, at my own christening, gave me the everlasting gift, spotless amid all spotted joys, of love for the fairy tale. It began in me quite early, before there was any separation between myself and the world. Eve's apple had not yet been eaten; every bird had an emperor to sing to and any passing ant or beetle might be a prince in disguise.

This undifferentiated world is common to all children. They may never have heard of the fairy tales but still be on easy terms with myth. St George and King Arthur, under other names, defend the alleyways and crossroads, and Beowulf's Grendel, variously disguised, breathes fire in the vacant lots. Skipping games, street songs, lullabies, all carry the stories in them. But far above these, as a source of myth, are the half-heard scraps of gossip, from parent to parent, neighbour to neighbour as they whisper across a fence. A hint, a carefully garbled disclosure, a silencing finger at the lip, and the tales, like rain clouds, gather. It could almost be said that a listening child has no need to read the tales. A keen ear and the power to dissemble — he must not *seem* to be listening — are all that is required. By putting two and two together — fragments of talk and his own logic — he will fashion the themes for himself.

For me, the nods and becks of my mother's friends, walking under parasols or presiding over tinkling tea-tables, were preparatory exercises to my study of the myths. The scandals, the tight corners, the flights into the face of fate! When eventually I read of Zeus visiting Danaë in a shower of gold, Perseus encountering the Gorgon, or the hair-breadth escapes of the Argonauts, such adventures caused me no surprise. I had heard their modern parallels over tea and caraway cake.

As for the Three Fates, I recognized them immediately as my great-aunts, huge cloudy presences — with power, it seemed, to loose and to bind — perched watchfully, like crows on a fence, at the edge of our family circle. One of them, it was said — or rather, it was whispered, the rumour being so hideous — one of them lived on her capital. What was capital, I wondered, wild with conjecture, full of concern. And the dreadful answer came bubbling up — it was *herself*, her substance! Each day when she disappeared to her room, it was not to rest, like anyone else, but secretly to live on her person, to gnaw, perhaps, a toe or a finger or to wolf down some inner organ. The fact that there was no visible sign of this activity did not fool me for a moment. A strange and dreadful deed was here and not to be denied. Aunt Jane, stealthily nibbling at her liver, was at once her own Prometheus and her own eagle. The myth did not need to be told me. It rose and spoke itself.

I might have saved myself anxiety by taking the question to my parents who would have expounded the role of capital in the world of things-as-they-are. But the grown-up view of things-as-they-are, limited as it is in dimension, lit by a wholly rational sun and capable of explanation, is different from that of a child. For a child this world is infinite, the sun shines up from the abyss as well as down from the sky, the time is always now and endless and the only way to explain a thing is to say that it cannot be explained.

I am glad, therefore, to have kept my terror whole and thus retained a strong link with the child's things-as-they-are, where all things relate to one another and all are congruous. Hercules, the Frog Prince, and Joseph in his coloured coat march with the child to Babylon by candlelight and back.

The boy who assured me that the Virgin Mary was the mother of Finn, the Irish hero — reasoning, perhaps, that all princely paladins must be born from a single stock — was in this world well within his rights. So, too, was the one who hoped — and not at all hopelessly — that since Castor and Pollux were turned at death into neighbour stars, the same courtesy might well be shown to himself and his nearest and dearest. And both would have had a brotherly feeling for the little girl who, assured at bedtime that she need not feel lonely — the One Above being everywhere — begged her mother earnestly to ask God to leave the room. 'He makes me nervous,' she protested. 'I would rather have Rumpelstiltzkin.' This form of thinking, which perhaps should properly be called linking, is the essence of fairy tale. All things may be included in it.

Perhaps we are born knowing the tales for our grandmothers and all their ancestral kin continually run about in our blood repeating them endlessly, and the shock they give us when we first hear them is not of surprise but of recognition. Things long unknowingly known have suddenly been remembered. Later, like streams, they run underground. For a while they disappear and we lose them. We are busy, instead, with our personal myth in which the real is turned to dream and the dream becomes the real. Sifting all this is a long process. It may perhaps take half a lifetime and the few who come round to the tales again are those who are in luck.

But love of the fairy tales, you may argue, need not require the lover to refashion them. Do they need retelling, you may ask. Does it not smack of arrogance for any writer to imagine he can put a gloss on a familiar theme? If I answer yes to both these questions I put myself in jeopardy. And yet, why should I fear? To be in jeopardy is a proper fairy-tale situation. Danger is at the heart of the matter, for without danger how shall we foster the rescuing power?

Besides, is it not true that the fairy tale has always been in a continuous process of transformation? How else can we account for the widely differing versions that turn up in different countries? One cannot say of any of the Sleeping Beauties in this book that here is the sole and absolute source, if, indeed, such a thing exists.

The idea of the sleeper, of somebody hidden from mortal eye, waiting until the time shall ripen has always been dear to the folkly mind — Snow White asleep in her glass coffin, Brynhild behind her wall of fire, Charlemagne in the heart of France, King Arthur in the Isle of Avalon, Frederick Barbarossa under his mountain in Thuringia. Muchukunda, the Hindu king, slept through eons till he was awakened by the Lord Krishna; Oisin of Ireland dreamed in Tir na n'Og for more than three hundred years. Psyche in her magic sleep is a type of Sleeping Beauty, Sumerian Ishtar in the underworld may be said to be another. Holga the Dane is sleeping and waiting, and so, they say, is Sir Francis Drake. Quetzalcoatl of Mexico and Virochocha of Peru are both sleepers. Morgan le

Fay of France and England and Dame Holle of Germany are sleeping in raths and cairns.

The theme of the sleeper is as old as the memory of man. Where it first arose we do not know. One can never find where myth and fairy tale begin any more than one can find wild wheat growing. They are not invented, that is certain. They germinate from seeds sown by an unknown hand. 'The Authors,' as the poet William Blake has said, 'are in Eternity,' and we must be content to leave them there. The story is, after all, what matters.

It is true, of course, that all of the five versions gathered here can be dated; that is, we know when they were first published. The Italian Gianbattista Basile's *Pentamerone* which gives us *Sole, Luna, e Talia* belongs to the early part of the seventeenth century; Charles Perrault's *La Belle au Bois Dormant*, the French version, to the latter part. Grimm's *Dornroschen* first found its way into print in Germany in the early nineteenth century, Bradley-Birt's *The Petrified Mansion*, from Bengal, and Jeremiah Curtin's *The Queen of Tubber Tintye*, from Ireland, in the nineteenth century's closing years. But every one of these historically authenticated persons was a collector, not a creator. They retold, in their own words, stories that were told to them. But the theme itself, the theme of the sleeper, has no relation to historical fact; it comes from afar, from the world's storehouse of fairy tale which is somewhere beyond the calendar.

This being so, I have grouped the stories of the Sleeping Beauty, not in order of precedence — there is no way of knowing which came first — but in relation to each other. For instance, *The Petrified Mansion* and *The Queen of Tubber Tintye* have in common the fact that in both versions animals as well as humans fall under the spell of sleep. There is a further link between these two in that in neither story is there any foretelling of the heroine's fate, nor any mention of the spinning motif. In turn, *The Queen of Tubber Tintye* has an element in common with *Sole, Luna, e Talia*, for in both tales the Prince 'steals the fruit of love' while the Beauty lies asleep. Perrault rectifies this by providing a chapel and a priest so that hero and heroine may be lawfully married. Even so, *Sole, Luna, e Talia* and *La Belle au Bois Dormant* have several similar characteristics. In each the fate of the Beauty is foretold, by astrologers in Basile, by the Fairies in Perrault; in each, two children are begotten; in each the Prince is provided with an ogress relative who orders the children to be slain and served up in a stew — in Basile a wife, in Perrault a mother.

The last motif does not appear in *Dornroschen* — indeed, as the Brothers Grimm so clearly saw, it is not necessary to the fundamental theme and probably does not belong to it. But in Grimm the spindle is retained from *La Belle au Bois Dormant;* so also are Perrault's Fairies, though these are transmogrified in the German version into Thirteen Wise Women.

In this latest, and best-known, telling of the story it is possible to see how over the centuries it has been refined and purged of dross. It is as though the tale itself, through its own energy and need, had winnowed away everything but the true whole grain. By the time it was told to the Brothers Grimm, its outer stuff, worked on by time and the folkly mind, had become transparent and complete, nothing too much, nothing too little. Bradley-Bird's stark narrative has been elaborated; Jeremiah Curtin's over-wordiness has been curbed; Basile's gross justification for his gross events — that fortune brings luck to those that sleep — is seen for the graceless thing it is and dropped accordingly; Perrault's sophistries fall away and the story emerges clear, all essence.

It is this version, this clarification of the tale on which I have built what one may call the Sultana's interpretation. It was written not at all to improve the story — how could one improve on the Brothers Grimm? — but to ventilate my own thoughts about it. To begin with, I was at pains to give it a faraway setting — a vaguely Middle-Eastern world — to lift it out of its well-worn rut. I needed to separate it from its attic clutter — the spinning wheel, the pointed witch cap and all the pantomime buffoonery — in order to see its meaning clear. The story in its present guise may be thought of as a series of reflections on the theme of the Sleeping Beauty, particularly as it appears in *Dornroschen* (Rose in the Thorns or Briar Rose).

The opening theme is a familiar one. The King and the Queen, like our Sultan and Sultana, are longing for a child. This situation is so often and so insistently restated in the fairy tales that we cannot but take notice of it. What is it telling us? That in fairy tale, compared with the rest of the teeming world, the characters are less fecund? Surely not. The child is withheld in order to show the need for what the child stands for — the new order, the renewed conditions, the throwing forward of events, the revivifying of life. Once this need is made clear the longing is allowed to bear its proper fruit. In Perrault, after 'prayers, pilgrimages, vows to saints,' the Queen at last conceives. But note what happens in Grimm. A frog brings her the reassurance. Within a year, she will bear a child. A messenger flies from the dark waters where all things have their beginings. In effect, her own unconsciousness speaks.

So, in due time, the child is born, the new events begin to gather, and the story is on its way. The christening, the first rite of passage in any life, has now to be performed. And since the good graces of the fairy world are essential to any mortal undertaking, the Wise Women are sent for. Here now is the first hint of danger, the hand-sized cloud in the sky. For while there are thirteen Wise Women in the kingdom, the King has only twelve gold places. What a foolish short-sighted man to put himself in such a position!

But we must not forget that there has to be a story. A fairy tale, like any other, has its own organic life that may not be shortened or cut down before its allotted span. Where would the story be if the King had been wiser and had had a little forethought? Or if, going back a little further, the child had not been born? To find the meaning we need the story and once we have accepted the story we cannot escape the story's fate.

Well, what does the King do? In Perrault he provides seven gold cases for seven Fairies, believing that the eighth Fairy was under a spell or dead or somehow harmless. (It is typical of Perrault that for all his sophistry he was unaware that creatures of the fairy world are known to be immortal.) Grimm merely notes, without attempting to solve the problem, that as there were only twelve gold plates one of the thirteen Wise Women would have to stay at home. In our version, the Sultan, indeed, senses the danger but washes his hands of responsibility and leaves the matter to chance. He could, perhaps, have borrowed a plate or sent for a goldsmith and had one made. But the story had to have its way and the Thirteenth Wise Woman her opportunity.

The appearance of this lady at the christening is the great moment of the tale, the hook from which everything hangs. Properly to understand why this is so we must turn to Wise Women in general and their role in the world of men. To begin with they are not mortal women. They are sisters, rather, of the Sirens, kin to the Fates and the World Mothers. As such, as creatures of another dimension, myth and legend have been at pains to embody them in other than human shape — the winged female figures of Homer, the bird-headed women of the Irish tales, the wild women of ancient Russia with square heads and hairy bodies and the wisplike Jinn of the Middle East who were not allowed grosser forms than those of fire and smoke. It was to do away with their pantomime image and give them their proper weight and authority that our version provided the Wise Women with their hairless heads of gold and silver and made their golden and silver feet hover a little above the earth as the gods do on the Greek vases. And in dressing them in the colours of the spectrum, the aim was to suggest that the Thirteen are parts of the single whole and the opposites complementary.

For it should be remembered that no Wise Woman or Fairy is in herself either good or bad; she takes on one aspect or the other according to the laws of the story and the necessity of events. The powers of these ladies are equivocal. They change with changing circumstances; they are as swift to take umbrage as they are to bestow a boon; they curse and bless with equal gusto. Each Wise Woman is, in fact, an aspect of the Hindu goddess, Kali, who carries in her multiple hands the powers of good and evil.

It is clear, therefore, that the Thirteenth Wise Woman becomes the Wicked Fairy solely for the purpose of one particular story. It was by chance that she received no invitation; it might just as well have been one of her sisters. So, thrust by circumstance into her role, she acts according to law.

Up she rises, ostensibly to avenge an insult but in reality to thrust the story forward and keep the drama moving. She becomes the necessary antagonist, placed there to show that whatever is 'other,' opposite and fearful, is as indispensable an instrument of creation as any force for good. The pulling of the Devas and Asuras in opposite directions churn the ocean of life in the Hindu myth and the interaction of the good and the bad Fairies produces the fairy tale. The Thirteenth Wise Woman stands as a guardian of the threshold, the paradoxical adversary without whose presence no threshold may be passed.

This is the role played in so many stories by the Wicked Stepmother. The true mother, by her very nature, is bound to preserve, protect and comfort; this is why she is so often disposed of before the story begins. It is the stepmother, her cold heart unwittingly co-operating with the hero's need, who thrusts the child from the warm hearth, out from the sheltering walls of home to find his own true way.

Powers such as these, at once demonic and divine, are not to be taken lightly. They give a name to evil, free it, and bring it into the light. For evil will out, they sharply warn us, no matter how deeply buried. Down in its dungeon it plots and plans, waiting, like an unloved child, the day of its revenge. What it needs, like the unloved child, is to be recognized, not disclaimed; given its place and proper birthright and allowed to contact and co-operate with its sister beneficient forces. Only the integration of good and evil and the stern acceptance of opposites will change the situation and bring about the condition that is known as Happy Ever After.

Without the Wicked Fairy there would have been no story. She, not the heroine, is the goddess in the machine. Her hand is discernible in every event that leads up to the denouement; the departure of the protecting parents from the palace on the day of the birthday, the inner promptings that lead the Princess to climb the fateful tower, and who can deny — though it is never explicitly stated in any of the three versions dealing with the spinning motif — that the Thirteenth Wise Woman and none other is the old woman with the spindle? Fairy tales have a logic of their own and that the Wicked Fairy should take upon herself this role is a logical assumption. So mighty a character would inevitably play her part out to the very end.

For me she has always been unique among the shadow figures of the stories. As a child I had no pity for the jealous queen in 'Snow White' or the shifty old witch in 'Rapunzel.' I could cheerfully consign all the cruel stepmothers to their cruel fates. But the ill luck of the Wicked Fairy roused all my child's compassion. She was, in a sense, a victim. For her alone there was no gold plate — all she could do was accept the fact. But there was a certain nobiliby in her acceptance. Without complaining, well aware of the fact that things must go wrong that they may come right, she undertook the task that made her the most despised figure in all fairy tale, the one least worthy of forgiveness. All I could do, in the face of the tragedy, was to comfort myself with the thought that in another story, at another time, the Thirteenth Wise Woman would be avenged. Her luck would at last come round again: chance would give her a golden plate, chance would give her the possibility of playing the part of the Good Fairy.

But it is not only the nobility of the Wicked Fairy that makes 'The Sleeping Beauty' unique among fairy tales. The story also contains the one hero who appears to have no hero's task to perform. The Prince has to slay no dragon in order to win the hand of the Princess. There is no dwarf or talking animal to befriend, no glass mountain to be climbed. All he has to do is to come at the right time. The Grimm version alone mentions the fact that the hedge was hung with the corpses of those who had tried to break through before the hundred years were up, thus pointing an admonitory finger at the truth that to choose the moment when the time is ripe is essentially a heroic deed. So, all unarmed, the Prince arrives. The time, the place, and the man coincide. He walks through the bowing, flowering hedge as easily as Arthur, the Once and Future King, pulls the royal sword from the stone. The Prince is the sole hero of fairy tale for whom it is a question not of doing but of being. In a word, he is himself his own task. Only such a one, Perrault and Grimm both wordlessly tell us, can give the kiss that will break the spell.

But if the Prince is a mysterious figure, how much more so is she who is the crux of the story, the maiden of surpassing beauty asleep behind her wall of thorns, she whom men from the beginning of time have pondered on and treasured. I say the beginning of time with intent, for when a woman is the chief character in a story it is a sign of the theme's antiquity. It takes us back to those cloudy eras when the world was ruled not, as it was in later years, by a god but by the Great Goddess. Here, as with the Prince, is a heroine who has ostensibly nothing to do, nothing to suffer. She is endowed with every blessing by grace and happy fortune, no slights or indignities are put upon her as is the case with her sister heroines, Snow White, Cinderella, Little Two-Eyes, or the Goose Girl. She simply has to follow her fate, prick her finger, and fall asleep. But perhaps — is this what the story is telling us? — perhaps it is not a simple thing to faithfully follow one's fate. Nor is it really a simple fate to carry such a wealth of graces and to fall asleep for a hundred years. These two elements in the story, the unparalleled beauty and the long deep sleep, are what light up the mind and set one questioning. One thing is certain. She is not merely a pretty girl waiting, after an eon of dreams, to be wakened by a lover. That she is a symbol, the core and heart of the world she inhabits, is shown by the fact, clearly stated in *The Petrified Mansion, The Queen of Tubber Tintye, The Sleeping Beauty in the Wood,* and *Dornroschen,* that when she sleeps, all about her sleep, when she wakens, her world wakes with her. One is reminded of the Grail Legend where, when the Fisher King is ill, his whole court is out of health and the countryside laid waste; when the King recovers, the courtiers, too, are whole again and the land begins to blossom. And there is an echo of this in the Norse sagas. We are told that when Brynhild (herself one of the world's sleepers) 'lifted her head and laughed the whole castle dinned.'

A symbol indeed. But what does it mean? Who is she, this peerless beauty, this hidden sleeping figure that has kindled the imaginations of so many generations and for whom children go about on tiptoe lest she be too soon wakened?

There are those who see the tale exclusively as a nature myth, as the earth in spring, personified as a maiden, awaking from the long dark sleep of winter; or as a seed hidden deep in the earth until the kiss of the sun makes it send forth leaves. This is undoubtedly an aspect of the story. But a symbol, by the very fact of being a symbol, has not one sole and absolute meaning. It throws out light in every direction. Meaning comes pouring from it.

As well as being a nature myth, it is also possible that there are elements of a secret and forgotten ritual in the theme, reminders of initiation ceremonies where the neophyte dies — or sleeps — on one level and awakes on another, as chrysalis wakes into butterfly. Or again it may be that since all fairy tales hark back to myth we are present here at the death and resurrection of a goddess, of Persephone down in the underworld biding her time till she returns to earth.

We can but guess, for the fairy tales never explain. But we should not let ourselves be fooled by their apparent simplicity. It is their role to say much in little. And not to explain is to set up in the hearer or the reader an inner friction in which one question inevitably leads to another and the answers that come are never conclusions. They never exhaust the meaning.

The latest version of the story, true to the law of the fairy tale, makes no attempt to explain. One could call it perhaps a meditation, for it broods and ponders upon the theme, elaborating it here and there with no other thought than of bringing out what the writer feels to be further hidden meanings. For instance, the Beauty, who has never before been given a name, is here called Rose — having regard not only to the Grimms' *Dornroschen* but also to Robert Graves' Druidic language of the trees in *The White Goddess*, where he speaks of the 'erotic' briar. And further to underline this aspect, she is given a dove which in myth was sacred to Aphrodite, the Greek goddess of love; and a cat which was sacred to Freya, Aphrodite's Nordic counterpart. To these a lizard is added, not merely to provide the necessary fairy-tale third but to be assimilated to the symbol of the spindle which is nothing if not erotic.

All the known versions of the story have in them this strong element of eroticism. Indeed, it can be said with truth that every fairy tale that deals with a beautiful heroine and a lordly hero is, among many other things, speaking to us of love, laying down patterns and examples for all our human loving.

The Sleeping Beauty, therefore, is not alone in this. What makes it unique is the spell of sleep. Brooding upon this, the why and the wherefore, we become, like the Sultana of the present version, full of wonder at her daughter's story. For inevitably, if the fairy-tale characters are our prototypes — which is what they are designed to be — we come to the point where we are forced to relate the stories and their meanings to ourselves. No amount of rationalizing will bring us to the heart of the fairy tale. To enter it one must be prepared to let the rational reason go. The stories have to be loved for themselves before they will release their secrets. So, face to face with the Sleeping Beauty — who has long been the dream of every man and the hope of every woman — we find ourselves compelled to ask: what is it in *us* that at a certain moment suddenly falls asleep? Who lies hidden deep within us? And who will come at last to wake us, what aspect of ourselves?

Are we dealing here with the sleeping soul and all the external affairs of life that hem it in and hide it; something that falls asleep after childhood, something that not to waken would make life meaningless? To give an answer, supposing we had it, would be breaking the law of the fairy tale. And perhaps no answer is necessary. It is enough that we ponder upon and love the story and ask ourselves the question.

First published as the Afterword to 'About the Sleeping Beauty', Collins, 1977.

The Shortest Stories in the World

IF YOU reply to a child's request for a story with the old jingle

'I'll tell you a story
Of Jack o'Manory,
And now my story's begun.
I'll tell you another
Of Jack and his brother
And now my story is done.'

that child will, very naturally, feel defrauded. After all, he had been expecting heroes, villains and princesses; witches galore and wolves and ogres; even, perhaps a rabbit who lost both shoes and a blue jacket in escaping from Mr Macgregor's garden. And now he has been fobbed off with a crisp negative, a mere six-legged rhyme. If he doesn't decide, there and then, never to speak to you again, you can count yourself lucky.

If, on the other hand, you respond with 'Yes, I will tell you the shortest story in the world' and *then* declaim *Jack O'Manory,* he may very possibly be enchanted. He will see the fun and wit of it and enjoy the way it flashes by, like a shooting star in the night. The long train of witches and heroes can wait while the sudden movement is savoured. He has, in effect, *had* his story.

When I was young I had a great-aunt who could make those sudden moments of the nursery rhymes even more dramatic. From my point of view, she improved upon them.

'Little Bo-peep, has lost her sheep
And can't tell where to find them,
Leave them alone and they'll come home'
— pause for effect —
'Saying "What a thoroughly careless
and forgetful little girl!"'

The expected 'Wagging their tails behind them' seemed to me altogether too dull and sheepish compared with that devastating dénouement.
Or

'Augustus was a chubby lad
Fat, ruddy cheeks Augustus had
And everybody saw with joy'
— pause again —
'The disgusting over-fed unhealthy-looking child!'

Away with 'The happy, hearty, healthy boy!' I preferred the quick exposion of laughter of that interpolated line. Moreover, I was enjoying the experience with somebody else, and a grown-up to boot; a grown-up who either liked children or accurately remembered her own childhood, I never quite knew which. And now I come to think if it, the nursery rhymes, improved upon or not, are always communications between grown-up and child for they belong to the earliest years before the alphabet has appeared, when old and young are young together — or old together, whichever you like. The generations cannot help meeting in them since the material of the Shortest Stories comes out of antiquity and tradition and is handed on from grandmother to grandchild. The lessons they propound — and there *are* lessons if you look for them — go back to the drying of the flood. They carry in their miniscule pockets the origins of all the novels and dramas in literature.
Take, for instance, this affecting tale.

'Solomon Grundy
Born on a Monday
Christened on Tuesday,
Married on Wednesday,
Took ill on Thursday,
Worse on Friday,
Died on Saturday,
Buried on Sunday,
And that was the end
Of Solomon Grundy.'

Isn't it a newspaper in little, a scenario for a Dickens novel? Could Tolstoi have done better? Did Shakespeare know of it when he wrote the seven ages of man?

Or think of

'Goosey, Goosey Gander
Whither shall I wander?
Upstairs and downstairs,
In my lady's chamber.
There I met an old man
Who wouldn't say his prayers —
I took him by the left leg
And threw him down the stairs.'

What a sense of — and doubtless founded upon — scandal! Of course the old man would not say his prayers — it was not the proper place. And what was he doing in my lady's chamber, anyway? No wonder Goosey Gander, careful mother — or chaperone, perhaps — incontinently got rid of him.

Think of that celebrated lullaby to which so many millions of infants have been — indeed, are being at this very moment — hushed into happy sleep.

'Rock-a-bye, baby, on the tree top.
When the wind blows, the cradle will rock,
When the bough breaks, the cradle will fall,
Down will come baby, cradle and all.'

If one takes those words at face value, they sound like a mournful little ditty, for the nursling's life — wind and branches being what they are — appears to be in the greatest jeopardy. But babies being what *they* are, all-wise and not yet grown into ignorance, know better. They are well aware that the song is saying 'Let storms rage and forests shatter, Mother will save you, child, so sleep!' And, even so, on another level — and one cannot avoid levels in nursery rhymes, fairy tales or myth — the song is speaking of the dangers, accidents and difficulties that beset the human creature from the very outset of its life till the moment of its death. Over and over again the nursery rhymes assure us that nothing is easy. If it is, it is merely a matter of luck. Little Tommy Tucker has to sing for his supper. He doesn't get it for nothing (after all, we ask for the gift of daily bread, not a whole week's rations). Cock Robin (All the birds of the air/Fell a-sighing and a-sobbing/When they heard the bell toll for poor Cock Robin) was killed by the arrow of his brother, the sparrow. 'Oranges and Lemons,' after enumerating so euphoniously the words spoken by the church bells of London, ends with

'Here comes a candle to light you to bed
And here comes a chopper to chop off your head.'

And 'Lord Rendal,' with his wonderful elegiac refrain that, in spite of its sombreness, children love, dies because his sweetheart has given him a broth of poisonous eels.

'What colour were they, Rendal, my son,
What colour were they, my pretty one?
They were spicket and sparkit, mother,
O spicket and sparkit, mother!
Make my bed soon, for I'm sick to my heart
And I fain would lie down.'

Poor Rendal! Wicked sweetheart! Implacable nursery rhymes!

Even the ladybird (originally Bird of the Virgin Mary and in America ladybug), smallest of creatures, does not get off lightly. Sometimes, too, called God's Little Cow, she eats the aphids that make the leaves of the rose curl up and, as a reward for this, it has from antiquity been the custom for humans to set her on a finger and warn her —

'Ladybird, ladybird, fly away home,
Your house is on fire and your children are gone.
All except one and her name is Ann
And she is under the frying pan.'

Mannhardt, the German folklorist, asserted that the rhyme goes back to mythological times and that it was, in fact, a charm intended to speed the sun across the dangers of sunset; in effect, to save the sun from burning up in its own glow. The sunset is the 'house on fire' and the ladybird is sent to save it. In this regard it is still customary in the East to utter a prayer to the setting sun in order to ensure its safe return. Who has not felt in childhood the anxiety of the sun's going? 'But how do you *know* it will come back?' I used to ask my parents. 'It always does,' they replied, serenely. And, since parents are a child's first gods, I had to content myself with their dictum, but tremblingly, as an article of belief, and not as something securely known.

And what about the rhyme of 'London Bridge?' All through that story runs the uneasy fear that, no matter what one builds it of, it will still be falling down. 'Bricks and mortar will not stay, Iron and steel will bend and bow, Silver and gold will be stolen away.' And why? Because we have forgotten what our mythological fathers knew about the Devil, who is said to have no love of bridges.

His business is with separation, and bridges join things together; they lead from one shore to another and, indeed, from earth to heaven. Break them and men will fall into Hell, or at least be drowned in the river. There are folkoristic grounds for the belief that in ancient times bridges had human corpses — particularly corpses of children — built into them to ensure their safety. There is a tradition in the City of London that even the latest of London bridges has been sprinkled with human blood. But if the rhyme poses the problem, it also, luckily, solves it. A child can feel safe in his bed if he sings it to the last verse.

'Set a man to watch all night,
Dance over, my lady Leigh,
Set a man to watch all night,
My fair lady.'

This idea of the watchman is common to all traditions. Only the one that stays awake can save a bridge or a falling world.

So, you see, the nursery rhymes are not all guileless simplicities. Some of them carry a weight of meaning that comes from man's earliest times. 'Eena, Meena, Myna, Mo' which is now used in various versions for deciding who is going to be It in a game, is supposed originally to have been a Druidic counting out formula for choosing human sacrifices. Of course, we in England, when we want to describe the antiquity of a thing or a saying, tend to put it down to the Druids. For a long time we laid Stonehenge at their door — and it is morally, or immorally, certain that they did use it for their gruesome festivals — until a professer at M I T got to work on it with a computer and came up with the conclusion, apparently conclusive, that Stonehenge was an astronomical observatory long before the Druids were even thought of.

But if Stonehenge outdates the Druids, the myths outdate Stonehenge. They came from a time that never was and is always and were, as Coomaraswamy suggests, not invented by but rather communicated to man. And the Shortest Stories in the world are an essential part of the myth.

Take the tale of 'Jack and Jill' which is known to every two-year-old. At first reading it seems simple, even naive. But then one finds oneself facing an enigma. Why *up* the hill? It is axiomatic that, since water runs downwards, wells are always sunk in the lowest possible location. Could it have been some special kind of water that was found on a hilltop, water that had to be climbed for? Where is the Well at the World's End situated or the Well of the

Water of Life? In valley or on mountain? Perhaps Baring Gould in his *Curious Myths of the Middle Ages* was edging his way towards the antiquity of the theme when he suggested that it preserved within it the Scandinavian myth of the two children, Hjuki and Bill, who were caught up by Mani, the Moon, as they were taking water — or perhaps stealing is the right word here — from the sacred well Byrgir. Norwegians, Swedes and Finns believe that they see the children when the moon is full carrying a pail on a pole between them. This, of course, does not explain it, it merely points to the myth. We, on the other hand, see a man in the moon — sometimes he even has a dog. And the Japanese see a hare. So far as it is known, however, the men who actually walked on the moon failed to catch a glimpse of any of these figures. But, mythologically speaking, I wouldn't put it past these figures to be there. Old Wives Tales are not always wrong. Wasn't it J B S Haldane, the scientist-philosopher, who said that the universe might prove to be not merely queerer than we imagine but queerer than we *can* imagine.?

Who, for instance could have invented 'Hey diddle diddle/The cat and the fiddle'? You may, if you're looking for explanations remind me that in Egypt the cow is a goddess called Hathor and connected with the sky, but to drag this in would, to my mind, be pulling the long bow, even though the long bow is itself straight out of myth. But why did she jump over the moon and the dish elope with the spoon? The irrelevance! The magic! The ill-logic! Let us not ask for explanations. Here, sense and non-sense are dancing together. That should be enough.

Indeed, these two dancing opposites — whose opposition is more apparent than real — are to be found in all the nursery rhymes, even in those that do not rhyme but depend for their cumulative effect on repetition. Think of *The Old Woman and her Pig*, for instance. You remember how

> *'The ox began to drink the water,*
> *The water began to quench the fire,*
> *The fire began to burn the stick,*
> *The stick began to beat the dog,*
> *The dog began to bite the pig,*
> *The little pig jumped over the stile,*
> *And the old woman got home that night.'*

And this tallies with the long sequence of mishaps that occurred because the Rat ate the Malt that lay in the House that Jack built.

These stories have both come a long way, perhaps from those ubiquitous Druids! And the newer religions, as they had done with the primitive gods and the so-called heathen sacred places, were very quick to absorb them. A version of 'The House that Jack Built', having to do with pears that would not drop from their tree, was taken over by the Christian church and, according to Eckenstein — one of the great authorities on nursery rhyme — was annually recited at harvest time at the feast of the Holy St Lambert. And there is a Hebrew chant that closely resembles the *Old Woman and her Pig* which is still recited as part of the ceremonial of Passover. It is called the *Had Gadyo*, and begins

> *'A kid, a kid, my father bought,*
> *For two pieces of money.*
> > *A kid, a kid*
>
> *Then came the cat and ate the kid,*
> *That my father bought*
> *For two pieces of money.*
> > *A kid, a kid.'*

and so on, through staff, fire, water, ox, butcher, angel of death and the Holy One who, of course, vanquishes the angel and so the charm is unwound.

Opinions differ as to meaning. I like very much — arrogantly, perhaps, because it sorts with my own feeling — the idea of a learned rabbi who interpreted it as showing how each creative power is kept within its bounds by a power that stands above it; the kid eaten by the cat, the water lapped up by the ox, the angel of death annihilated.

And there are those other cumulative songs, the number chants, or, as they are sometimes called — for these, too, religion purloined from myth — the Chants of the Creed. 'The Twelve Days of Christmas,' secular as it apparently is, belongs among the Christmas carols. And what we now know as 'Green Grow the Rushes-O', also chanted at the Passover under the title of 'He who knows', is a mixture of religious and mythological elements and, like its fellows, is not only a lesson in counting but — looked at from its inner side — a manual of traditional instruction.

> *'I'll sing you one-O*
> *Green grow the rushes-O!'*

and so on up to the mythical twelve and down again.

'*Twelve are the twelve apostles.*
Eleven are the eleven who went to heaven (i.e. all except Judas)
And ten are the ten commandments.
Nine are the nine bright shiners (constellations),
Eight are the Gabriel hunters (mythological hounds, the sound of whose baying is the wind),
Seven are the seven stars in the sky (planets)
And six are the six bold rainers (the Pleiades, bringers of rain).
Five is the symbol at your door (the Pentagon, symbol of man, hung by primitive folk over the lintel)
And four are the gospel makers (Matthew, Mark, Luke and John).
Three, three are the rivals (the Trinity; the three forces — active, passive, and reconciling — through which all things are created; Brahma, Vishnu and Shiva),
Two, two are the lily-white boys (Castor and Pollux, the eternal twins, the opposites)
A-clothed all in green-O,
One is one and all alone
And ever more shall be so.'

When I was a child, I brooded long upon that One. Was it God? Was it myself? I have now come to the conclusion that it is both. Essential aloneness is to be found at either end of the spectrum. 'I'll sing you one-O' is a riddle that takes a lifetime to find out the answer.

Riddles, anyway, are part of nursery lore and originally were mythologically used as a method of instruction. Remember the riddle of the Sphinx — 'What goes first on four legs, then on two and then on three?' and how Oedipus answered it at the outset of his fateful rule in Thebes. 'A man!' he said. And the Sphinx was routed.

But who could know, without screwing up his mind into knots, that

'*What God never sees*
What the King seldom sees
What we see every day
Tell me this riddle, I pray!'

means an Equal?

Mother Goose, however, has easier and more secular questions up her sleeve — or wing.

'As I was going o'er London Bridge
I met a London scholar,
He took off his hat and drew off his glove
And what was the name of that scholar?'

The answer, of course, is in the question and I leave you to solve it for yourselves.

As for

'Hitty, pitty within the wall
Hitty, pitty without the wall.
If you touch Hitty pitty
Hitty pitty will bite you!'

the solution here is a nettle. Why Hitty pitty? No one knows. It is just a rhyme that has no reason and perhaps, indeed, that is the reason that children love repeating it.

But to my mind the best and perhaps the most widely spread of the little rhymes is 'Humpty Dumpty.' Until Lewis Carroll made so much of it in *Through the Looking Glass* the answer was not so generally known, though the riddle comes into every tradition. The egg has always represented the origin of life. Aristophanes wrote of the fabulous, heaven-born bird that laid it. In Hindu story, the golden egg from which will come Prajapati, the god of creation, floats on the primal waters. The world-egg breaks in the Finnish *Kalevala*, its upper part becoming the sky, the lower half the earth. In Tibet, it is said, certain statues represent the Buddha holding a shattered egg-shell — from non-existence the world has come into manifestation, ignorance has become enlightenment. So much for the egg's macrocosmic content. But it bears, too, its microcosmic meaning. Can you think of a better way to tell children — or grown-ups, for that matter — that there are some things that all the king's horses and all the king's men cannot put together again; things that, for all our grieving, may be broken beyond mending? It can be a bitter lesson.

But now, with so many stories told, it surely is time for bed.

'Little Nannie Netticoat,
In a white petticoat
And a red nose,
The longer she lives, the shorter she grows.'

in other words, a candle, is waiting to light our way.

We could suitably end with 'Now I lay me,' which may be, in one form or another, as old as time itself. And if the line 'If I should die before I wake' smacks too much of nursery rhyme sombreness — some children anxiously question it — here is a happier subsitute, not known, I think, to Mother Goose, which was taught to me in my childhood. It goes

> *'Lord, keep us safe this night*
> *Secure from all our fears.*
> *May angels guard us while we sleep*
> *Til morning light appears.'*

So good night. Sleep well and happy dreams!

First published in 'Games' magazine.

Admit One

'TAXI! Hi; Taxi!'

A voice called. An arm waved. A cab, answering the signal, pulled up beside the kerb and a shabby, undistinguished-looking man, hatless and without luggage, stepped forward to give the direction.

'Heaven,' he said. 'No need to hurry.'

The driver eyed his prospective fare with some uncertainty.

'It's a long trip, sir,' he admonished him. 'You sure you got the fare?'

'I have enough,' said the man, and got in.

At length — a long time or a short time, it doesn't matter — the cab arrived at its destination. The passenger descended, paid the amount shown on the clock and gave a modest tip. Then, taking from his pocket a slip of paper, he walked toward the pearly gates and gently pulled the bell-rope.

Somewhere within a bell jangled, leisurely footsteps answered its call, and a key turned rustily in a lock that clearly needed oiling. At the same moment, the cabby gave vent to an angry shout.

'Hey!' he yelled. 'This tip won't do! I thought there was only one of you. I hadn't bargained for twins or triplets, or quintuplets — or whatever you call 'em.'

He waved his hand at the door of the cab from which was issuing a bevy of men, each of them an identical image of the passenger who had hailed it — facially, at any rate, but in the matter of dress and bearing, far more prosperous and important.

One wore a top hat, another a bowler, a third a mortar-board. There were fur-coated men, men in silk gowns, men in well-cut city suits, all of them laden with possessions — suitcases, umbrellas, golf-clubs, satchels. A cleric fingered the cross on his chest; a man wearing ear-rings and a velvet cape swaggered forth, swinging a cane; another humped a brass trumpet and tootled a triumphal march as he walked toward the gates.

'One got in and all these got out! Wot you goin' to do about it?' the cabby demanded of his original fare.

'Nothing. I've given you all I had. I'm not responsible for these people — at least, not any more.'

'Well, somebody's responsible! I'll have my rights or I'll go to headquarters.'

'You are *at* headquarters,' said a voice. And there was St Peter, with his keys, pushing open the creaking gates.

The shabby man stepped up to him and held out his slip of paper. 'H'm,' said St Peter, looking it over. 'This is a Ticket of Admission. Name of applicant — Mr X. But there seem to be so many of you!' He glanced enquiringly at the jostling crowd that was now surging about him. 'You all seem exactly alike to me. Which one is Mr X?'

The fares that the cabby had not bargained for set up an instant clamour.

'*I* am! *I* am! *I* am! *I* am!' they cried in important voices.

'But this ticket says Admit One. You cannot all be Mr X. I shall get into terrible hot water if I let the wrong man in. Explain yourselves, I pray you!'

'I am a learned man! I am a bishop! I am in the *Guinness Book of Records!* I am an actor! I am a saint! Admit me, I am Mr X!' Each man loudly declared himself, beating his breast as he did so.

St Peter regarded them thoughtfully. 'A distinguished assembly, indeed,' he observed, as his gaze moved through the crowd. 'But there is one who has not yet spoken. Who are *you?*' he enquired of the first man, whom the others, in their enthusiasm, had rudely elbowed aside.

The man smiled. 'I *was* Mr X.,' he said, calmly. 'As such, I paraded through the world and the world, as it seemed to me, applauded. But I have divested myself of so much,' he made a slight gesture toward the others, 'that I feel now I have no name at all — indeed, that I do not need one. I do not say I am nobody, mind you. That would be making too great a claim. And yet, there's a sense of nullity — the fairy tales call it Nix-Nought-Nothing — a nullity in which something moves. What that something is, I do not know. I have become a simple man and cannot put a word upon it.'

'Let us not philosophize,' said St Peter. 'I am a simple man myself, for all I have heard the cock crowing. Yet I, too, believe that something moves. There's a fellow here who understands things.

His name, when he had one, was Augustine. You can have a chat with him about it. For, clearly, the ticket belongs to you. So, come in, ex-Mr X., and welcome!'

The shabby man stooped and took off his boots. Then, diffidently, but with dignity, he stepped over the threshold. As he did so, a cry went up from the throng at the gate. It sounded like a long-drawn 'I!' of reiterated self-assertion. Or was it, rather, the Hebrew 'Aie!', ultimate word of lamentation, that swelled and waned and was silent? St Peter drew the gates towards him and thrust his head through the gap.

'Go round to the kitchen door, driver. They'll give you some bread and a sup of wine.'

'You mean — I don't have to take them back, all that lot?' the cabby enquired, with a sweeping wave of his hand. Then he stared. His mouth fell open. His hand was waving at nothing.

'They've disappeared! Luggage and all! But where could they have gone?' he demanded. 'They can't just vanish into thin air!'

'They can. And they have, my good man. Though air is perhaps too substantial a word.'

'What! Here today and gone tomorrow?'

'No. Here today and gone today.'

The cabby, puzzled, shook his head. 'Wonders will never cease!' he declared.

'Never. Thank Heaven!' St Peter grinned. And he pulled the gates to with a clang and turned his key in the lock.

Only Connect

IT WAS suggested to me when the Library of Congress did me the honour of asking me to address you that I should talk about how *Mary Poppins* came to be written. Now, I know that there are many people who can talk, and at great length, on subjects of which they are totally ignorant. But I'm not one of them. I can't speak of what I don't know and this is not from an excess of modesty but from lack of relevant data. Any work of fiction, any work of imagination, has, inevitably, something of the quality of poetry, or of those strange flashes of realization that happen for no apparent reason or rhyme — it can't be described. Words are like the notes on a piano, instruments of communication, not the poem — or the music — itself. Once a piece of work is finished, it has said all there is to be said. My instinct is always to whittle down, not to enlarge upon, and hasn't your own poet, Randall Jarrell, said — I forget the exact phrase for the moment — that a writer must remain silent about the way in which he writes? Even what he writes. Nothing, however, prevents a writer from speaking about the earth — the compost, as it were — from which his work arises. He can't help knowing something about that because it is, of course, his very self.

And this brings me to my title. I don't have to tell you where it comes from. When I was at Radcliffe last year students from that college and Harvard used to crowd into my small apartment once a week and the talk was so good, they were all so alive, so open to ideas, and so ready to fight me for them. I liked that. And I remember that on one occasion I said — and it still seems to me true — that thinking was linking. At that, one marvellous girl blazed out at me, 'Yes! Only connect!' and began searching for pencil and paper. But I begged her not, for the life of her, to write it down in a notebook. E. M. Forster had made the connection already, and now it was really her own. Once you write things down you've lost them. They are simply dead words on dead paper.

But 'Only connect' was the exact phrase I had been leading up to and it has been precious to me ever since I read *Howards End*, of which it is the epigraph. Perhaps, indeed, it's the theme of all Forster's writing, the attempt to link a passionate scepticism with the desire for meaning, to find the human key to the inhuman world about us; to connect the individual with the community, the known with the unknown; to relate the past to the present and both to the future. Oh, it's a marvellous phrase and I seized upon it for this lecture because — well, what else *is* there to seize upon? This question of linking is, anyway, very close to me and since that is what I am talking about tonight inevitably I have to go back to the past.

You remember Blake's 'Little Black Boy'? 'My mother bore me in the Southern wild.' In that sense I was a little black boy too, for I was born in the subtropics of Australia. Not that I spent all my life there, only my young years, and mostly far from cities. I lived a life that was at once new and old. The country was new and the land itself very old — the oldest in the world, geologists say, and in spite of all the brash pioneering atmosphere that still existed, even a child could sense the antiquity of it. We had also strong family traditions; we couldn't escape them, caught as we were between the horns of an Irish father and a mother of Scottish and Irish descent. It was simple, not rich, not centred at all round possessions or the search for status symbols. It seems to me that there were few *things* of any kind — furniture, of course, clothes and food, all the modest necessities. But of toys, and personal treasures, very few. If we wanted them we had to invent them, not by parental edict but from necessity. And there were very few books: Dickens and Scott, of course, Shakespeare, Tennyson, and some of the Irish poets. I ate my way through these like a bookworm not because of any highbrow leanings but simply because they were books. But for the children who, as far as I can remember, were seldom specially catered for, it was the grown-up world that was important. There was a modest hodge-podge of good and bad: Beatrix Potter, simple (even babyish) comics, an odd book that nobody else seems to have heard of called *The Wallypug of Why*, Ethel Turner's stories, *Alice*, Kingsley's *Heroes*. Hawthorne I never met till I was grown up and it seems to me, as I read him now, though perhaps I wouldn't have thought so then, that he rather talks down to children, 'tinifying,' if I may coin the word, and inventing dear little curly-haired daughters to make people like

Midas more acceptable. Kingsley doesn't do those things. He gives you the myths straight.

Then, too, we had something that no child could find today, not anywhere in the world. We had penny books. You could buy a fairy tale for a penny — that's how their lore went into me. And just as good, perhaps even better at that age, you could buy a *Buffalo Bill*. I don't know whether anybody in this audience remembers such books? Indeed, not long ago — for it seemed so unlikely — I began to wonder whether I hadn't made them up. It was a great relief to me when Rosamond Lehmann, the novelist, assured me that I hadn't. 'Of *course* we had penny books,' she said, and we dreamed over them together. Oh, why didn't I keep them? What grown-up, with no eye for the future, tossed the raggedy little morsels — as I myself have done since with many a child's tattered paper treasure — into a nearby dustbin? Last year, when I was in Toronto visiting the Osborne collection of children's books that goes back to the 17th century, I eagerly searched the glass cases. 'If only,' I said, quite by chance, 'I could see a penny book.' A conspiratorial, Guy Fawkes sort of look passed between the librarians, and one hurried away and quickly came back with something held secretively behind her. She put it on the case before me and there was a *Buffalo Bill* — almost, it seemed, the very one, in the faded blacks and blues and reds that I had so long remembered. On the back of the cover was the advertisement for the two-and-sixpenny alarm clock that I had saved up for long ago but never quite achieved. And there, also — much more important — was the air rifle for nineteen-and-elevenpence that would kill an elephant at five yards. Alas, I never got that, either. What would I have done with it, if I had, you may ask. I never had a moment's doubt about what I was saving for. It was to slay the enemies of Ireland! The sorrows of the 'most distressful country' got into me very early — how could it help doing so with my father's nostalgia for it continually feeding the imagination? My body ran about in the Southern sunlight but my inner world had subtler colours, the greys and snows of England where Little Joe swept all the crossings and the numberless greens of Ireland which seemed to me to be inhabited solely by poets plucking harps, heroes lordily cutting off each other's heads and veiled ladies sitting on the ground keening.

I think, perhaps, if there was any special virtue in my upbringing, it lay in the fact that my parents, both of them, were very allusive talkers. Neither of them ever read anything that didn't very quickly come out in conversation and from there pass into the family idiom. If my father discovered a poem he liked, even a piece of doggerel, it would presently be, as it were, on the breakfast table. Many a phrase, as ordinary to me then as the daily porridge, began its life, as I later learned, as a quotation from a poem or snatch from a ballad. As an instance, my father, who was a great lover of horses — and tricky, dangerous horses at that — would call out, whenever he returned from riding or driving, 'Bonnie George Campbell is home!' And my mother from somewhere in the house would always answer 'Thank God!' But *who* has come home, I used to wonder, for my father was neither George nor Campbell. It was not until much later, when I began to read the Scottish ballads, that I understood. You remember it?

> *Booted and saddled*
> *And bridled rode he,*
> *To hame cam' his guid horse*
> *But never cam' he.*

For all Bonnie Georges that come safely home the Lord should, indeed, be praised.

'Oh, what can ail thee, knight-at-arms?' my mother would sometimes say to a weeping child. Who was this knight, I often wondered. And yet, when you come to think of it, all children are knights-at-arms at times, alone and palely loitering. It is then they need to be comforted. But sometimes my father would prevent that. 'No, no,' he would say, 'let her weep. You know we need the rain.' Thinking of this, with hindsight, I see how really antique that was, that we cannot really escape the myths, even if we wish to. You can call it, perhaps, sympathetic magic. And it is a fact that still, in countries suffering from drought, a cup of water is poured on the ground in the hope of bringing rain. In Sumeria, the oldest civilization the world knows, the rain god was invoked by the pouring of a cup of wine. I remembered this recently when a journalist, who had been talking to people in Ireland about the assassination of President Kennedy, told me that one old man had said gravely, 'We cried the rain down for him that night.' What an epitaph! The rain cried down!

Then, too, there were maxims galore and proverbs and aphorisms. I was so often told — being a passionately lazy child — to 'Make an effort, Mrs Dombey,' that I began to think that Dombey was one of my own names. How could I know it was out of Dickens?

Then, there were other, closer, connections with myth. In those lucky days there was always help to be had in the house. Such people are wonderful meat for children. The life they live, from the child's point of view — because to him it is strange and unknown — seems to be filled with all the glamour that his own dailiness lacks. One of them — Bella, or was it Bertha? — had a parrot-headed umbrella. This fascinated me. On days out, it swung beside Bella's furbelows — she was far more elegant, I then thought, than my mother — and was carefully put away in tissue paper on her return, while she told us the always fantastic story of what she had done and seen. Well, she never *quite* told — she did more, she hinted. 'Ah,' she would say, looking like Cassandra, 'if you could know what's happened to me cousin's brother-in-law!' But all too often, when prayed to continue, she would assure us, looking doomed and splendid, that the story was really beyond all telling and not for the ears of children. Oh, those inadequate ears of children! We were left to wonder, always mythologically — had he perhaps been chained to the mast because of someone's siren voice? Was his liver being slowly eaten by a baldheaded local eagle? Whatever they were, the things she didn't tell, they were always larger than life.

Once, however, she spoke plain. 'I saw Paddy Liston in the gutter,' she said, 'and him as drunk as an English duke!' Well, what a sight for the inward eye! It filled our imagination to such an extent that now I can never think of our poor, probably sober, dukes without seeing them en masse under tables, robed and crowned and in the last stages of alcoholic dissolution. We didn't, as you see, need television! In a world where there are few possessions, where nobody answers questions, where nobody explains — I say this with joy not sorrow! — children must build life for themselves. One child is forced this way, one another. I went into imagination and poetry — perhaps I should more modestly say versifying — and never with grown-up approbation. Come to that, I never sought it.

'Hardly W B Yeats,' said my father once, when my mother showed him a scrap of mine. And remembering it now I feel bound to agree with him, though at the age of seven it would have been hard even for *Yeats* to be W B Yeats. My father, as you see, perhaps because he was so far away from her, was in love with Cathleen ni Houlihan. Nothing that Ireland did was wrong, nothing that other countries did was completely right. Even his maxims came from Ireland. 'Never put a baby in a drawer,' was one of them. But who would ever do such a thing? Even if he saw a doll in a drawer, he would pluck it out, saying 'Remember Parnell!' We had never even *heard* of Parnell and I had to wait to make the connection till I read a life of him a few years ago. Soon after he was born his mother, called away on some pretext, put him down quickly and came back to discover that her baby had disappeared. She looked everywhere, servants searched the house, gardeners rummaged in the shrubberies — no sign of Charles Stewart Parnell. I hope I'm not inventing it, but I think the police, too, were sent for. And while they were once more searching the nursery a mewling little sound came from the bureau. And there was Charles Stewart, six weeks old and at his last gasp because his mother, absent-mindedly dumping him into a open drawer had, also absent-mindedly, shut it! I am sure my father knew this story. Where else could the maxim have come from?

So you see, I was drenched in the Celtic twilight before I ever came to it. Indeed I only came to it when it was over and had practically turned into night. I had dreamed of it all my life and although my father was long dead, I had to test what my childhood had taught me. So the first thing I did on arriving in England was to send a piece of writing to AE (George Russell), who was then editor of *The Irish Statesman*. With all the hauteur of youth I deliberately sent no covering letter, just a stamped addressed envelope for return. And sure enough the stamped envelope came back, as I had fully expected it to do, but inside — instead of my manuscript — was a cheque for three guineas and a letter from AE. It said 'If you have any more, please let me see them and if you are ever in Ireland let us meet.' So, you see, even if I hadn't been already going to Ireland I would have been off on the next train.

That was how I came under the wing of AE and got to know Yeats and the gifted people in their circle, all of whom cheerfully licked me into shape like a set of mother cats with a kitten. As you can imagine, this was blessing and far beyond my deserving. But I was not the only kitten, no young person was ever sent empty away, the riches were poured out upon all. It was strong meat, this first introduction to my father's country, among the poets and the makers of history. Perhaps it was just as well that my first contact with my Irish relatives should take me down several pegs. I needed it. They, I discovered, were not at all in love with Cathleen ni Houlihan. Living cheek by jowl with her, they saw her without any trappings. Irish to the marrow, full of local lore and story, lovers of horses and the countryside, they weren't at all sure that life depended on poetry and they took the Celtic Renaissance with more than a grain of salt. 'I don't like you gallivanting around with men who see fairies,' said one. 'And the thought of you, a young girl, in Fleet Street, that terrible place — it's beyond thinking about!' From his description of it, I saw myself suffering nameless indignities at the hands of newspaper tycoons or being dragged up dark alleys by drunken reporters, and looked forward to it all with the greatest enthusiasm — though of course I didn't say so. 'And you'll meet such frightful people,' he said. 'There's one who lived down the road a way — old now, of course, but a terrible great boastful fellow. If you meet him, be courteous, but do not pursue the acquaintance. His name is Shaw, George Bernard Shaw.'

Gradually I learned to dissemble my enthusiasm for all that the elderly relatives of my father's generation found so reprehensible. One of them even remarked approvingly, 'You're not nearly so mad as you used to be.' Yet, he was the one who, on his death-bed, hearing his wife asking the doctor if he was likely to last till the next morning, remarked sardonically, 'I don't need to. I've seen plenty of mornings. All I want to know is, will I live to hear the result of the boat race?' Among last words this spartan, if eccentric, phrase deserves, I think, a place.

Not so mad as I used to be? Little did he know! It was coming back from visiting him that one of what he would have called my maddest moments occurred. I knew that on the way back to Dublin the train would pass Lough Gill. And I remembered that in Lough Gill lay Yeats' Lake Isle of Innisfree. So I leapt from the carriage and charged a boatman on the lapping shore to take me there.

'Ach, there's no such place,' he said.

'Oh, but there is, I assure you. W. B. Yeats wrote about it.'

'And who would he be?'

I told him.

'Ah, I know them, those poets, always stravaiging through their minds, inventing outlandish things. *We* call it Rat island!' Rat Island! Well!

So we set out, under grey hovering clouds, with me in the bows and a young priest, who suddenly arose out of the earth, it seemed, joining us in the stern. At last, after a rough passage, there was Innisfree. No hive for the honeybee and no log cabin but of course I hadn't expected them. They were only in the bee-loud glade of Yeats' stravaiging mind. But the whole island was covered with rowan trees wearing their red berries like jewels and the thought suddenly came to me — a most disastrous one, as it turned out

— 'I'll take back some branches to the poet.' In no time, for the island is diminutive, I had broken off pretty nearly every branch from the rowans and was staggering with them towards the boat. By now a strong wind had sprung up and the rain was falling and the lake was wild. Those Irish loughs beat up into a great sea very quickly. As we embarked, the waves seemed as high as the Statue of Liberty and I wished I'd had more swimming practice. Then I noticed, between one trough and the next, that the priest, pale as paper, was telling his beads with one hand and with the other plucking off my rowan berries and dropping them into the water. 'Ah, Father,' said the boatman, pulling stertorously on the oars, 'it's not the weight of a berry or two that will save us now.' He gave me a reflective glance and I got the idea, remembering that in times of shipwreck women are notoriously unlucky, that he was planning to throw me overboard, if the worst came to the worst. I wished *I* had a string of beads!

However, perhaps because of the priest's prayers, we came at last safely to shore. I hurried through the rain with my burden and took the next train for Dublin. The other passengers edged away from my streaming garments as though I were some sort of ancient mariner. I should never have started this, I knew, but there is an unfortunate streak of obstinacy in me that would not let me stop. From Dublin station, through curtains of cloud — taxis did not exist for me in those days — I carried the great branches to Yeats' house in Merrion Square and stood there, with my hair like rats' tails, my tattered branches equally ratlike, looking like Birnam come to Dunsinane and wishing I was dead. I prayed, as I rang the bell, that Yeats would not open the door himself, but my prayer went unheard.

For an articulate man to be struck dumb is, you can imagine, rare. But struck dumb he was at the sight of me. In shame, I heard him cry a name into the dark beyond of the house and saw him hurriedly escape upstairs. Then the name came forward in human shape and took me gently, as though I were ill or lost or witless, down to the basement kitchen. There I was warmed and dried and given cocoa; the dreadful branches were taken away. I felt like someone who had died and was now contentedly on the other side, certain that nothing more could happen. In this dreamlike state, I was gathering myself to go — out the back way if possible — never to be seen again. But a maid came bustling kindly in and said — as though to someone still alive! — 'The master will see you now.' I was horrified. This was the last straw. 'What for?' I wanted to know. 'Ah, then, you'll see. He has his ways.'

And so, up the stairs — or the seven-story mountain — I went and there he was in his room with the blue curtains.

'My canary has laid an egg!' he said and joyously led me to the cages by the window. From there we went round the room together, I getting better every minute and he telling me which of his books he liked and how, when he got an idea for a poem — there was a long momentous pause, here. He was always the bard, always filling the role of poet, not play-acting but knowing well the role's requirements and giving them their due. He never came into a room, he *entered* it; walking around his study was a ceremonial peregrination, wonderful to witness. 'When I get an idea for a poem,' he went on, oracularly, 'I take down one of my own books and read it and then I go on from there.' Moses explaining his tablets couldn't have moved me more. And so, serenely, we came to the end of the pilgrimage and I was just about to bid him goodbye when I noticed on his desk a vase of water and in it one sprig of fruiting rowan. I glanced at him distrustfully. 'Was he teaching me a lesson?' I wondered, for at that age one cannot accept to be taught. But he wasn't; I knew it by the look on his face. He would do nothing so banal. He was not trying to enlighten me and so I was enlightened and found a connection in the process. It needed only a sprig, said the lesson. And I learned, also, something about writing. The secret is to say less than you need. You don't want a forest, a leaf will do.

Next day, when I was lunching with AE, he said to me, 'Yeats was very touched that you brought him a sprig of rowan from Innisfree.' So I had to tell him the whole story. You couldn't be untruthful with AE. 'I hope,' he said slyly, 'when you go to Dunfanaghay [his own favourite part of Ireland] you won't cut down all the willows for me. What about the tree spirits? Remember the dryads!' Dryads! I'd grown up on a diet of mythology and on Innisfree I'd forgotten it all. It was AE who had to remind me, AE whose thought was crystal-clear and hard — and still had room for dryads. These men — he, Yeats, James Stephens, and the rest — had aristocratic minds. For them, the world was not fragmented. An idea did not suddenly grow, like Topsy, all alone and separate. For them, all things had antecedents and long family trees. They saw nothing shameful or silly in myths and fairy stories, nor did they shovel them out of sight in some cupboard marked Only for Children. They were always willing to concede that there were more things in heaven and earth than philosophy dreamed of. They allowed for the unknown. And, as you can imagine, I took great heart from this.

It was AE who showed me how to look at and learn from one's own writing. 'Popkins,' he said once — he always called her just plain Popkins, whether deliberately mistaking the name or not, I never knew. His humour was always subtle — 'Popkins, had she lived in another age, in the old times to which she certainly belongs, would undoubtedly have had long golden tresses, a wreath of flowers in one hand, and perhaps a spear in the other. Her eyes would have been like the sea, her nose comely, and on her feet winged sandals. But, this being Kali Yuga, as the Hindus call it — in our terms, the Iron Age — she comes in the habiliments most suited to it.'

Well, golden tresses and all that pretty paraphernalia didn't interest me; she could only be as she *was*. But that AE could really know so much about it astonished me, that he should guess at her antecedents and genealogy when I hadn't thought of them myself — it put me on my mettle. I began to *read* the book. But it was only after many years that I realized what he meant, that she had come out of the same world as the fairy tales.

My childish love for the tales had continued to increase in me — Tolkien says somewhere that if you are natively attached to the fairy tales (lots of people are not and there's no blame in that), that habit grows on you as you grow older. And it has certainly grown on me. 'Only connect' comes strongly into this. Not long ago, I read in the *New York Times* about how the eels from America and Europe make their way to the Sargasso Sea to mate and lay their eggs, the journey for American eels taking one year, for Europeans two. Afterwards, they make their long way back to their respective homes and apparently feel it was worth it. Well, for me the tales are a sort of Sargasso Sea and I am a kind of eel. And all these years of pondering on the fairy tale, first of all for love of it — because to learn about anything, it seems to me, you have to love it first — and later because I became enthralled by it. All this pondering has led me to believe that the true fairy tales (I'm not talking now about invented ones) come straight out of myth; they are, as it were, miniscule reaffirmations of myth, or perhaps the myth made accessible to the local folkly mind. In the nineteenth century, as you know, Andrew Lang and all his fellow pundits treated them as the meanderings of the primitive intelligence — and therefore, apparently, suitable for children! Then the anthropologists had a go at them and later they descended, if I may so put it, to the psychoanalysts. But none of these seem to have been able to exhaust their meaning; there is still plenty left. They're like the magic pitcher in the Greek myth of Baucis and Philemon — you remember it retold in Hawthorne? — no matter how much milk you poured out, it was still full to the brim. This, of course, is where Jack's magic purse comes from; whenever you take out the last coin there is always another there.

Of course, you may ask — indeed, people are always asking — who invented the myths? And do you think they are true? Well, true? What is true? As far as I am concerned it doesn't matter tuppence if the incidents in the myths never happened. That does not make them any less true, for, indeed, in one way or another, they're happening all the time. You only have to open a newspaper to find them crowding into it. Life itself continually re-enacts them. Not long ago, staying with friends in Virginia, I watched from the terrace as two little girls of six and four performed the rite of burial over a dead bird. I guessed that they did not want to touch it but they gathered all their grandfather's flowers and covered the body with them. Over these they laid branches and set a fence of sticks around them. Then they stood up and began to dance, not wildly, not gaily, not childishly, but formally, with measured steps. After that they knelt down — one on either side of the grave — were they praying? I couldn't see — and then they leaned across the sticks and gravely embraced each other. They had never been to church or a funeral, never before seen anything dead, knew nothing about the rite they were enacting out of ancestral memory, and the whole performance was true. I don't insist that you make anything out of it, but it meant something to me — the assurance that the myths and rites run around in our blood; that when old drums beat we stamp our feet, if only metaphorically. Time and the past are getting at us. The Australian aborigines have a word for this. For any happening further back than a grandmother their memories cannot go, any event further forward than a grandson, they cannot pretend to envisage. Beyond these times, when knowing is relatively possible, they can only reach by speaking of what lies there as the Dreaming. 'It is gone into the Dreaming,' they say of the past. 'It will come in the Dreaming,' they say of the future.

There is a wonderful Japanese phrase, used as a Zen koan, which says, 'Not created but summoned.' It seems to me that this is all that can be said of the myths, 'They are in the Dreaming. They are not created but summoned.' But it is the fairy tale, not the myth, that is really my province. One might say that fairy tales are the myths fallen into time and locality. For instance, if this glass of water is myth, and I drink it, the last drop — or the lees of the wine — is the fairy tale. The drop is the same stuff, all the essentials are there, it is small, but perfect. Not minimized, not to be made digestible for children. I think it is more and more realized that the fairy tales are not entertainments for children at all. In their primal state, that is. They've been bowdlerized and had the essentials removed in order not to frighten — but to my mind it is better not to tell them at all than to take out all the vital organs and leave only the skin. And what *isn't* frightening, after all? What *doesn't* carry a stern lesson? Even the nursery rhymes present us with very difficult truths. And they, too, like the fairy tales, have long family trees, though it would not be easy, I admit, to prove it legally.

Take Humpty Dumpty. All the king's horses and all the king's men couldn't put him together again. That some things are broken irrevocably, never to be whole again, is a hard truth and this is a good way of teaching it. Away back in Egypt, the myth was telling the same thing. You remember how, when the body of Osiris was cut up and scattered, his sister-wife Isis searched the world for the 14 pieces, trying to re-member him and always unable to recover the 14th. I'm not trying here to suggest that whoever wrote 'Humpty Dumpty' had Isis and Osiris in mind. Of course not. I merely make the connection between them. And what about the cow that jumped over the moon? In Egypt the sky was always thought of as a cow, her body arching over the earth and her four legs standing firmly upon it. Again, it is I who make the link, not the writer of the rhyme. 'How many miles to Babylon?' What is that telling us, I wonder, with its three score and ten, the life of man? There is a gloss upon this rhyme that makes it perhaps a little clearer.

> *How many miles to Babylon?*
> *If it's three score and ten*
> *Bury me under the cold gravestone*
> *For my time is come, but make no moan,*
> *I shall be back by candle-light —*
> *Many times again!*

You may think this is hocus-pocus and mumbo jumbo — and well it may be, except to me — but if you look in the Oxford dictionary, you will find that hocus-pocus itself derives from *hoc est corpus* — and we are, after all, talking here about the body, if I may so put it, of an idea. Mumbo jumbo has, alas, no known derivation.

It is a figure supposed to have been invented by African chiefs in order to keep their wives properly disciplined and to give them a sense of awe. As for fee fi fo fum, you must go back to ancient Greece for that. It was the great incantation of the Erinyes, the triple furies born from the drops of blood of Cronus; and the Old World rang with it as they pursued their prey. What a long and circuitous way it took before it found a home in our Western nurseries!

You may, of course, feel that this is drawing a long bow. But, as I see it, what is a long bow for but to be drawn? And our phrase 'the long bow' itself comes from the great bow of Philoctetes, one of the Argonauts, who inherited it from Hercules. A man had to be a hero inwardly and outwardly to be able to draw that bow.

Or it may be that you will categorize all this as 'old wives tales.' But I am one who believes in old wives' tales and that it is the proper function of old wives to tell tales. Old wives have the best stories in the world, and long memories. Why should we treat them with contempt? The tales have to be told in order that we may understand that in the long run, whatever it may be, every man must become the hero of his own story; his own fairy tale, if you like, a real fairy tale. Hans Andersen, for me, in spite of the fact that he often used old material, is an inventor of fairy tales; so is Oscar Wilde. They both have an element of nostalgia in them, a devitalizing element that the true tale never has. Perhaps those that most clearly derive from myth, those that clearly show their antecedents, are the Greek stories, the Norse tales, and Grimms. These are old trees, rooted in the folk, full of meaning and ritual; they retell the myths in terms that can be understood by unlettered people. For originally they were for the listener rather than the reader; they came long before books. Every one of these tales, it seems to me, is asking something of us, telling us something about life. Of course I am now on my hobbyhorse and anyone who wishes may get up and shoot at me or at any rate ask a question. I am not here to stand and assert but to share my questioning with you.

Doesn't it seem to you, too, that there is more in the tales than meets the eye? Think of all those stories of the three brothers, who go off in search of various treasures. As a child, naturally, I thought of them as separate entities — the eldest so handsome, always delayed at the crossroads, or prevented from going farther because of some temptation. He's handsome and brave, and relying on this, he assures himself that when the time comes, he'll find the treasure. Then the second, sure of his cleverness, a cleverness that proves to be groundless, also fails in the quest. Lastly, the third brother sets out, realizing his ignorance, knowing himself a simpleton. And so he is. Simple and humble, willing to accept help from anyone who will give it. You'll remember the story of 'Puddocky,' a prime example of this. I always loved that youngest son. Nowadays, however, I think of the brothers, not as single adventurers, but as three stages of one man. In the beginning he sets out bravely, young and handsome, and quickly gets to the end of that; but 'I'm still clever,' he thinks to himself; yet soon he finds even that's not true. He ends by knowing he knows nothing. And once he knows nothing he begins to know something and from there it is really only a step to happy ever after.

The fairy tales also tell us a great deal about women — or, perhaps about woman and her role in life, the triple role of maiden, mother, and crone. Each one of us, of course, begins as a maiden and whether she becomes a physical mother or not makes no difference, the role of mother is the next step, the flowering of the bud. Last of all comes the grandmother — again, not the physical grandmother, but the stage where the flower withers into seed pod. To become a crone, it seems to me, is the last great hope of woman, supremely worth achieving. An old woman who remembers, who has gathered up all the threads of life and sits by the fire with her hands in her lap — not doing anything any more — what a marvellous thing! This is what it is to become wise. There you sit in your rocking chair as in the fairy tales — I hope I shall, anyway — aware of all you have learned and garnered and having it available in case the young ones want it. You will not force it on them, but simply tell it. That's what the crones — all those good and bad fairies — are doing in the tales.

Of course, it is not always easy to see the relation between the fairy tale and the myth. They do not *all* insist on telling you of their great-grandparents. But many of them have lineaments that loudly proclaim their breeding. Cinderella, for instance, whose story is so ancient that she is found in one guise or another in practically every mythology known to man. She has been grossly ill-treated, however, by writers of pantomime and by illustrators who retell the tales in terms of their own illustrations. Chop off a nose or leg, what does it matter? All tellers of the Cinderella story, ever since Perrault himself retold it, make the mistake of assuming that it is because she wishes that she goes to the ball. If that were so, wouldn't we all be married to princes? No, the wishing has much more behind it; it must be so if the happy ending is to be achieved.

The Grimms come near to the true theme. There, it is not because she wishes but because she has performed the necessary rites at her mother's grave, and because, above all, she has accepted her fate, that she meets the little benevolent bird who gives her the golden gown and all the magnificent rest. And then, the story has so many sisters. There is a book — the author's name is Cox — which has more than three hundred versions of the Cinderella story. But I like to make my own connections. Would you not say she was the girl in 'King Cophetua and the Beggar Maid'? Isn't she, as near as makes no matter, patient Griselda? And who but Cinderella is Lear's Cordelia, with those two monstrous sisters? Going back to myth, you will find her in the garb of Sita, the prototype of all feminine virtue in the epic of the Ramayana, in India, which is as old as history.

And what about that recurrent theme where a character in the story agrees — for a price — to give the villain the first thing that runs to greet him on his return home? It's a wonderful story. You find it in 'The King of the Golden Mountain' and 'The Singing, Soaring Lark' and it goes back to Methuselah, or at any rate the Old Testament, in the story of Jephthah's daughter. None of the true stories was born yesterday; they all come from far and have a long way yet to go. One that was dear to me as a child — I still think it most beautiful, even though others protest that it is brutal and bloody — was 'The Juniper Tree.' There is a wicked stepmother, of course, who, when the little stepson bends down to get an apple from a chest, drops the lid and cuts his head off. Even now I never bend over a chest without making quite sure that the top won't fall on me. And so the story goes from bad to worse. Sitting the body at the table, with the head balanced on top of it, she orders the little sister to call her brother to supper. Naturally, he does not answer, so the little sister gives him a shake and down falls the severed head. And now worse hurries on to worst. The stepmother cooks the child in a stew and gives this meal to the father when he comes home from work. 'Ah,' he exclaims, 'how truly delicious. I feel as though it were all mine.' As, indeed, of course, it is.

Eventually the little watching bird puts all to rights, the little sister is freed of her supposed guilt, the little boy comes alive again, the stepmother — and serve her right! — is finished off with a millstone. It sounds, I admit, like a mess of horrors. But it never bothered me at all. Knowing the power of the little bird I never doubted that the boy would be safe. If, indeed, the father ate him, it was inevitable, even natural, that the boy would somehow, and in good time, return to his proper shape. After all, hadn't Cronus, the father of the gods, eaten up his children? Son after son was born to Rhea and each time Cronus said 'He'll supplant me!' and promptly swallowed him down. But with her last child Rhea grew cunning, swaddled a stone and gave it to her husband who, feeling — though erroneously — that it was all his, let it go the way of the others. Thus Zeus was saved to become king of the gods. And, once on his throne he, himself, performed the same act — or an aspect of it — when he took his unborn son Dionysus into his own thigh — his mother having been burnt to death — and at the full period of nine months brought him forth, unharmed and perfect.

And then there are the countless stories that warn against trying to see too much; of the demon lover who persuades the maiden to marry him on the understanding that she must never, once the night falls, attempt to look at him. And always the maiden — who could help it? — always the maiden fails. Either she is persuaded by her family as — again! — in 'The Singing Soaring Lark' and 'Melusine' or she is overcome by curiosity, as in 'Cupid and Psyche'. And as a result he disappears or has to go through grave vicissitudes before he comes to himself once more. This theme comes directly out of myth, it goes back to the farthest limits of time when Semele, not knowing that her bridegroom was divine, yet suspecting it, begs him to grant her one boon, that she may see him in all his splendour. Reluctantly Zeus unveils himself and she, unable to endure the lightning, is herself turned to ash. The story is a warning, repeated down the centuries, through myth, folk and fairy tale, that it is dangerous to look upon the face of the god. Seek him rather with the inward eye.

'Rumpelstiltzkin' was another of my favourites, for its meaning lay very close to me. Everyone knows the story of how the miller's daughter, in order to become a queen, promises the little old man her first child if he will spin her straw into gold. Of course he does it. It is no problem. To him they are one and the same. But when the child is born she cannot bear to part with it and he agrees to let her off if she can discover his name. So for three days she tries this and she tries that, always unsuccessfully, and he warns her that when tomorrow comes he will take the child away. In despair, she sends riders far and wide, east of the sun and west of the moon. Only one comes back with a clue. 'In the land where the wolf and the hare say goodnight to each other, I came upon an old man, jumping up and down and singing "My name is Rumpelstiltzkin." And so, the next day, making a great pretence of it, she asks the old man 'Is it Tom, is it Dick, is it Harry?' No! 'Then is it Rumpelstiltzkin?' And with that he shrieks a great 'Yes!', stamps his foot into the earth and tears himself in two. His name is known, therefore he is finished. This role has been played out.

This idea of the secrecy of the name, the taboo against making it known, goes back to man's very early days, to the time, perhaps, when he had no name. During the war I spent two summers with the Navaho Indians and when they gave me an Indian name they warned me that it would be bad luck both for me and the tribe if I ever disclosed it to anyone. And I never have. For one thing, I do not want to receive or give bad luck, and for another I have a strong atavistic feeling — one, I think, that is strongly shared by unlettered people all over the world — that to disclose one's name, or take another's before the time for it is ripe — well, it's dangerous. I tremble inwardly and withdraw when my Christian name is seized before I have given it, and I have the same hesitancy about using that of another person. An Indian — or a gypsy — would understand this very well. It is a very ancient taboo and I relate it — though I don't suggest that anyone else relate it — to the earliest times when men built altars 'To the Unknown God.' If I were ever to build an altar, I would put that inscription above it.

In making these connections, I do not want to assert or impose. But, in fact, all things are separate and fragmentary until man himself connects them, sometimes wrongly and sometimes rightly. As far as I am concerned, it is all a matter of hint and suggestion, something seen at the corner of the eye and linked with another thing, equally fleeting. You remember Walt Whitman's poem, 'On the Beach at Night'. 'I give you the first suggestion, the problem, the indirection.' Isn't that wonderful? Turn your back on it and you'll find it! It's like Shakespeare's 'By indirection find direction out.' And with these quotations I connect Swift's dictum 'Vision is the art of seeing things invisible.' Doesn't this relate to the unknown name?

But now let me make one last link. I was rereading recently how Aeneas came to Campania — which is now Naples — seeking some means of getting into contact with the ghost of his father, Anchises. First, for piety, he prays at the temple of Apollo, begging the god to inspire the Cumean Sybil, whose cave is at hand, to help him on his way to the underworld. Nearby is the great forest where lies the terrible Lake of Avernus over which no bird flies, and at the edge of that is the rift between the great rocks that guard the way to the realm of Pluto. You know the story. She tells him to break from one tree in the forest a small golden branch. With that in his hand he will be able to descend into the depths. So, holding the branch before him as an amulet, he begins the dreadful journey. Of course, the whole of Frazer's *Golden Bough* is about this branch and many of the fairy stories repeat it; 'The Shoes That Were Danced to Pieces,' for instance, where the 12 princesses are followed each night to the underworld by a soldier who breaks off a little golden branch to bring back as a sign that he has, indeed, been there.

Not for nothing, I thought, as I read again of Aeneas, were those four sites so close together — the temple of Apollo, the cave of the Sybil, the Lake of Avernus, the Land of the Dead. It is inevitable that they should touch and interpenetrate each other, not only in myth, but in life. Life, in a sense, *is* myth, one might say; the one is a part of the other. In both of them the good and the bad, the dangerous and the safe, live very close together. And I remembered, as I thought about this, how Aeneas had begged the Sybil to speak her oracle in words and not, as was her usual practice, to write it on leaves that would blow away. That struck a chord in me, for I knew a story where this had actually happened. In this story, the wind blows leaves into the hands of two children. And on each leaf a message is written. One says 'Come' and the other 'Tonight.' Now, the story I'm talking about is 'Hallowe'en.' It is in *Mary Poppins in the Park*. And there is the Sybil disregarding Aeneas by writing the oracle down on leaves! And I thought I had invented it! There's a poem by Rupert Brooke, one verse of which says:

> There's wisdom in women, of more than
> they have known,
> And thoughts go blowing through them,
> are wiser than their own.

Truly, I had far wiser thoughts than my own when I wrote that story. You may remember — though why should you? — that it is about a party in the park where all the shadows are free. They go out to enjoy themselves and leave their owners at home. The only one whose shadow refuses to go without her is — guess! — Mary Poppins.

I find another connection here in the fact that tonight happens to be Hallowe'en. In ancient times this used to be the festival of the dead. I think it was one of the Popes, Boniface IV, perhaps, in the seventh century, who decided to do away with all the pagan saturnalia and turn it from what it so significantly was, into a commemoration of the saints and martyrs. But in spite of him the myth never lost its mystery; men needed the festival rites for the dead; they needed to find a way out of grieving that would ease their fear that the spirits of the dead might come back to earth and haunt them. They put on masks and disguised their faces, wrapping themselves, to cheat the ghosts, in the garments of black that became for us, their late descendants, simply mourning clothes. The wake that the Irish hold for the dead is part of this ancient saturnalia. It gives an opportunity and a justification for the living to turn their faces again to life: it also provides a propitious moment, a ritual moment, one could say, a kind of crack through which some element of the unknown can be brought into the known.

Is anyone thinking of saints and martyrs on this Hallowe'en, I wonder? And who knows, when they leave this hall, that their shadows will be with them? For me the fairy tales are abroad tonight. Good fairies and demons, Beauty and the Beast — they are all knocking at the doors, rattling their money boxes and holding out grubby hands for candy. It's a pagan festival still, be sure, swinging between trick and treat, angel and devil, yes and no. It is a night of ghosts and shadows, a night that links the past and the present, a night perhaps when that crack between known and unknown cold open, and we could believe the old Greek poet, Aratus, when he declared: 'Full of Zeus are the cities, full of Zeus are the harbours, full of Zeus are all the ways of men.'

If it was true then it is true always, time cannot change the timeless. It could be — could it not? — *this* city, full of lighted, grinning pumpkin faces; *that* harbour out on Chesapeake Bay; *we* men — if we could only connect. What do you think?

First published in 'The Quarterly Journal' (Library of Congress, USA), 1967.

Printed in Great Britain
by Amazon.co.uk, Ltd.,
Marston Gate.